Leading Health Care Organizations

Leading Health Care Organizations

Edited by

Sue Dopson
Saïd Business School
Fellow of Templeton College
University of Oxford

and

Annabelle L. Mark
Professor of Health Care Organization
Middlesex University Business School

First published 2003 by
PALGRAVE MACMILLAN
Houndmills, Basingstoke, Hampshire RG21 6XS and
175 Fifth Avenue, New York, N.Y. 10010
Companies and representatives throughout the world

PALGRAVE MACMILLAN is the global academic imprint of the Palgrave
Macmillan division of St. Martin's Press, LLC and of Palgrave Macmillan Ltd.
Macmillan® is a registered trademark in the United States, United Kingdom
and other countries. Palgrave is a registered trademark in the European
Union and other countries.

ISBN 1–4039–0270–4

This book is printed on paper suitable for recycling and made from fully
managed and sustained forest sources.

A catalogue record for this book is available from the British Library.

Library of Congress Cataloging in Publication Data
    Leading health care organizations / edited by Sue Dopson and
    Annabelle L. Mark.
        p.   cm.
    Includes bibliographical references and index.
    ISBN 1–4039–0270–4 (cloth)
    1. Health services administration—Great Britain.   2. Leadership—
    Great Britain.   3. Health services administration.   I. Dopson, Sue.
    II. Mark, Annabelle L.
    RA395.G7L43 2003
    362.1'068—dc21   2003043602

10   9   8   7   6   5   4   3   2   1
12   11   10   09   08   07   06   05   04   03

Printed and bound in Great Britain by
Antony Rowe Ltd, Chippenham and Eastbourne

For William Dopson and Louise Mark

Live the Question Now

I want to beg you as much as I can to be patient
Toward all that's unsolved in your heart,
And to learn to love the questions themselves,
Like locked rooms,
Or like books that are written in a foreign tongue.

Do not seek the answers that cannot be given you,
Because you would not be able to live them,
And the point is to live everything.

Live the questions now,
Perhaps you will then, gradually,
Without noticing it,
Live along some distant day
Into the answer.

Rainer Maria Rilke

Contents

Foreword: Why Leadership is Important (and How to Choose the Right Book on It Before 2035)

Given the enormous numbers of books on leadership (10,398 on Amazon.co.uk and 12,173 on Amazon.com on 23 October 2002), one might be forgiven for asking whether the title is, at best, irrelevant and at worst arrogant. Unfortunately, two aspects of the answer might suggest otherwise. First, there is very little consensus amongst leadership researchers as to whether leadership does indeed make a difference. Second, if it does, there is very little agreement amongst the book authors as to how that difference might be made more tractable. Indeed, we can't even agree on what leadership is, never mind whether it is important or how it can be improved. Some of that diversity of opinion is contained in this edited collection, but let me say straight away that you will undoubtedly learn more about leadership from this collection than from most of the books available at Amazon.

Of course, it could be that some of the Leadership authors and researchers are right and the rest are wrong, but the difficulty is deciding which is which. We could simply sit down and read all the books to evaluate their utility and then implement whichever we thought most appropriate. But at the rate of one book a day it would take you 33 years just to read the current list on Amazon.com and by 2035 we can rest assured that even more material will await us. Moreover, if the current crop of books is anything to go by then we still will not be in a position to implement 'the' answer because leadership studies do not appear to be edging incrementally closer to an agreed formula. On the contrary, we are witnessing a constant expansion in alternatives; in an inversion of Darwinian selection and species reduction we seem to be in the midst of a cornucopia of variance. Of course, this may be what is required: it is just possible that each leadership situation is so unique that we require thousands of alternative models to explain them all. But, even if this is true, it provides little help to those seeking some crumb of comfort in their leadership struggles because nobody has time to read through the corpus of material in search of the right model for them.

Alternatively, perhaps the confusion is a consequence of different definitions of leadership. For some leadership theory relates to the heroic and charismatic models initiated by Thomas Carlyle in the nineteenth century, though this implies that anyone not in a crisis situation and therefore not able to save their colleagues, department, hospital, company or country, can never embody the true essence of leadership. Yet, as Max Weber argued in his original work on charisma, there are only a handful of these kinds of people around in the world at any one time – and many of these appear to believe themselves (following Nietzsche) 'to be on the side of angels' and hence extraordinarily dangerous to our well-being.

This heroic model of leadership, then, is both dangerous and dangerously naïve – but it is common. In a conversation with an MBA class the topic of the football World Cup and England's performance under Sven-Goran Eriksson came up. England had just defeated Argentina and I asked the class what kind of a leader Eriksson was. 'He is a god' came an instant reply from an English supporter. 'So what will happen', I responded, 'if England lose against Brazil in their next match?' 'We will crucify him' came the response. Now this little exchange encompasses several critical aspects of the problem of leadership. First, we assume that leaders can make a crucial difference to organizational performance – even though we should recognize that more often than not their role is as much to play the scapegoat after defeat as the lion after success. Second, we attribute to leaders an infallibility that is impossible to attain let alone maintain. Thus rather than insisting that leaders are, like the rest of us, fallible, prone to error and in some way or other imperfect, we desperately want them to be infallible. If this was not the case then it becomes difficult to explain why we are so unsympathetic to those who make mistakes. When, for example, David Beckham was sent off in the previous World Cup for tripping an Argentinean player it was almost as if the god had turned into the devil – the player who could have won the cup on his own is now held to be wholly responsible for the team's defeat. Yet it was the team's response that led to that defeat because several teams have players sent off but retain their shape, their self-belief and go on to win – as indeed the Brazilian team did against Turkey this time round.

This dichotomous approach to leaders – from god to devil – is captured both by the notion of 'crucifying' Eriksson after a defeat, and by the fragility of our respect for them. Yet we simultaneously know that individual leaders are not wholly responsible for our collective failure. Indeed, we know that individuals are destined at some point to err in their judgement, to make a mistake or to fail. Intriguingly, then, while we should be concerned with constructing procedures and systems for limiting the impact of the inevitable mistakes made by leaders, and from stopping them making mistakes where possible, we tend instead to relieve ourselves of responsibility by seeking out the scapegoat. And for this all to make sense we have to rationalize our approach to a position where leaders are perfect, mistakes should not be made, and where we play no active role in the process – and therefore take no responsibility for it.

It does not take a genius to recognize that in almost every case where organizations fail, whether that is a surgical team, a hospital unit, a company or a country, it is rarely the consequence of one leader's actions. Indeed, usually the subsequent enquiries reveal a whole host of people and procedures that could and should have stopped the problem either from emerging in the first place or from spreading in the second. So what stops them? Inevitably there are many complex reasons and causal factors in most cases, but just as inevitably there are people who could have stopped the rot but who chose not to. Often these silent witnesses fear for their own jobs, reputations and the like, but it may well be that the overwhelming issue is the power of leadership and the hierarchy of leaders. In short, we allow them to do things that they should not be allowed to do because we are embedded in the value system that attributes greatness and infallibility to them – we are, therefore, part of the problem – unless we dissent.

Ironically, dissent is usually regarded as a problem for leaders, and certainly many of the leadership texts concentrate on methods to generate consent. But we know that throughout history leaders have found it relatively easy to construct systems of consent – often in support of the most horrendous and barbaric acts. So the problem remains, if leaders are imperfect but they require our consent, what kind of consent should they receive? They might well prefer acquiescence, since this would allow them significant freedom of action but acquiescence can easily lead to irresponsible followership, where followers allow leaders to 'mislead' them. In this situation what leaders actually develop is 'Destructive Consent' because their followers merely consent to being misled. On the other hand, what leaders should perhaps be considering – in recognition of their limited skills and resources – their fallibility – is 'Constructive Dissent'. Here, followers have the best interests of the organization at heart – but are willing to voice their dissent if and when they believe leaders to be heading in the wrong direction.

Deep within this approach is a recognition not simply that formal leaders are fallible and not helped by irresponsible followers but also that leadership is not a phenomenon that we can define as 'something that formal leaders do'. On the contrary, leadership in this approach is not a position at all but a process, not a noun but a verb. And if the 'doing' of leadership is manifest by the behaviour of many people in organizations, and not just formal leaders, then we need to rethink the answer to the question: is leadership important? We might agree that formal leaders act more as scapegoats than heroic problem-solvers, we might also agree with Tolstoy that formal leaders are pushed along by their organizations more than they actually pull their organizations along, but none of this suggests that leadership is unimportant. Without scapegoats how would we account for organizational failures – except by that most uncomfortable procedure of looking in the mirror to see who is responsible?

Thus we are inexorably driven to the conclusion that leadership is critical but it may have little to do with (formal) leaders. If that is the case then what has been called 'deep' or 'distributed' leadership may be one solution to the impossible task of reading all the books. In effect, rather than worrying about who the leader is, or which book has the answer, we should all concern ourselves with ensuring our own responsibilities for leadership – whether in follower/constructive dissenter mode or in leadership mode – to maximize the possibilities of collective success and minimize the probabilities of individual failure.

Perhaps, after all though, there is a book that can help us all resolve this leadership enigma – but it is not a book entitled *Leadership – The (pick any number) Ways to Success*. Rather it is Conrad's *Heart of Darkness*. In the story (also reconstructed as the US/Vietnam movie *Apocalypse Now!*) Kurtz is the company envoy deep along the Congo river who has apparently taken leave of his senses and Marlow is sent from London to discover the truth and, if necessary, resolve the problem. But as the journey progresses it becomes apparent to Marlow that far from Kurtz being the individual problem, it is the company – including Marlow – and all its accompanying culture, which incorporates the real responsibility for Kurtz's descent into irrationality.

If we transport this metaphorical journey back to our leadership problem we have a very uncomfortable reflection: we may blame our own Kurtzes for leading us astray, for failing us, for beguiling us with their promises of fame and fortune or immortality in paradise amongst the angels, but it is we who have allowed our leaders to become the scapegoat and for allowing them to take the responsibility when things went well, even though it is clear that leadership is a collective not an individual achievement.

This realization about collective responsibility seems, at last, to have taken institutional root and some of the research involved in this collection reflects that connection between followers and leaders. But there is no 'party line' to be towed here and that, in itself, is a manifestation of the extraordinary complexity that sits with leadership. Only when we accept that there is no perfect or universal solution to this problem, and only when we become comfortable with the paradoxes and anxieties that this generates, we will stop fretting so much about choosing the right book before 2035 and get back to trying to make our worlds better places when we leave them than when they found us.

Templeton College   KEITH GRINT
University of Oxford

Notes on the Contributors

Jeffrey Alexander is the Richard Carl Jelinek Professor of Health Management and Policy in the School of Public Health, University of Michigan. He holds both a PhD and Master's degree in Health Services Administration from Stanford University. His teaching and research interests focus on organizational change in the health care sector, multi-institutional systems, governance of health care organizations, and physician participation in institutional management and policy-making.

Pauline Allen is a Lecturer in organizational research at the London School of Hygiene and Tropical Medicine and an academic member of the National Co-ordinating Centre for NHS Service Delivery and Organization R&D Programme. She is also qualified as a solicitor, although she no longer practices. Using economic and legal approaches, her research interests include contracts, looking at both formal and informal relationships; and professional and legal accountability.

Charlotte Ashburner is working on a three year action research project to improve care for older people in collaboration with City University, London.

Paul Bate is Professor of Health Services Management in the Medical School, University College London. A social anthropologist by background, he has long experience of working with clinicians, senior managers and staff at all levels of the NHS, as well as other leading public and private sector organizations in the UK and abroad. The main focus of his work is change, especially big change, change management and leadership development, and in these areas he has acted as consultant and policy advisor, action researcher, strategist and educator. The range of organization settings has been varied, including health service trusts – the most recent being the University College London Hospitals currently engaged in a major change project around modernization and one of the biggest Public Finance Initiatives (PFI) projects in Europe – the ILO (Geneva), Eli Lilly, BR, BP, and Gerling International (Cologne). He has been working closely with the NHS Modernization Agency, evaluating the Collaboratives (work that will now be extended to a UK/US cross-cultural project funded by the Nuffield Trust), directing the NHS Chief Executives Programme, 'Leading Change, Delivering the

Future', and working on new models for modernization based on Social Movement Theory. Paul is the author of three major books and numerous articles in top-ranked journals, and his latest book *Strategies for Cultural Change* was short-listed for the MCA Best Management Book of the Year Prize.

Joan Bloom is a Professor at the University of California, Berkeley. She has been studying the Colorado Medicaid experiment in mental health for the past 10 years. She is particularly interested in how changes in organizations affect staff and patient outcomes.

Stephen Campbell is a Research Fellow at the National Primary Care Research and Development Centre (NPCRDC), Manchester University. His research interests focus on the quality of care in general practice, including access, clinical care, practice management and user/patient evaluations as well as strategies for quality assessment and quality improvement within practices and Primary Care Trusts.

Simon Carmel is a Research Fellow in the Health Services Research Unit at the London School of Hygiene and Tropical Medicine. He is currently completing his doctoral thesis, which is an ethnographic study of the organization of work in intensive care. His research interests are in the areas of high-technology medicine, knowledge in clinical practice, inter-professional working relationships, and the application and development of qualitative approaches to health services research.

Ann F. Chou is an Assistant Professor in the School of Public and Environmental Affairs at Indiana University in Indianapolis. She studies organizational issues around implementation in mental health and cancer care delivery.

David A. Chambers is currently the Programme Official for the Dissemination and Implementation Research Programme, part of the Services Research and Clinical Epidemiology Branch at the National Institute of Mental Health (NIMH) in the United States. His work has focused on how change occurs in clinical practice, how new practices are introduced into real-world clinical settings, and how health information is disseminated to multiple audiences. Prior to his work at NIMH, Dr Chambers was a member of a research group in Oxford that evaluated several National Health Service initiatives, each aiming to translate research findings into clinical practice.

Barbara Coyle is an anthropologist with an interest in the professional sub-cultures of health care settings, and for the last five years she has worked with the Centre for Clinical Governance Research at the University of New South Wales and the Centre for Clinical Management Development at the University of Durham.

Alison Evans Cuellar is an Assistant Professor of Health Policy and Management at Columbia University in New York. Her research interests centre on organizational attempts to integrate and the affects on health service delivery, costs and quality of care.

Geraldine Cunningham Geraldine was appointed to the Royal College of Nursing in 1994 to undertake a national research study evaluating the effects of a needs-led development programme on a sample of ward leaders, senior nurses, their teams, and the quality of patient care. The research received the prestigious European Baxter Award for Excellence in Health Care Management in 1997. Geraldine is currently leading the RCN Clinical Leadership Programme, which commenced in April 1999 and is now running in over 140 organizations in 6 countries. The next phase of the work is to develop the programme across clinical teams, due to start in January 2003. She has special interest in personal development, patient narrative and observation of care.

Pieter Degeling is Professor of Health Management and Director of the Centre for Clinical Management Development at the University of Durham. Prior to 2002 he was Professor of Health Management in the School for Health Services Management at the University of New South Wales and was Foundation Director of its Centre for Clinical Governance Research. He has published extensively on health care reform, clinician management, clinical pathway development and implementation and clinical governance.

Philip Dewe is Professor of Organizational Behaviour and Head of the Department of Organizational Psychology, Birkbeck College, University of London. After a period of work in commerce in New Zealand he became a Senior Research Officer in the Work Research Unit, Department of Employment (UK). In 1980 he joined Massey University in New Zealand and headed the Department of Human Resource Management until joining the Department of Organizational Psychology, Birkbeck College, University of London in 2000. Research interests include work stress and coping, human resource management issues and the employment of the older worker.

Sue Dopson is a Fellow of Templeton College, Oxford University and teaches Organizational Behaviour at the Said Business School. She is a postgraduate tutor, teaches on Management Development programmes for various companies and works on the College's Strategic Leadership Programme. As a member of the Oxford Health Care Management Institute (OHCMI) she is involved in the development of courses for the NHS and a number of research projects, including the evaluation of projects aimed at improving clinical effectiveness, exploring issues of getting the results of medical research evidence into clinical practice, and more general research in the area of NHS management. She has published on the changes in the management of the NHS, the changing nature of middle management, management careers and developments in public-sector management.

Amanda Evans works as a part-time Research Associate for King's College, London. In the past she has held a number of senior nursing roles involved in management and practice development including the development of a pioneering intermediate care unit within an acute NHS Trust.

Naomi Fulop is a Senior Lecturer in Health Services Delivery and Organizational Research and Director of the National Co-ordinating Centre for Service Delivery and Organization R&D at the London School of Hygiene and Tropical Medicine. Dr Fulop's research interests are in the area of service delivery and organizational issues in health care, most recently on relationships between, and configurations of, health care organizations. Recent and current topics include the impact of vertical and horizontal integration of health care, learning between health care organizations, and the concept of turnaround in health care organizations.

Ben Gray has researched and published extensively on health and social care. His studies range from service evaluations to focusing on users' views in mental health, as well as refugee studies, child protection, oncology care, emotions in organizations and multiple sclerosis. Studies conducted with families, children and ethnic minorities are a key theme throughout all these projects.

Keith Grint is Director of Research at the Said Business School and Fellow of Templeton College, Oxford University, where he teaches organizational behaviour and leadership. His publications include: *The Sociology of Work: An Introduction*, Polity Press (1991), 2nd edn (1998); *The Gender–Technology Relation* (ed. with Ros Gill), Taylor & Francis (1995); *Management: A Sociological Introduction*, Cambridge: Polity Press (1995); *The Machine at Work* (with Steve Woolgar), Polity Press (1997); *Leadership* (edited), Oxford University Press (1997); *Fuzzy Management*, Oxford University Press (1997); *The Arts of Leadership*, Oxford University Press (2000); and *Work and Society: A Reader* (ed.) Polity Press (2000). He is currently completing a book on *D-Day and Leadership* and editing the *Encyclopedia of Leadership*.

David Guest is Professor of Organizational and Human Resource Management and Head of the Management Centre at King's College, London. Prior to joining King's, he was Professor of Organizational Psychology and Head of the Department of Organizational Psychology at Birkbeck College. He has written and researched extensively in the areas of human resource management, employment relations and the psychological contract, motivation and commitment, and careers. His current research is concerned with the relationship between human resource management and performance; the individualization of employment relations; flexibility and employment contracts; and the career implications of new roles and employment arrangements.

Shirley Halliwell has been a research technician at the National Primary Care Research and Development Centre (NPCRDC) since 1994, having previously worked as a market researcher. Besides clinical governance, she has contributed to research on skill mix and direct payments to disabled people, and to NPCRDC's national database.

Alexandra Harrison worked as a health care professional and manager in other provinces in Canada before joining the University of Calgary in Alberta. She is the Director of Postgraduate Medical Education at the University of Calgary and also teaches graduate courses on the health care system and health care management. Her research interests include medical education, as well as the design, management and evaluation of health care organizations and systems.

David Hunter was appointed Professor of Health Policy and Management at the University of Durham in December 1999. He previously held this title at the University of Leeds where, from 1989 to 1997, he was Director of the Nuffield Institute for Health. David's research interests lie in the management of primary care, strengthening the public health function, managing clinical work, and health care rationing. He has published widely in these fields.

Andrew Hutchings is a Lecturer in Health Services Research in the Department of Public Health and Policy, London School of Hygiene and Tropical Medicine. He has a background in management science, public finance and medical statistics and he previously worked for the Audit Commission and District Audit. His research interests include quality improvement and service delivery and organization.

Rick Iedema has published widely in the areas of social linguistics and culture change. He is a Senior Researcher in the Centre for Clinical Governance Research at the University of New South Wales and is a Senior Lecturer in the School of Community Medicine and Public Health in the Faculty of Medicine at the University of New South Wales.

John Kennedy is a statistician with an interest in social policy and the organizational change implications of health care reform. Since October 2001 he has been a Research Fellow at the Centre for Clinical Management Development at the University of Durham.

Annette King is a Senior Research Officer in the recently established Office of Government Chief Social Researcher, Strategy Unit, in the Cabinet Office. Previously, she was a Research Fellow in the Health Services Research Unit, London School of Hygiene and Tropical Medicine and the Department of Sociology, University of East London. She has worked on research in comparative social policy, on issues of organization and management of UK health services, and is currently conducting research into the use of policy pilots in Government. Her research interests include the use of qualitative research methods in social policy and evaluation approaches to public policy.

Linda Latham joined the Health Services Management Centre, University of Birmingham, in May 1999 as a Research Fellow working full-time on research and development in relation to clinical governance. Prior to this time, she enjoyed a long association with the NHS which dated back to 1976. Linda has practiced as a clinician in both primary and secondary care settings and gained experience in operational and strategic management. Linda also held a short service commission in the Princess Mary's Royal Air Force Nursing Service. More recently Linda has been involved in the commissioning and development of secondary care services in both Oxfordshire and Shropshire.

Fiona Lee is Associate Professor of Organizational Behaviour and Human Resource Management and Associate Professor of Psychology at the University of Michigan. Dr Lee holds a PhD in Social Psychology from Harvard University. Her research focuses on how complex events are understood and communicated within organizations, and how these interpretations affect working relationships, risk-taking, learning, impressions and performance.

Richard Lichtenstein is an Associate Professor in the Department of Health Management and Policy in the School of Public Health at the

University of Michigan. He received a Bachelors Degree in Industrial and Labour Relations at Cornell University and received both the Master of Public Health (MPH) and the Doctor of Philosophy (PhD) degrees in Medical Care Organization at the University of Michigan. His research focuses on health care professionals' job satisfaction and a variety of issues relating to multidisciplinary teams in health care.

Annabelle L. Mark is Professor of Health Care Organization and spent the first ten years of her career as a manager in the UK National Health Service. Since 1985 she has been working as an academic at South Bank and Middlesex Universities. She teaches organizational behaviour and health management to post-experience students. She is a Fellow of the Institute of Health Services Management, a Fellow of The Royal Society of Medicine and Research Associate of Oxford Health Care Management Institute Templeton College Oxford. Her research interest and publications include the changing professional roles in healthcare in particular doctors in the management role, demarketing and managing demand, emotion in healthcare, and the development of NHS Direct. She is also the founding academic of the conference Organizational Behaviour in Healthcare which has its fourth meeting scheduled for 2004 at the University of Calgary, Alberta.

Martin Marshall is Professor of General Practice at the National Primary Care Research and Development Centre (NPCRDC) and a part-time GP in an inner-city practice. His research interests are the policy aspects of health care quality – quality indicators in primary care, public disclosure of information about performance, and the relationship between organisational culture and quality improvement. He advises the Commission for Health Improvement, the NHS Modernization Agency, the National Clinical Assessment Authority, the National Patient Safety Agency and the National Primary Care Collaborative.

Sara Lister is the Assistant Chief Nurse, Royal Marsden Hospital, as Head of School, Royal Marsden School of Cancer Nursing and Rehabilitation. In this dual role Sara's primary purpose is to enable nurses to enhance further the care they give to individuals with cancer. As Assistant Chief Nurse she leads practice development, research, clinical audit and professional development across the Trust. This includes editing *The Royal Marsden Manual of Clinical Nursing Procedures*. As Head of School she is leading the establishment of a patient focused service-led education centre, the key purpose of which is the development of expert clinical practitioners in the specialized field of cancer care. Integral to both these roles is a commitment to supporting nurses in their own personal emotional labour. She spent two years working as a senior national facilitator with the Royal College of Nursing Clinical Leadership Programme. The experience of working across many different NHS Trusts has been good preparation for her current post leading research, practice and professional development at the Royal Marsden Hospital.

Sharyn Maxwell is an economist with an interest in the incentives required to address culture change implications of health care reform. Up until the end of 2001 she was a researcher with the Centre for Clinical Governance Research at the University of New South Wales. In March 2002 she was appointed as a Research Fellow at the Centre for Clinical Management Development, University of Durham.

Craig Mitton holds a Canadian Health Services Research Foundation Post-doctoral Fellowship. The first year of this award was taken up at the Centre for Health and Policy Studies at the University of Calgary, and the second year in the Division of Health Sciences at Curtin University, Perth, Australia. His main research interests are in priority-setting and resource allocation in health organizations, and in the economic evaluation of technologies, services and treatments.

Gale Murray is the Founding President and CEO of The Change Foundation. The Foundation, established by the Ontario Hospital Association in 1997, has a mandate to improve health and health care delivery through applied research and analysis, development and education programs and grants to charities. As hospital restructuring has been a major health care delivery change in the last few years, much of the Foundation's attention has been focused here. Gale has co-authored a number of reports on the financial position of Ontario hospitals, an assessment of hospital restructuring as well as alternative strategic paths for Ontario hospitals. Her current research interest is on demand management in health care and strategies to manage demand. Gale brings to her research broad-based public and private sector experience in health care management and planning including six years as the CEO for VON (Ontario). She has also served as the Executive Director of the Manitoulin and Sudbury District Health Council, and as the Regional Director for Extendicare for Northern Ontario. Earlier in her career worked in the Department of Social Services in New Brunswick. Gale holds a Master's degree from the University of Toronto in Political Economy and a BA from York University in Political Science.

Sue Nash is Head of Nursing and Clinical Services in one of the Nuffield Hospitals, an independent not for profit organisation. Her special interest apart from the pursuit of excellence in the provision of patient care is the personal development of clinical staff, she has had extensive experience of operational management in the public and voluntary sectors including 20 years of nurse leadership and management at ward, unit and hospital level.

Charles Normand is Professor of Health Economics at the London School of Hygiene and Tropical Medicine. His research interests centre on evaluation of service developments, ageing and health care provision, financing of services and service delivery and organization. He was a non-executive director of the Central Middlesex Hospital from 1991 to 1999. He is a co-investigator on the Department for International Development Health Systems Development Programme, working in Bangladesh, Uganda, South Africa and Russia.

Tumutual Norton has worked for over 20 years in the field of children and youth services. Previous to joining the staff of the Department of Mental Health, Mrs Norton worked for six years at the Department of Human Services, Division of Youth Services. During the past 16 years her work has focused on development of a system of care for youth with serious behavioural or emotional disorders and their families. Mrs Norton holds an undergraduate degree from Tougaloo College and an MA degree in Guidance and Counselling from Ohio State University.

Riccardo Peccei is Reader in Organizational Behaviour and Human Resource Management at King's College, London. His research interests include the study of the transformation of work and employment relations in the service sector, the impact of HRM on organizational performance and employee well-being, and the nature and consequences of employee empowerment, partnership and participation in contemporary organizations. He is currently working on the impact of organizational demography on employee satisfaction and commitment at work, on the antecedents and consequences of information disclosure, and on the continuing evaluation of the impact of the role of nurse/midwife/health visitor consultant in the NHS.

Susan Pickard is a graduate of modern history (1987) and in social anthropology (1988) from University of Oxford and holds a PhD in social anthropology from the University of Bristol (1994). She has taught and researched at the Universities of Salford, Birmingham and Manchester on various aspects of primary care delivery including quasi-markets and the role of contracts, lay involvement in decision-making and in quality, priority setting and the experience of lay care-giving.

Gerasimos Protopsaltis was a Research Fellow in the Health Services Research Unit, at the London School of Hygiene and Tropical Medicine until October 2002, working on two projects: (i) evaluating the impact of NHS trust mergers and reconfigurations in London – a process analysis of NHS provider organizations, and (ii) turnaround management situations – what lessons can be drawn from the experience of changing the management of failing organizations or those in a state of crisis. His first degree was in Sociology and Industrial Psychology at the University of Natal-Durban, from where he also holds an honour's degree in Sociology. He attained his MA in Sociology and Health Studies from the University of Essex, researching the social factors influencing adolescent suicide. His research interests centre on health service delivery and organization. He has now relocated and is working in Athens, Greece.

Sally Redfern is Professor of Nursing at King's College, London and former Director of the Nursing Research Unit at King's. She was previously Senior Lecturer in the School of Nursing and Midwifery at King's. Her research interests include service organization and delivery issues in nursing and health care, with a focus on quality of practice. Her current research is concerned with the evaluation of the role of consultant nurse/midwife/health visitor, and the processes involved in changing practice to improve quality of care and outcomes for patients and staff in health care settings for older people.

Glenn Robert is Senior Research Fellow at the Centre for Health Informatics and Multiprofessional Education at University College London. He previously worked at the Health Services Management Centre, University of Birmingham. His research interests centre on quality and service improvement in health care, with a focus on policy implementation and securing change within local health care organizations. Dr Robert is currently working on a cross-cultural research study of 'high performing' health care organizations in the UK, US and the Netherlands.

Anne Rogers is Professor of the Sociology of Health Care at the University of Manchester. Her research interests are in the sociology of mental health and illness, self-care and patient involvement in the National Health Service.

Martin Roland trained at Oxford University and entered general practice in 1979, initially in London, then Cambridge, and now in inner-city Manchester. He became Professor of General Practice at Manchester University in 1991, and Director of the National Primary Care Research and Development Centre (NPCRDC) in 1999. His research interests include quality of care, with a particular focus on developing ways of measuring and improving the quality of primary care; back pain in general practice; hospital referrals; use of time in general practice; and out of hours care.

Patrice Rosenthal is Senior Lecturer in Organizational Behaviour and Human Resource Management in the Management Centre at King's College, London. She previously worked in the Industrial Relations Department of the London School of Economics, where she was Seear Fellow in Human Resource Management. Her research interests include the changing nature of front-line service work, with a focus on the design and impact of quality interventions in service organizations. She has also written on gender and management. She is currently researching customer orientation in public-sector organizations.

Brenda Scafidi is Director of the Division of Children and Youth Services at the Department of Mental Health. Dr Scafidi has worked for 37 years in the fields of education and mental health in Mississippi, Florida and Louisiana. She has taught elementary through university levels and administered school and other related services and programmes in Mississippi, Louisiana and Florida for children and youth with a variety of special needs. For the past 20 years her work has focused on youth with serious behavioural or emotional disorders and their families. Dr Scafidi holds a Doctoral degree in special education from USM, a Master's degree in remedial/clinical reading from USM, and a Bachelor's degree in elementary education from MUW.

Rod Sheaff is a researcher in health policy and organization at the National Primary Care Research and Development Centre (NPCRDC) University of Manchester. His main current research interest is in health system reform and policy implementation. He has worked as researcher, educator and consultant in various health systems, especially in central and eastern Europe. His background in political theory gives him a wider interest in the New Public Management and the political economy of the public sector, which his books *Responsive Healthcare* and the *Need for Healthcare* reflect.

Bonnie Sibbald was born in Canada and trained as a human geneticist at McGill, Queens and London Universities, before moving into research in British general practice. She is Professor of Health Services Research and Deputy Director of the National Primary Care Research and Development Centre (NPCRDC), University of Manchester. Her interest in health care organization and delivery in general practice currently focuses on the general practice workforce, in particular skill mix and general practitioner recruitment, retention and distribution. In 1996 she was made an Honorary Fellow of the Royal College of General Practitioners for her contribution to the development of academic general practice.

Pam Smith is Professor of Nurse Education and Director of the Centre for Research in Nursing and Midwifery Education at Surrey University. Pam's teaching and research interests are in emotions, care and organizations; health promotion, primary care and inner-city regeneration; chronic illness management; education of health and social care professionals; qualitative research methodologies and practicipatory research methods. She is co-convenor of the emotional labour research interest group and ESRC seminar series with Dr Stephen Smith, Brunel University, Professor Michael Rustin, University of East London, and Dr Del Loewenthal, University of Surrey.

Stephen Lloyd Smith is a member of the School of Business and Management at Brunel University, where his teaching includes a long-standing module in the management of emotional labour. He is also part of the Centre for Research in Emotion Work (CREW). He and Pam Smith have co-organized several workshops and conferences in emotional labour, linking Brunel, South Bank University, the University of East London, Surrey University and Warwick University. Recent publications include 'Arlie Hochschild: Soft Spoken Conservationist of Emotions', 'The Theology of Emotion', 'Towards a Manifesto for Feelings' and 'If you Love your Work, Do you thank a Careers Counsellor?' (with Fiona Douglas), published in *Soundings* (issues 11 and 20), and 'Emotion and Labour in Cultural Comparison' in M. Stroinska (ed.) (2001) *relative Points of View; Linguistic Representations of Culture*, Oxford: Berghahan Books.

Peter Spurgeon is Professor of Health Services Management at the Health Services Management Centre, University of Birmingham. He is a previous Director of the Centre and is now Director of Organizational Development and Leadership. He has particular interests in service reconfiguration and the role of clinicians in management. He has led HSMC's three-year research study into the implementation of clinical governance in secondary and primary care trusts.

Sharon Topping is an Associate Professor of Management at the University of Southern Mississippi. She recently was a NIMH Post-Doctoral Fellow at the Cecil G. Sheps Center for Health Services Research at the University of North Carolina-Chapel Hill and the Duke Medical School. Prior to receiving her PhD in Health Care Administration at the University of Alabama at Birmingham, she had over 15 years experience in the accounting and consulting business. Dr Topping has published numerous papers, chapters and cases in management and health care journals and books, and has been principle investigator or co-investigator on a number of NIH grants. She is currently principal investigator on a National Institute of Mental Health grant examining the use of multidisciplinary, interagency teams to coordinate mental health services for children and youth particularly in rural areas.

Rhiannon Walters is a specialist in public health and health promotion with skills in research methods and epidemiology. She specializes in health policy, bringing evidence-based interventions into practice, and the evaluation of complex multi-sectoral interventions. She was Information Officer at the Faculty of Public Health Medicine from 1989 to 1996, worked for the consultancy London Health Economics Consortium to 1996, where she specialized in public health and health promotion projects, and has worked independently since 1999.

Rebecca Wells is an Assistant Professor in the Department of Health Policy and Administration at Penn State. Dr Wells holds both a Master's in health services administration and a PhD from the University of Michigan. Her research interests focus on both internal and inter-organizational sources of knowledge diversity within organizations, particularly health care providers that serve vulnerable populations.

Jenifer Wilson-Barnett is Professor and Head of the School of Nursing and Midwifery, King's College, London, Fellow of the Royal College of Nursing and Fellow of King's College. After being a medical ward sister and completing her PhD, she became the first Lecturer in Nursing at the University of London (Chelsea College) and was awarded a Chair in 1986 at King's College, London. Her work includes research on psychological care for people with chronic disorders, providing nurses with skills to support patients and families, and evaluating new and expanding roles for nurses.

Mark Winters is a freelance anthropologist with an interest in identity and culture. For the last three years he has worked with the Centre for Clinical Governance Research at the University of New South Wales and the Centre for Clinical Management Development at the University of Durham.

Introduction

This is the third book arising from the third International Conference on Organizational Behaviour and Health Care. The original purpose of the Conference is to offer a forum for people working in the field to meet and discuss their work in specific terms, as well as debate broader yet related issues such as the use of methodology and research design in health care studies. In the preface to the first volume of this series (Mark and Dopson, 1997), Rosemary Stewart, a founding academic in the field noted:

> there is little sense of a developing body of knowledge in health care management, which starts from early research that is recognized as the foundation for later work, and from which major new developments can be traced.

The most recent conference in this series, held at the Saïd Business School, University of Oxford, offers reasons to be more cheerful. The papers selected for inclusion in this book are characterized by a concern to use existing literature and theory to inform writing, and a willingness to be explicit about research design and methods used. The conference was organized around the theme of leadership in health care. It sought to attract international contributors and papers that addressed three areas:

- *The nature of leadership in health care.* Who occupies the role? What predisposes this fact? Is it for example, profession, personality or politics?
- *Leading health care organizations.* Are they different? if so can we determine any commonalities which make them so? , and to what extent is this information transferable?
- *Taking health care forward in the twenty-first century.* What will be the context of healthcare delivery in the future? Will leadership change the culture or will the culture change the leadership required?

The Parts of the book are organized around these themes, and a brief summary of each chapter is given below.

The nature of leadership in health care

Rod Sheaff and colleagues suggest that English GPs continue to regard leadership by fellow doctors as a lesser evil than managerial leadership. They go on to argue that professional networks continue to influence GPs more than general managers. Indeed professional leaders are adopting increasingly active forms of professional self-regulation to preempt managerial encroachment.

Stephen Smith and his colleagues consider the problems of leading the Royal College of Nursing (RCN) leadership programme through its rapid development to a clearer understanding of what it does, rather than just what it says it does. This is advanced by introducing and facilitating ideas around communication of emotion. In particular the chapter considers the nature of feelings which enable aspects of the leadership programme to be explored via the non cognitive to arrive at new understandings about the programme and how it can be discussed and advanced further. It makes explicit the high level of the non-cognitive which needs to be explored if a true understanding of leadership is to be embraced.

Rebecca Wells and her colleagues focus on the nature of leadership in mental health care. Mental health has long relied on interdisciplinary treatment teams to deliver complex services, effectively dispersing leadership across a diverse range of individuals. The diversity of these teams is both an asset and a challenge, as some members may react to differences by disengaging from group processes. In the chapter, two theories are used to examine variation in individual staff member integration within interdisciplinary teams: social identity and status characteristics. A sample of US Veterans Administration (VA) psychiatric teams is the context for examining how demographics affected who engaged in team decisions – who spoke up and were rewarded for their contributions – and who receded. This study implies that relational demography needs to consider the status connotations of comparisons as well as to incorporate both their local and societal bases. These insights will help managers understand how to empower people to lead at all levels of the organization.

Peter Spurgeon's chapter considers leadership in the context of the implementation of clinical governance in the British NHS. It locates the definition and development of clinical governance as part of the agenda to improve quality in health care. The two key innovations in this policy are summarized as, increased visibility and accountability now vested in the role of the Chief Executive. Two examples of implementation are then briefly described in relation to the transactional and transformational leadership model. It is argued that while the requirements of the latter style are understood and accepted by the leaders concerned, problems with implementation are shown to relate to a lack of transactional activity.

Simon Carmels' contribution presents an ethnographic analysis of an intensive care unit (ICU) and considers inter-professional working and clinical leadership in this setting. Close examination of medical work in this area suggests that clinical leadership in the ICU is provided by the consultant clinicians' ability to manage organizational and clinical uncertainty, and to encourage and train other staff in such management. More specifically, Carmel provides rich ethnographic material to suggest ways in which consultants demonstrate their leadership in both transactional and transformational ways.

Leading health care organizations

Bate and Robert consider the knowledge management practices of leading private-sector organizations and assess their likely relevance to those leading NHS reform. They raise many questions about what the NHS must do to encourage the growth and development of communities of practice and to ignite the spontaneous informal processes that create the energy for successful change efforts. Whilst the literature on knowledge management suggests that knowledge dissemination and transferability only occur when there is a collective identity, and the existence of a wider social network, the research on NHS collaboratives discussed in the paper suggests neither seem to be fully present. Collaboratives are discussed as 'information rich but knowledge poor'.

In recent years, multidisciplinary, interagency teams have become an important strategy used to coordinate services, particularly in the delivery of mental health care. Despite this importance, little is known about how these teams operate and what makes them effective. Topping and colleagues set out an in-depth, three-year exploratory study. The chapter reports on the first year's findings. The focus is on multidisciplinary, interagency teams used to coordinate services to children and youth with serious emotional disorders in Mississippi. This chapter identifies factors that facilitate and hinder the operation of these teams, while also developing a conceptual model specific to multidisciplinary, interagency teams. A major contribution of the work is a better understanding of the input characteristics, pattern of relationships, and types of process behaviours that are needed for these teams to become effective and take a lead. In so doing, it provides valuable information to those managing health care organizations in the twenty-first century on how to better use teams to coordinate services and provide effective care.

Degeling and colleagues' chapter compares the Australian and UK experiences of implementing health care reform over the last 20 years to bridge the promised performance gap. A useful exploration of leadership definitions and policy purpose shows some theoretical as well as practical contradictions, arising in part from an over instrumental approach to both. However it is through an experimental exploration of the role of followership that some explanations prove more forthcoming, in particular the understanding that differing professional groups impose a differential set of expectations on their leader/managers, which these leaders know they ignore at their peril. It is argued that attempts to change perceptions of these groups has fallen on deaf ears because of a failure to understand the webs of meaning associated with both roles and contexts.

The problems of leading health care through the challenge of changes to resource distribution are explored in the chapter by Harrison. Two case studies of attempts to implement Programme Budgeting and Marginal Analysis (PBMA) in the reorganized health care systems of Alberta in Canada, are described. The analysis of the cases highlights the organizational behaviour aspects of a PBMA 'Calgary' framework that have emerged from this research project. The findings have parallels in international comparisons of the PBMA resource allocation process as well as lessons that are relevant to understanding leadership in health care organizations. These are most notably the need for a willingness to make decisions sometimes in spite of, rather than because of, the evidence which is only ever partial. This must be supported by the teams involved, who need an interest in the outcomes, which are led by an appropriate champion with a clear implementation brief.

Taking health care forward in the twenty-first century

The changing role boundaries in nursing are explored in Sally Redfern and her colleagues' chapter, which sets out the UK experience in introducing Consultant posts in nursing. The research reported is based on an evaluation of the first 32 posts in the UK. What becomes evident as the project proceeds is the similarity in objectives and outlines which has been experienced before in attempts to enhance the role of nurses, notably after the Salmon Report in the 1960s. Differing definitions and expectations of the role both within the profession and from other stakeholders, notably those within the organization, are leading to role confusion and overload. However, the need to address opportunities for career progression in the profession is supported by the calibre of recruits willing to take the risk. What is emphasized to the reader, is the continued internal professional focus for the role when, in fact, some organizational leadership rather than just professional leadership for its implementation may be required.

Chamber's and Dopson's chapter analyses a series of evidence-based change projects in the US and the UK in an effort to understand the influences on leading the implementation of change in health care settings. The authors explore the concept of evidence-based medicine and the underlying assumptions. The chapter develops the conceptual model used to explore change associated with the work of Pettigrew, Ferlie and McKee (1992). Significantly, the chapter reminds us of the complexity of leading changes in health care settings where a key part of that leadership challenge is leading health care professionals.

Murray points out that it is difficult for leaders to know where and when an innovation will occur. In response to this dilemma, a number of countries' health jurisdictions and organizations have utilized the development of scenarios to assist a better understanding of the future of health services. She documents a scenario system used in Ontario, Canada. From these scenarios she considers what hospital enterprises of the future might look like and the leadership challenges that ensue. These scenarios include: reformed cathedral, focus factory, mall, broker, and fire-station models. The strengths and potential difficulties of each model are explored.

Fulop's chapter reviews a programme of mergers of health care organizations in the UK which arose as part of the government's new agenda following their election in 1997. There are no real surprises in the findings so far, that mergers are disruptive, dubious of purpose and fail to improve or even maintain service outcomes at least in the short and medium term. (Cautionary warnings to this effect from Alan Langlands the Chief Executive of the NHS at the time of their introduction fell on deaf ears.) The reasons may be that the motives and agendas of the various stakeholders include what the chapter terms 'unstated drivers' which have political and individual purpose at odds with organizational and patients' interests. The leadership skills in these circumstances may be more about leading away from such strategies as through them.

Cuellar's chapter considers the development of appropriate organizational forms for community mental health services in Colorado, USA, and compares different types of financing and contracting arrangements to improve effectiveness. Many of the issues raised by these alternative models are reminiscent of similar issues faced by the UK NHS. The data generated by the research indicates that from the employees' point of view, such changes do not result in any radical changes to perception about their work or role, or that of the organizations through which they provide care. It seems unlikely, therefore, that such changes will impact positively upon the client group, thus questioning the relevance of assumptions about organizational learning and effectiveness through such instrumental approaches.

We asked Keith Grint to consider the concept of leadership and its importance in the Foreword to this book. Reflecting on this volume of chapters, Grint concludes that the realization about collective responsibility seems to have taken institutional root, and that the research documented in subsequent chapters reflects the connection between followers and leaders. He concludes that only if we accept that there is no universal solution to the problem of leadership and the paradoxes and anxieties this generates can we get back to trying to make our worlds better places when we leave them, than when they found us.

Grint reminds us that there is no shortage of texts in this area, indeed he estimates some 10,398 books exist. There is, however, a profound lack of clarity about the term leadership. Stogdill (1974) points out 'there are almost as many definitions of leadership as there are persons who have attempted to define the concept'. Simply put, leadership research findings are characterized by those who are optimistic and see that there are well-established contributions to our knowledge. These include the two categories of leader behaviour – interpersonal relations, and task accomplishment; there is no ideal leader personality and different situations require different leader behaviours. There are, however, those who are more pessimistic, such as Quinn (1980):

> Despite the immense investment in the enterprise, researchers have become increasingly disenchanted with the field. The seemingly endless display of unconnected empirical investigations is bewildering as well as frustrating.

This is perhaps because there is a growing realization that the contextual aspects of leading, as demonstrated through the three themes explored in this book, is where the road to better understanding lies (Spreitzer and Cummings, 2001).

We hope this edited collection is not just adding more paper to the debate, but that as a result of reading it you feel more able to reflect on the undoubted complexity of leading in health care settings.

References

Mark, A. and Dopson, S. (1997) *Organisational Behaviour in Health Care: The Research Agenda* (Basingstoke: Macmillan – now Palgrave Macmillan).

Quinn, J. B. (1980) *Strategies for Change: Logical Incrementalism* (Homewood, IL: Irwin).

Pettigrew, A., McKee, L. and Ferlie, E. (1992) *Shaping Strategic Change* (New York: Sage).

Spreitzer, G. M. and Cummings, T. G. (2001) 'The Leadership Challenges of the Next Generation in the Future of Leadership', in W. Bennis, G. M. Spreitzer and T. G. Cummings (eds), The Future of Leadership (San Francisco: Jossey-Bass).

Stogdill, R. M. (1974) *Handbook of Leadership: A Survey of Theory and Research* (New York: Free Press).

Acknowledgements

The following people served on the conference advisory panel and were involved in the refereeing process for contributions now appearing in this book:

Professor Ewan Ferlie, Imperial College, London
Professor Louise Fitzgerald, De Montfort University
Professor John Gabbay, University of Southampton
Dr Louise Locock, Department of Social Policy and Social Work, University of Oxford
Dr Rosemary Stewart, Templeton College, Oxford

We are particularly grateful to Stephan Gant, Templeton College, who provided invaluable administrative support, and Marilyn Lyne, the conference organizer at the Saïd Business School, University of Oxford in compiling this book. We are also grateful to all those who took part in what was a successful third conference, the chapter contributors for their patience with us as editors, and their work dealing with copyright clearance.

Part I

The Nature of Leadership

1
Medical Leadership in English Primary Care Networks

Rod Sheaff, Anne Rogers, Susan Pickard, Martin Marshall, Stephen Campbell, Martin Roland, Bonnie Sibbald and Shirley Halliwell

Leadership in the medical domain has an ambivalent character. On one hand, salaried doctors (for example, hospital doctors in Germany, most Scandinavian primary care doctors) are members of organizational hierarchies whose top-level leaders are lay managers and policy-makers, even if that leadership control is mediated through senior medical managers (for example, a Clinical Director, *Chefarzt* or *Glavvrach*). Where doctors work under contract to a public body (for example, British and Italian GPs), sick-fund (*Kassenärzte* in Germany and their equivalents in the Netherlands, France, Belgium and other EU countries) or commercial insurer (in Switzerland, USA), these bodies are formally the contract principal and the doctors their agents. Either way, the doctor is formally subordinate to lay 'leaders'. On the other hand, such leadership as lay managers can exercise through these channels coexists with a professional leadership, organizing their fellow-professionals through an independent professional network. Typically these professional networks comprise national and local organizations for professional registration, quality and ethical control, education and negotiations with government and payers; and individual subscribers. This professional leadership has in many health systems greater influence over rank-and-file doctors than lay leaders of the doctors' employing or sub-contracting bodies do. Many governments have tried to incorporate these professional networks into the aforementioned health system governance structures under lay leadership (Freidson, 1994; Johnson *et al.*, 1995; Stacey, 1992; Starr and Immergut, 1987; Harrison and Dowswell, 2002; Thompson, 1987). The professional network assists in implementing public policy, in particular regulating the quality and probity of doctors' practice, in return for legal privileges, material benefits and governmental non-interference in its internal affairs.

Recently another kind of network has appeared in health systems alongside the medical professional network. Provider networks are a way of managing services which, although public-funded, are jointly provided by several separate public bodies or a mix of public and private organizations. Such provider networks exist in housing, education, social care, public transport and health care (Kickert *et al.*, 1997) in Europe and North America. In health care, local professional networks are also drawn into such provider networks as one component. Primary Care Groups (PCGs) and Primary Care Trusts (PCTs) in England are an instance. They are charged with coordinating local networks of health care organizations, including general practices, so as to ensure provision of NHS primary health services in compliance with national health policy. Such developments raise the question of how the relationship between professional and lay leaderships in these new provider networks differs from that in hierarchical and contractual contexts. Accordingly, this chapter compares one account of how professional leadership occurs in a bureaucracy with evidence about how medical leadership is exercised in English PCGs and PCTs. Insofar as similar professional networks and provider networks are found in other health systems, the comparison may suggest implications for them too.

A social grouping can be defined as having a leadership insofar as a distinct subset of its members (the leaders) formulate policies and succeed in inducing the other members (the followers) to adopt and implement them, and to regard the leaders' role as legitimate. Then, managers can be defined as a specific kind of leader; those whose capacity to lead others stems from occupancy of 'middle' or 'high' positions in a formal organizational hierarchy. A professional leadership are those who *de facto* influence their colleagues' practice, whether or not through a formal line-management relationship. One account of professional leadership in a bureaucracy that is relevant to modern health systems is the theory of 'soft bureaucracy' (Jermier *et al.*, 1991; Courpasson, 1997, 1998, 1999, 2000). Jermier *et al.*, define 'soft bureaucracy' as 'an organization with a rigid exterior appearance symbolizing what key stakeholders expect but with a loosely-coupled set of interior practices' (1991, p. 170). Soft bureaucracy combines two elements: managers retain the capacity to exercise 'hard' governance, but 'soft' management practices attenuate and legitimate it in specific ways. That description certainly applies to the ways that leadership over doctors is exercised in many health systems.

In most health systems, general (that is lay) managers have powers of 'hard' governance over non-professionals. Managers can exercise leadership through local hierarchical supervision, by standardizing ('normalizing') working procedures and through payments and penalties, above all those which employees' contracts of employment provide for (Courpasson, 1997). They can dismiss staff. Nevertheless, subordinates consciously accept managerial domination as rational because they believe they will benefit from the resulting organizational efficiency. Even when hard governance is exercised, therefore, 'the problem of organizational leaders is to elaborate and reproduce specific sources of legitimacy within a 'bureaucratic' form of governance' (Courpasson, 2000, pp. 141–2).

Soft bureaucracies take this aspect of leadership much further; 'Organizations have not renounced the use of coercion for governing, but they apply it through different media, where power is systematically legitimized.' (Courpasson, 2000, p. 157). In soft bureaucracies, leadership has two main components. Firstly, leaders legitimate their leadership in not one but three specific ways:

1 a 'political' legitimation based on the subordinates' voluntary renunciation of power to managers as under 'hard' governance; but also
2 an instrumental legitimation, arguing that managerial decisions promote the organization's broad aims, which all organizational members accept; and
3 what Courpasson calls a 'liberal' legitimation in terms of surviving external threats.

Liberal legitimation is the basis of what Courpasson calls 'soft coercion'. Soft coercion consists of representing external threats to the organization's survival – typically, competitive threats – as necessitating and legitimating decisions (for example, to change working practices) which although disagreeable to employees will ensure the organization survives.

So far as professionals are concerned, the other method of leadership is what Courpasson (2000, p. 151) calls 'flexible corporatism'. General managers try to apply various managerial tools to professional work: more transparent definitions of professional success and failure, enabling individual performance appraisal; and assigning tasks, objectives and rewards individually to professionals. They do so, however, through intermediaries who have the necessary technical knowledge and legitimacy. The 'best' professional is made head of department with relatively weak powers over her co-professionals, functioning in a boundary role between general managers and rank-and-file members of her profession (Ferlie *et al.*, 1996). Leaders of local professional networks are eminently suitable candidates for such positions. Thus, although some health care professions are largely insulated from hard governance, '[managerial] domination remains possible and efficient, providing it is combined with the soft acceptance of a limited autonomy of experts' (Courpasson, 2000, p. 152).

All this presupposes bureaucratic governance structures. However, English GPs' wariness of entering salaried NHS employment and the power of their professional organizations made it politically impossible to establish PCGs (and subsequently PCTs) as anything other than provider networks. Although every general practice must be a member of its local PCG/T, most general practices remain organizationally independent, working under contract to the Department of Health not the PCG/T (although the PCG/T does reimburse most of their spending on buildings and support staff). PCGs had a Board and managerial infrastructure with the task of coordinating primary care and implementing government policy in primary care through, above all, general practices. At national level, GPs' professional networks were powerful enough to win GPs the right to elect the Board chair and the majority of members (the minority includes at least one nurse, social services and lay members). All PCGs had a clinical governance lead (usually a GP), as does each general practice. A PCG was thus a strongly professionalized network of general practices, other health care providers and health-related organizations (for example social services).

All PCGs have now (2003) become Primary Care Trusts (PCTs), the first 17 being established in 2000. The PCG Board retains its former composition and role but is renamed the 'Professional Executive'. It becomes accountable to a new body appointed by central government and called (confusingly) the PCT Board. PCTs have the option to make locally negotiated 'Personal Medical Services' (PMS) contracts with the independent GPs in their territory and to employ salaried GPs. However almost all GPs remain self-employed at present.

PCG/Ts have been called upon to implement 'Clinical Governance' (CG), a set of policies intended to level up the quality of clinical practice and establish firm organizational bases for regulating the quality of care. It greatly supplements a more traditional means of quality control (for example, professional licensing, patient complaints systems, negligence litigation (Dingwall and Fenn, 1992)) also found in many other health systems. National Service Frameworks (NSFs) stipulate minimum clinical standards and service availability for specific care groups (for example diabetics, elderly people), starting with coronary heart disease (Department of Health, 2000a) and mental health (Department of Health, 2000b). There will be regular appraisal and revalidation of NHS doctors, largely on the basis of their educational activities since their last revalidation, and arrangements for identifying doctors 'whose performance gives cause for concern' (Department of Health, 2000c). Clinical governance in English PCGs and PCTs thus offers opportunities to explore how medical leadership occurs and what relationships between medical leadership and general management exist within a provider network.

The following account draws upon case studies of six PCGs and six PCTs during 2000. Semi-structured interviews of key informants at PCG or PCT level were triangulated with documentary evidence (managerial reports, organization charts, administrative data, maps), national policy documents, the English National Primary Care R&D Centre's database and Tracker survey of PCG/Ts (Wilkin *et al.*, 2000). As concrete activities to compare across the sites, we focused on implementation of the NSFs for coronary heart disease (CHD) and mental health. The former is specific, detailed and leaves little scope for local interpretation or discretion in how it is implemented. The mental health NSF is rather the opposite. The resulting descriptions show how general managers and professional leaders said they were *attempting* to lead local rank-and-file GPs. Whether they actually succeeded in changing GPs' clinical practice is another matter and the subject of ongoing research. Sites differed in how far they extended the clinical governance of primary health care into mental health services; whether R&D activities were included; and how far nursing and lay representatives participated in clinical governance. However, PCG/Ts' overall organizational framework, legal personality and basic institutional structures, both managerial and professional, are stipulated in legislation and policy guidance and are nationally uniform. That warrants the cautious analytic generalization (Yin, 1989) that the patterns of leadership seen in the study sites are likely to be found in other English PCG/Ts.

Clinical leadership in PCGs and PCTs

The leadership stratum in PCG/Ts consists of the PCG Board or PCT Professional Executive (as the case may be). General practitioner (GP) doctors are the most powerful group, followed by NHS managers (Wilkin *et al.*, 2000). This leadership had typically already been active in medical audit or GP fundholding. It was selected by other GPs, often in behind-the-scenes negotiations which made the formal elections to the PCG Board a forgone conclusion (Sheaff *et al.*, 2002). It included a clinical governance 'lead' GP and a clinical governance group or committee. All the study PCG/Ts also had a prescribing subcommittee. Because prescribing was everywhere a major clinical governance issue, the clinical governance lead was invariably a member. They also coopted existing GP groups (for example, locality groups, medical audit groups, former fundholder networks) for clinical governance purposes. Around this core were two peripheries. The inner periphery consisted of all GPs; whilst membership of the outer periphery was less stable. It varied for work concerning coronary heart disease, prescribing, mental health services, services for other care groups or negotiating with NHS hospital and community health services trusts, making some groups, organizations and (non-medical) individuals 'semi-detached' from the network.

GP leaders had few means, however, for exercising power and creating obedience through hierarchical supervision, coercing or punishing uncooperative GPs (for example, by financially penalizing them). Unlike nursing and paramedical staff, only a handful of salaried doctors (mainly in community and psychiatric services, and locums) are directly employed by PCTs. In the absence of any formal hierarchical relationship with most GPs, one might have expected PCTs to use locally-negotiated relational contracts as a substitute, effectively constituting line-management arrangements under another name (Bennet and Ferlie, 1996). However, PMS contracts were not used that way in the study sites. Neither were other payments (for example, reimbursement of expenses) used to influence clinical governance activity at practice level.

Nevertheless, leadership activities fitting the description of 'soft governance' were found, sometimes in attenuated forms. Although the evidence-based medicine is underdeveloped in primary care, some clinical management norms (that is impersonal definitions of acceptable standards of clinical practice) besides the first two NSFs did exist, promulgated mainly by the Department of Health, NICE, the Cochrane Centre, Royal Colleges and other national expert bodies. (Other NSFs have since appeared.) GPs preferred the more prescriptive, specific cardiac NSF (see below) and had done much more to implement it than its mental health counterpart. Insofar as relevant management norms existed, managers were in a weak position to apply them. The main obstacle was GPs' unreceptiveness to what they perceived as *managerial* norms. Instead, CG leads encouraged GPs to adopt self-imposed targets (for example, site B encouraged GPs to write their own SSRI (venlafaxine) prescribing guidelines). The same applied to management tools. Existing audit and education activities, including the Medical Audit Advisory Groups created in 1990, were relabelled as 'clinical governance' or reconstituted as part of Personal or Practice Development Plans. Clinical audit was the main clinical governance technique but several sites also participated in the National Primary Care Collaboratives, a set of regional networks aimed at promoting 'best practice' in specific clinical tasks. Multi-PCG/T clinical audits also occurred, especially for coronary heart disease. Clinical governance leads encouraged GPs to volunteer for particular projects (for example, developing new clinical protocols or referral routes).

As for assigning tasks, objectives and rewards on an individual basis, the study PCG/Ts were just starting to develop local indicators of individual clinicians' work performance. A typical report was:

we did a baseline survey of all twenty-six practices, that involved quite a detailed questionnaire, half day visit to every practice and that was primarily action just to communicate with practices, to support the lead within each practice and to look at what resources there were. Not, not really standards of care, but more things based around clinical risk, I guess, and then [we] came up with one or two recommendations. (CGL, site E)

Likewise:

now there is an agreement that all CG audit data will be made available to all of the PCT team. Practices get a PCT average and 20 sets of scores (one for each practice in the PCT) with their own data identified. So the CG lead knows who is lagging behind. (CGL, site I)

By making the quality of clinical practice more transparent, PCG/Ts were enabling individual GPs to benchmark their own practice against that of other local GPs. CG leads' regular visits to individual practices were an important occasion for discussing such matters and if necessary utter the 'quiet word' of warning which Rosenthal (1995) and others describe. Overt competition between individual GPs was not in evidence. Such individual rewards and penalties as existed were the subtle incentives of peer pressure and of comparison with colleagues.

All three forms of legitimation which Courpasson attributes to soft bureaucracies were evident, but in distinctive forms. Both documents and CG leads themselves tended to represent clinical governance tasks in very instrumental, problem-solving terms, assuming that deviations from evidence-based guidelines, especially for coronary heart disease, would be clinically and scientifically indefensible. CG leads told us that most GPs found the coronary NSF easy to comply with and saw the reasons for it. Several said that their PCG/T already met its requirements. Mental health was another matter. That NSF seemed less familiar and: 'not necessarily woollier, but obviously much less...immediately directive. The mental health one wasn't quite so obvious' (CG lead, site E).

One NSF had clearer instrumental legitimacy than the other. Despite their initial tendency to see clinical governance as a threat, CG leads in several sites also argued much as follows:

> I think people [GPs] are less worried about [clinical] audit than they used to be. They used to see it very much as a threat, whereas now they actually see it as a means to an end...as a means of determining where they are and how, where they should be getting to, how far from the ideal they are. (CGL, site B)

Although clinical governance was legitimated in strongly instrumental terms, these terms were the technical, health effects of 'good' clinical practice not its contribution to other government or NHS management objectives.

Nevertheless, local clinical governance priorities generally reflected the most heavily nationally promoted policy initiatives, a fact which respondents explained by saying that national policies coincided with local health needs and priorities anyway. Our respondents expressed a variant of what Courpasson calls 'liberal legitimation' of clinical governance activity, arguing that GPs feared the 'threat' of NHS management 'policing' GPs' work:

> I think people [GPs] perceive the sort of wider government agenda as being much more about policing and...about holding people to account, and making doctors, or all clinicians really, act in certain ways and limiting clinical freedom. (CGL, site E)

Elsewhere:

> you see the government and the Region and leads all talk about no blame culture and yet every week there's something in the newspaper about this doctor did that and he's been struck off and this doctor's done that and he's going to be. So, the words from one side

and what we actually experience on a daily basis are not the same. (CGL, site M)

Some GPs reportedly reacted with scepticism and passive resistance: 'We do have practices who see it [clinical governance] as policing and who resist that to some extent' (CGL site D). In three sites, informants suggested that CG leads' visits to practices were not always welcome and that some practices fobbed off clinical governance leads with specious reports of clinical governance activity. We were told that sceptics or disengaged GPs were generally a minority, often of older GPs, although in site I, the largest practice in the PCT was described as sceptical.

A form of soft coercion was occurring. Several clinical governance leads and managers predicted that if GPs did not implement clinical governance voluntarily, the government would intervene more directly. As evidence they cited the numerous national policy initiatives relating to clinical quality (for example, the formation of NICE) and the extensive mass-media reports of serious failures in the medical self-regulation of clinical quality and safety (Klein, 1998). CG leads represented their own clinical governance policies as a 'filter' or 'buffer' protecting GPs from heavy-handed government and NHS management interventions, tacitly contrasting their own clinical governance proposals with a vague threat of worse alternatives. In these circumstances most (but not all) GPs were willing to share some of their decision-making with GPs in other practices and the PCG/T clinical governance lead.

PCG/Ts were also constructing a 'political' legitimation for their leadership. Their initial focus was simply on setting up the clinical governance network itself, consolidating the GPs' trust in other GPs, in clinical governance activity and CG leads:

> written down on paper in answer is that the priority areas we've chosen for clinical governance are coronary heart disease and mental health. I think the truer answer would be to say that the first priority for [site D] PCT in terms of clinical governance is co-operation and involvement. (CGL, site D)

Clinical governance leads went to some lengths to make the performance comparisons mentioned above non-threatening, encouraging self-criticism rather than external criticism of their work where possible, publishing 'success stories' alongside reports of problems, and keeping the latter anonymous or confidential (so that each doctor could compare his own work compared with others' but not identify other doctors' performance scores individually). To influence GPs' clinical practice they relied heavily on training, education and regular study sessions, financed by earmarked payments from the English Department of Health, because these activities were seen as practically helpful to GPs, not threatening. Our respondents repeatedly described clinical governance activities as being self-managed by GPs themselves. GPs were willing to legitimate a local medical leadership and renounce some of their power to it, but not the leadership of NHS managers. The political legitimation of clinical governance thus harnessed a specific occupational culture rather than an organizational culture (cf. Trice and Beyer, 1991).

Reflections and implications

These case studies suggest certain trajectories of change in the nature of leadership in English general practice. National professional bodies (the Royal College of General Practitioners, BMA, GMC) are not becoming any less active; indeed the methods of evidence-based medicine are being developed largely by these bodies and agencies such as NICE whose membership partly overlaps with them. Local professional networks, however, are strengthening themselves more. There, more comprehensive, continual, active and directive leadership activities are focusing on everyday clinical practice for the largest care groups. They greatly extend local professional leaders' earlier repertoire of limited, sporadic audits, educational activities and *ad hoc* responses to political events and the occasional lapse in medical ethics. Everyday clinical practice is becoming more open to local medical leaders' scrutiny. The spread of evidence-based medicine helps local professional leaders both to undertake this scrutiny and to legitimate it in technical, clinical terms.

   Leadership in medicine retains its ambivalent character. During the 1990s a stratum of professional leaders (the medical directors) mediating between general managers and rank-and-file doctors emerged in English NHS hospitals (Ferlie *et al.*, 1996) and abroad (on Canada, see Coburn *et al.*, 1997). English GPs continue to regard leadership by fellow doctors as a lesser evil than managerial leadership, and professional networks still influence them more than general managers, the nominal leaders of the NHS, do. As general managers attempt to strengthen their own leadership over medical activity, local professional leaders have to adopt increasingly active forms of professional self-regulation to preempt managerial 'encroachment'. Professional leadership then consists of some professionals exercising soft governance over others. Restratification is central to this process (Freidson, 1984; Coburn *et al.*, 1997) because co-professional leaders have a legitimacy in the eyes of GPs which general (lay) managers lack. But in becoming more transparent to local medical leaders' scrutiny, GPs' medical practice is also becoming more transparent, at one remove, to the general managers.

There appears to be a tendency for both lay and professional leadership in health care to be exercised increasingly through 'soft bureaucratic' methods, but in specific forms. Professional leadership relies heavily upon all three forms of legitimation. Its instrumental legitimation emphasizes clinical rather than managerial or public policy ends. Political legitimation takes the form of legitimation of local professional leaders rather than general managers. Professional leadership rests partly on soft coercion and thus 'liberal' legitimation, but the external threat that it invokes is a real or imaginary threat to professional autonomy, working conditions and financial interests, not commercial competition. Although indicators of individual work performance, and management norms and tools are underdeveloped in primary care, that position is changing. In the absence of competition between doctors, the benchmarking of clinical activity serves as a surrogate. By exposing the individual doctor's working conduct more fully to the increasingly collectivized professional leaders' 'gaze', benchmarking also helps establish a discipline in a Foucauldian sense of technically legitimated rules of professional practice which regulate the individual professional's work (see Flynn, 2001; Foucault 1967, 1973; Johnson, 1995). Because soft leadership does not rely heavily on hierarchical organizational structures it can occur in networks too. Indeed, leaders in networks depend upon it more than leaders in hierarchies do.

PCG/Ts are a specific kind of provider network. They have a clearly defined core body and they are funded publicly, not by members' contributions as professional networks are. GP membership is mandatory. Nevertheless, provider networks based on predominantly non-contractual, non-hierarchical relationships – including preexisting professional networks – and incorporating a dual leadership (both professional and general-managerial) are increasingly being constructed in other health systems, especially Germany, the Netherlands, Switzerland, Spain and the USA. Evidence-based medicine is an international movement, and economic and political pressures on general managers to make professions more accountable also exist in most countries. Of the trends outlined above, three are especially likely to be relevant beyond the UK. One is the centrality of evidence-based technical legitimation for attempts to exercise leadership of doctors organized through networks of independent providers. Well-developed clinical guidelines and protocols are a necessary for such leadership, although in primary care evidence-based medicine is as yet generally less developed than in secondary care. The second is a new form of symbiosis between professional and managerial leadership. If policy-makers and lay managers can sustain the impression that they are willing, if necessary, to intervene more actively in the management of medical work, that posture enables professional leaders to apply soft coercion and so exercise a closer, more active leadership over everyday medical practice. Looking further ahead, and thirdly, soft leadership through provider and professional networks complements and deepens the somewhat limited classical contractual relationship between independent doctors and public bodies (or sickfunds, HMOs or insurers). In attenuated forms, soft leadership instates many of the monitoring and control systems that medical employees in a bureaucracy are subject to. In that sense, soft governance might be regarded as a transitional or even a preliminary step towards the construction of more formal, integrated organizations in those parts of health systems which have hitherto been the preserve of independent professionals. An important medium-term policy question is therefore how far soft leadership does indeed anticipate the establishment of more conventional, hierarchical forms of leadership in those domains of medicine.

References

Bennett, C. and Ferlie, E. (1996) 'Contracting in Theory and Practice: Some Evidence from the NHS', *Public Administration*, 74: 1, pp. 49–66.

Coburn, D, Rappaport, S. and Borgeault, I. (1997) 'Decline vs. Retention of Medical Power through Restratification: An Examination of the Ontario Case', *Sociology of Health and Illness*, 19: 1, pp. 1–22.

Courpasson, D. (1997) 'Régulation et Gouvernement des Organisations. Pour une Sociologie de l'action Managérial', *Sociologie du Travail*, 39: 1, pp. 39–61.

Courpasson, D. (1998) 'Le Changement est un Outil Politique', *Revue Française de Gestion*, 120 (Sept–Oct.), pp. 6–16.

Courpasson, D. (1999) 'Entre Fascination et Denonciation. Sociologie et Management des Organisations', *Sociologie du Travail*, 41: 3, pp. 295–305.

Courpasson, D. (2000) 'Managerial Strategies of Domination: Power in Soft Bureaucracies', *Organization Studies*, 21: 1, pp. 141–61.

Department of Health (UK) (2000a) *National Service Framework for Coronary Heart Disease. Modern Standards and Service Models* (Leeds: DoH).

Department of Health (UK) (2000b) *National Service Framework for Mental Health. Modern Standards and Service Models* (Leeds: DoH).

Department of Health (UK) (2000c) *Protecting Patients, Supporting Doctors* (Leeds: DoH).

Dingwall, R. and Fenn P. (eds) (1992) *Introduction. Quality and Regulation in Health Care: International Experiences* (London: Routledge), pp. 1–11.

Ferlie, E., Ashburner, L., Fitzgerald, L. and Pettigrew, A. (1996) *The New Public Management in Action* (Oxford: Oxford University Press).

Flynn, R. (2001) *Clinical Governance and Governmentality*. BSA Medical Sociology Conference, York, 21 September 2001.

Foucault, M. (1967) *Madness and Civilization* (London: Tavistock).

Foucault, M. (1973) *The Birth of the Clinic* (London: Tavistock).

Freidson, E. (1984) 'The Changing Nature of Professional Control', *Annual Review of Sociology*, 10, pp. 1–20.

Harrison, S. and Dowswell, G. (2002) 'Autonomy and Bureaucratic Accountability in Primary Care: What English General Practitioners Say', *Sociology of Health and Illness*, 24: 2, pp. 208–26.

Jermier, J. M., Slocum, J. W., Fry, L. W. and Gaines, J. (1991) 'Organizational Subcultures in a Soft Bureaucracy: Resistance Behind the Myth and Facade of an Official Culture', *Organizational Science*, 2: 2, pp. 170–94.

Johnson, T., Larkin, G. and Saks, M. (eds) (1995) *Health Professions and the State in Europe* (London: Routledge).

Kickert, W. J. M. *et al.* (eds) (1997) *Managing Complex Networks* (London: Sage).

Klein, R. (1998) 'Competence, Professional Self-Regulation and Public Interest', *British Medical Journal*, 316, pp. 1740–2.

Rosenthal, M. (1995) *The Incompetent Doctor* (Buckingham: Open University Press).

Sheaff, R., Dickson, M. and Smith, K. (2002) 'Is GP Restratification Beginning in England?, *Social Policy and Administration*, 36: 7, pp. 765–79.

Stacey, M. (1992) *Regulating British Medicine* (London: Wiley).

Starr, P. and Immergut, E. (1987) 'Health Care and the Boundaries of Politics', in C. S. Maier (ed.), *Changing Boundaries of the Political* (Cambridge: Cambridge University Press).

Thompson, D. (1987) 'Coalitions and Conflict in the National Health Service: Some Implications for General Management', *Sociology of Health and Illness*, 9: 2, pp. 128–53.

Trice, H. M. and Beyer, J. M. (1991) 'Cultural Leadership in Organizations', *Organization Science*, 2: 2, pp. 149–69.

Wilkin, D., Gillam, S., and Leese, B. (eds) (2000) *The National Tracker Survey of Primary Care Groups and Trusts* (Manchester: NPCRDC, 2000).

Yin, R. K. (1989) *Case Study Analysis* (London: Sage).

2

'Cognitive Sculpting' the RCN Clinical Leadership Development Programme; Emotion-Strategies in Leadership Development*

Stephen Lloyd Smith, Charlotte Ashburner, Pam Smith, Geraldine Cunningham, Ben Gray, Sara Lister and Sue Nash

Introduction

The RCN Clinical Leadership Development Programme (henceforth, the Programme) has perhaps the most extensive coverage and most intensive methodology of leadership development in Britain. Beginning with 12 NHS Trusts, the Programme has reached 147 organizations, including Belgian and Swiss participants.

The 'lead facilitators' include both RCN officers and senior nurse practitioners. They promote and sustain 'transformational leadership' among nurses under 'an agenda of patient-centred care'. This is consistent with RCN attempts to alter the wider agenda in the British National Health Service, by displacing 'managerialist' and 'market' discourses, strongly identified with resentment, resignation, fatalism and a massive, unsustainable loss of qualified nursing staff from the public health care system. However, Fabricus has argued that 'the crisis in Nursing...is caused by a deficit in professional *self*-esteem...' suggesting 'that...low self-esteem is the *cause* rather than the *effect* of the crisis' (Fabricus, 1999, p. 203).

---

*Earlier drafts of this chapter were presented to *Emotional Labour 2001* at South Bank University, London, 12 July 2001; to the *Annual Conference of the British Academy of Management*, Cardiff University, 7 September 2001; and to the *Conference on Health Care Management*, Saïd Business School, Oxford, 21–22 March 2002.

Indeed a guiding principle of the Programme is that low esteem in nursing is something which nurses can correct, especially if they recognize that they can play an authoritative leadership role. Menzies-Lyth (1999) has reminded nurses that when she suggested nurses were 'managers' 40 years ago, this

> evoked a wave of outrage. The audience thought of themselves as caring professionals and disassociated themselves from managers who, in their fantasies, were ruthless, inhuman and authoritarian...Dislike of being a manager has not gone. It is expressed more subtly and insidiously, but nonetheless effectively...
>
> In the end, the responsibility for the quality of care lies with the nurse-manager [formerly]...ward-sister...The nurse's responsibility also to be a manager is rejected and projected into another 'non-caring' manager who is felt as hard, or even cruel...
>
> The problem seems to be...a failure to understand the difference between 'authoritarian' and 'authoritative'. (1999, pp. 8, 12, 207)

Transformational leadership of patient-centred care is the RCN's counter-discourse, and while detectable in health policy before the Blair government, it is more attuned to this government's concern with 'modernization', 'new ways of working' and 'strengthened leadership' elaborated in the National Plan for the NHS. Thus the Programme aims to empower clinicians in a 'political context of modernization'. The Programme may prove to have been the most intensive and far-reaching leadership development initiative in the UK public sector as a whole.

The facilitators subscribe to 'practising what you preach' and taking 'responsibility for selves'; that 'differences are to be valued', and that the Programme should create 'space for others to develop' and 'enlarge their own authority'. Facilitators have seen themselves 'not as experts training for "competencies"', but as 'craft workers'. Resisting the temptation to specify 'the right '"behaviours"' they prefer that nurses should identify and develop their own version of the problems they face and to devise and test their courses of action.[1] Strategies are seen as 'more important than transmitting a list of skills'.

Leadership development takes place over a minimum of several months, during which the Programme adopts a 'duty of care' towards its participants. While not opposed to one-off leadership development interventions that are also widespread in the NHS (such as LEO three-day workshops,[2] nor longer programmes offered by the King's Fund), the Programme prefers to sustain participants through a long period of what can be, and perhaps must be, an unsettling and upsetting experience. This is because it is not assumed that transformational leadership comes naturally, quickly nor effortlessly to the clinician (for a discussion, see Goodwin, 2000).

The facilitators caution that among nurses joining the Programme 'wellness is important'. Facilitators' duty of care encompasses making an assessment of whether each clinician is prepared for what they may face and to arrange counselling for those who are not. Once underway, facilitators need to avoid 'toxic handling' of anxiety that compromises the well-being of the participant.

Taking 'responsibility for selves' requires 'honesty and courage'. However, an adult sense of responsibility is reported as an invigorating alternative to placing blame on managers.

The problem

However, the focus of this chapter is not to extol the Programme but to report on an event that helped to resolve a problem encountered and to clarify the nature of the Programme. The authors include both clinicians and academics – the Programme director, the original lead facilitators, a professor of nursing, a lecturer in management studies and a research fellow. We had convened every three months as a focus group to explore the Programme and to identify how debates in emotional labour[3] might contribute to it.

Typically, we would discuss emotions in general, the theoretical dimensions underlying emotional labour, description of critical incidents experienced by the clinicians and their accounts of what they were doing. Discussion included how a facilitator saw herself as acting to 'contain' anxiety through 'good breast'[4] (after Bion, 1967, pp. 110–19), and how another was determined to fend-off the pressing demands of management upon her nurses so that they could retain some space for their own development. She did this by rejecting a management edict that all training days be cancelled for financial reasons, and by being prepared to meet the consequences. By not telling her nurses what she had been instructed to do, we concluded that she had 'contained anxiety' in another sense, by preventing its transmission to nurses.

We also noted many of the 'observations of care' and 'patient stories' that the Programme had collected. For example, the climate of care observed in a ward was disturbed by an uproarious corridor conversation between a specialist and his entourage of juniors, approaching to 'do the round'. This observation led to a discussion about the circumstances under which nurses should challenge doctors and to the legitimate function of 'joking behaviour' during anxious moments. The clinicians could remember many pranks played out on wards and acknowledged that hospitals were great sources of anxiety, often not 'contained' but 'detached' or 'denied' (Menzies, 1970; Dartington, 1993).

Broadly, the focus groups would run for two hours per session, beginning at a moderate pace, but usually pursuing several themes with growing excitement and invariably running out of time with much left to discuss. It was part of our agreement that each discussion was documented *verbatim* by the academic members who offered an additional written commentary upon it and forwarded this to members of the focus group in advance of the next meeting. Systematic documentation of our discussions was intended to be used to elicit craft knowledge about the emotion work carried out by the facilitators on the Programme. A summary report was also part of the agreement.

After discussions held over an 18-month period, the clinicians expressed dissatisfaction. The focus group discussions were lively and wide-ranging, but too elliptical or tangential to what they, the practitioners, were attempting to do in the Programme. They admitted to not reading the verbatim transcripts and academic commentaries because they did not lend themselves to application in practice and about which they therefore 'could not be enthusiastic about or get excited by'. Above all, they were concerned that they had not incorporated anything from the focus groups into the *practice* of the Programme, and that the *usefulness* of our discussions was thus hard to see.

No particular blame was attached but the clinicians felt the focus group had run its course and that its contribution needed synthesizing if it was to be 'useful to practitioners on the Programme'. In other words the problem was not that the academics were failing to learn from the clinicians – they now had many hours of transcript – but to *find a process that enabled practitioners to extrapolate from discussion with academics*. They asked for 'one last meeting' and that the academics find a different and more appropriate format within which to run it. Ours was a cooperative enquiry and we found a way of working at this problem.

A new process was suggested to replace round-table discussion. Originally designed to elicit senior managers' strategic thinking, 'cognitive sculpting', can be described as thinking through the hands collectively. The rather sparse, essential description of the Programme – that it '*develops clinical leadership by involving clinicians in moving emotional experiences while acknowledging and containing their anxiety*' – is the direct outcome of applying the process we shall now describe. As we were to find, thinking through the hands is quite unlike thinking around a table, and we commend it to practitioners in any field.

Cognitive sculpting

It has been noted that in after-dinner conversation people will use items from the table to illustrate the story they are relating (Sims and Doyle, 2001). The salt cellar might be made to stand for an individual, or an organization or an object in the story, a napkin might be laid out to represent a place. The pepper pot might stand for another individual, organization or place, and so on. Other items are commandeered to stand for other elements in the story and moved around to represent changing episodes. Both storyteller and listeners will have their eyes focused on the developing 'cognitive sculpture', following it metaphorically as a three-dimensional object.

Cognitive sculpting is effective, Sims and Doyle argue, because it enables adults (and children) to think the way we tend to think in any case, that is through *metaphors*. As a means of eliciting, developing and representing knowledge, cognitive sculpting grows out of the use of the sand tray in infant schools, and from 'project displays' more generally. The reader's appreciation of how cognitive sculpting works may be aided by his or her recollection of their use of sand trays. You may remember that the objects you chose were not treated as the real thing, but that they stood for your thinking in such a way as to be as good as 'for real' for the purposes of description. The sand tray is an absorbing place to be, because it is good to get one's hands on, or into, at the same time as we are elaborating it 'in our heads'.

So too in cognitive sculpting: part of the satisfaction is that the activity of the hands contributes to what can be thought, opening up new possibilities which might be less apparent than in thought alone. Indeed, it may be a serious mistake to picture cognition and learning as something that 'heads' and 'hands' – or for that matter the emotions of the 'heart' – each do *separately*. Instead, that understanding works best where thought, the bodily senses and the emotions are invoked simultaneously. Sims and Doyle (2001) come close to stating this:

> We argue that metaphor is fundamental to abstract and strategic thinking and knowledge; that metaphor and analogy underpin not only our most creative thinking, but also our most commonplace thinking, which, being commonplace, tends to go unnoticed.

[Metaphorical expression] aris[es] from basic, concrete thinking using body-kinaesthetic and image schemas to represent what we take to be our knowledge of the world, both inner and outer.

...cognitive sculpting [is] a technique to help...understand, develop, and communicate the metaphors we live by, as well as to create and negotiate new metaphors. (Sims and Doyle, 2001)

While principles and discoveries can be imagined in thoughtful pictures and mental symbols, cognitive sculptures have particular advantages. Although the meaning of objects may change, the sculpture has some degree of permanence from one moment to the next, and the objects in it have to be changed deliberately. They offer a ready means of access to the argument, besides words. Given permission, the argument can be entered by others who may reposition, add or remove objects to re-present the argument as they see it. The argument is also *objectified* allowing it to become less personalized – a particular advantage in handling difficult and sensitive issues or impasse. (This may have some similarity to the use of dolls in family therapy sessions.)

In contrast, in the boardroom or in a round-table discussions of business (such as our focus group), playing with objects is discouraged as it may be seen as distracting and 'unprofessional'. Sims and Doyle suggest that this is a pity for many reasons that we can now anticipate. First it may inhibit the formation of metaphorical thinking – the widespread tendency to discuss one thing in terms of another wholly unrelated object or property. Second, because there is nothing tangible to focus on, a round-table discussion may focus on the person more than on the story. In fractious organizations this is not just a recipe for getting stuck, but may provoke a downward spiral of worsening relations. Third, as Sims and Doyle point out, it is difficult to offer or to understand arguments without picturing them. Thus economists picture an 'increase in demand' graphically as a line sloping upwards from left to right, over time, on the horizontal axis; with any given 'level' of demand being represented on the vertical axis as reversible between low demand and high demand above it, that is spatially.

Notice in the above how words act as metaphors – 'level', 'recipe', 'stuck', 'downward spiral', 'rising demand', 'high', 'low' 'above' – and how readily these metaphors 'come to hand'. Many anthropologists or linguists such as Miller (2001) have observed that all languages each seem to have a place (*sic*) for space and time metaphors which form a 'cognitive bedrock' for native speakers:

the codes, the syntax and morphology, by which speakers talk about the world can be inspected and reveal that the syntax and morphology, and even vocabulary, that are used for talking about spatial relations are also used for talking about non-spatial relations of all sorts. Many central grammatical structures in many languages are based on constructions relating to location or movement. (Miller, 2001, pp. 19–37)

English examples include '*in* January' '*at* Christmas' '*over* the coming year', but Russians have markedly different temporal/spatial expressions such as: 'the concert begins *through* ten minutes', rather than '*in* ten minutes' as *in* English. Our point here is that cognitive sculpting is *in keeping with the rich spatiality of language*: if language is spatial, how satisfying then to underline discussion by exploiting the spatial possibilities offered by cognitive sculpting.

Children draw emotional pleasure from play and this pleasure reinforces discoveries both about each other and about wider worlds. Play is invariably a spatial and temporal simulation of the parts of the world they are interested in exploring. Restricted opportunities for play may inhibit the development of the capacity to learn and the development of what Kelly (1991) calls 'psychological space'[5]. Those who are – so to speak – well-travelled in psychological space have a high capacity for making 'implicative links' or to 'construe creatively'. For children and for adults, then, playing with space and time enables learning and if children are fortunate they will have a lot of outdoor space in which to dramatize their discoveries. Educationalists accept that 'deep' learning is effected by making links between complexes of knowledge, understanding, practice and enjoyment (restated by Holt, 1995). This finding is in keeping with the link-making process and serious-fun of cognitive sculpting.

The parallels with play are strong because toys make ideal items for cognitive sculpting: a box full of numerous items to choose among and in which to find ready-to-hand metaphorical parallels. Sims finds that ambiguous objects have a plasticity of meaning that makes them easier to use, such as a miniature rugby ball which is really an alarm clock and various, similar, *kitsch* gift-shop items, manufactured for amusement. What is also needed is some simple rules that are easy to practice:

- The key rule is *that no participant in the discussion can speak except with specific reference to an object* that they have selected to place as part of the sculpture, *or to an object that is already part of the sculpture.*

Participants are free to change the function served by any object, to provide a commentary upon it, to rearrange it in juxtaposition to other objects, or to remove it, if any of these actions suit the argument they are trying to develop. But they *must only talk with an object in hand*, picking it up before they speak and putting it down afterwards.

- A large number of objects that are easy to handle should be available. Forty objects or more would be useful, as the more there are, the greater the chances that discussants will be able to seize on one which closely represents what they are thinking.
- Finally, there should be willingness to play.

It struck us that cognitive sculpting might provide a good format for our last RCN focus group meeting.

The sculpting session

The authors convened at a change to their more usual venue – at Brunel University, 15 February 2001, rather than at the RCN Institute in central London. A much longer period of time was allowed than usual – most of the day. David Sims took a few minutes to explain the principles behind cognitive sculpting – as above – and some of the ways in which it had been used. Although it had been used on a one-to-one basis as an alternative to management research interviews, he only recommends its use in larger groups. Sculpting sessions are often photographed or recorded on video for later analysis – freeing members of the need for note-taking and allowing the discussion to be revisited later. A plastic crate containing many objects was provided and a camera. The group was left to begin the process after not more than 10 minutes of instruction. The crate included around 40 disparate objects including an unfinished piece of knitting, a plastic 'super-woman' doll, a bent plastic tree, the miniature rugby ball with built-in alarm clock, a comb, a silvery disc, a ladybird fridge-magnet, a plastic grid with no obvious function, a silver coaster, a ruler, an expired passport, dolls clothes, a stick and so on.

Choosing to work while sitting on the carpet, we began speaking to the question of 'clinical leadership development'. It did not take long to begin the process and only one reminder was needed to 'always speak through an object'. In about 40 minutes we had placed nearly all the available objects on the floor in a semicircle, measuring approximately one metre long by half a metre across, developing our sculpture anti-clockwise in loose serial association from one object to the next.

The participants are agreed on the next, key moment: one of the nurses exclaimed that the sculpture we had created was 'just like all the discussions that we always have in the focus group'. 'One thing leads to another and to another' in a series of imaginative steps that showed 'no particular direction'. Our sprawling discussion was only too palpable in a sprawling sculpture: many thoughts, many objects, but nothing clear-cut. For the academics, permission to wander is sanctioned in the interests of coming across new ideas and to allow themes to emerge; but the practitioners experienced it in a different way. It was frustrating: '*just what we need* to *avoid...**again**!*' This insight was acknowledged and accepted unanimously and instantaneously, and with an emphatic but theatrical gesture of irritation, a second clinician brushed our discussion aside with a back-sweep of the left hand, done with a flourish. Each joined in, picking up the objects as quickly as possible and 'flinging' them into the box to begin again – indeed, so glad to get rid of the first sculpture that none remembered to photograph it.

Our second sculpture was sparse, containing a few objects that showed many cross-connections and interrelationships. It was discovered that few were needed. Each participant will have their own detailed recollection of how it was fashioned, but the second sculpture represented the realization that:

> Leadership facilitation involves emotional labour, incorporated in strategies that elicit emotions in others for the purpose of prompting transformational leadership in them. We [each facilitator] are doing this all the time and in many ways. And we each work using different palettes.

A coaster was picked up to represent 'a mirror needed for understanding' and 'the process of reflection'. A second practitioner added a plastic grid to signify a sieve and the third picked up a plastic circle of beads to represent a finer sieve. 'Sieving' was necessary to remove the extraneous discussion. A university member grasped a piece of wood to represent his 'grasp' of the clinical leadership development programme, which was enabled 'only when a programme facilitator and clinical leader came to speak to our MBA students at Brunel [recently]'. The clinical leader had said that it was *anger* at her manager's evaluation of her that had prompted her to ask herself why she was seen that way, why she had allowed herself to be seen that way and to change her leadership style altogether. This suggested to him that 'what the programme was all about was using emotional labour – or rather *emotion work* – to prompt change'.

In the second sculpture the Programme's measurement tools (listed above) were represented by a ruler and a thermometer. The passport represented legitimacy or 'licence' to practice the Programme in an ethical and responsible way. There was emphatic agreement around promoting understanding of the careful and ethical use of authority. The bent-over plastic tree represented a subject taking part in the Programme, who might be 'less than well'; the ladybird to 'eat the aphid' nuisance as a 'specialized gardener for the sick', but also to represent the nursery rhyme with its alarming lyrics about 'burning houses and children all gone'. Some unfinished knitted fabric represented 'vagueness' and 'concealment', the plastic model of the woman with long hair and star-spangled cloak represented the leader of the Programme. A need to 'nourish and nurture' was symbolized by a plastic hamburger. A smiling pink plastic snail was made to stand for slow but substantive development in transformational leadership. Each of these items were meaningful to the facilitators in terms of how they think about what they do and as a means of describing individual differences of approach.

One of the practitioners said that she now saw that the focus groups had allowed the facilitators to discuss emotions and had provided her with the insight that the clinical leadership programme created a space that allowed emotions to surface in participants. There are certain tools used in the Programme that were known to elicit strong emotional reactions. Both lead and local facilitators then worked in conjunction with these emotions through Action Learning Sets to engender change and development. There was a discussion as to whether this had been deliberate in the planning of the Programmes. These tools had been adopted because they appealed to the lead facilitators and because they were found to serve a useful purpose. Planning was too strong a description of why each device had been incorporated. Why the need for an emotional challenge? Its latent function was now becoming more manifest.

After a sandwich lunch we moved off the carpet and from the sculpture to conventional cognitive mapping – writing and drawing on flip-charts and white-boards, covering most available surfaces, but in a markedly more coherent discussion than on previous occasions, to reflect on the single question, 'What is it that we do?'

Three hundred and sixty-degree appraisal is unsettling and the Action Learning Sets could only be placed in the care of trained facilitators because of the painful issues that can emerge within them. The 'palette' referred to involves different ways of 'reframing' or 'modelling'. A sketch of a bucket and sponge represented the 'use of wet or dry sponges'. A dry sponge was needed as a sponge which was already wet could 'contain no anxiety'. Facilitators needed 'awareness of the dangers of toxic handling', which may risk 'leaking'...'even flooding intensity'. Their palette might include 'explicating ground rules', 'exposing, debunking, deconstructing and reconstructing fantasy', 'demystifying', 'creativity', 'collage', 'metaphor', 'support', 'feeding', 'risk-taking [facilitators] – pres*ent* as a gift; present as in 'being'; pres-*ence* as in 'the presence of the actor', needing to avoid the dangers of 'spoon feeding'.

'Containment' returned as central to one facilitator's 'palate' of approaches, but not to another's. One of the facilitators dwelt on the 'bucketful of emotions' in the subject, which organizations ignore at their peril, and which entail a complex connection between the subject's role, their authority, and their *capacity* to manage, including to 'manage upwards'. Positive experience was had in 'helping people to step out of the box'. Facilitators – and developing clinical leaders – needed to have some capacity for absorbing the anxieties of change.

The discussion also covered 'ownership issues' which the Programme's Steering Committee[6] has returned to several times. Because the Programme methodology was powerful, it could be danger-ous if used inexpertly. Just what form of licensing, accreditation or recognition is appropriate in protecting subjects, in maintaining quality control, and in maintaining the financial and managerial viability of a rapidly growing Programme from the RCN's point of view? Formal recognition and entry obtained 'by the front door preferably to the back door' was most likely to generate critical mass and to sustain the Programme's strategies at a particular location...but there were *so many* locations.

Discussion

Cognitive sculpting enabled both a richer and clearer discussion, not least because it removed some of the frustration that had been experi-enced by the practitioners, unblocking an impasse and enabling the facilitators to talk in a flowing way about what it is that they do. Metaphors were drawn in detailed diagrams which included containers, buckets, a ball with a bell and sponges, the outcome of which was to establish that Action Learning Sets have to be governed by rules which can be elicited from facilitators. The RCN has since reviewed the way it may control the Programme internationally without it collapsing inwards under its own success.

We are also in a better position to revisit and draw on the documentary record we made of the round-table focus-group discussions, in a way that was not possible before this event. The RCN's Steering Group has since reflected on the Programme's strategic research questions, and their full-time researchers, appointed in recent months, are now in a position to formulate their strategic approach in the light of the essence of the Programme, now explicated. In particular, the essential differences between the Programme and LEO interventions are clear.

Having found a format for discussion that practitioners and academics can communicate through, our next task is to become redundant and move on. This is true for both the academics in drafting conference papers and other publications, and for Programme facilitators who must judge the right time to leave those who have been through the Programme to get on with developing their leadership skills unaided. Some lead facilitators have moved on to other projects. New facilitators have been recruited.

Our experience as a focus group and the practices adopted by the RCN Clinical Leadership Development Programme, remind us that learning is more than cerebral – which seems the more usual model (Cohen and Sproul, 1996; Easterby-Smith, Burgoyne and Araujo, 1999) – or visual (Morgan, 1986) or even 'hands-on', but an ensemble of these. This is nowhere clearer than among emotional labourers in general and nurses in particular. Closer contact with the emotional labouring professions promises to enrich our approach to learning.

Returning to a wider analysis of nursing, the Programme raises interesting questions about the relationship between institutional divisions of labour and individual dispositions towards authority. To what extent does a capacity for transformational leadership challenge unfortunate organizational structures? To what extent does responsibility for correcting organizational failure belong with individuals? There would seem to be grounds for optimism in that the promotion of leadership, or perhaps, more basically, of 'adulthood' among nurses, will present a major challenge to that malaise which Anton Obholzer identifies with

a split between clinicians and managers...splitting...in which managers would be shielded from the social consequences of their financial actions as clinicians would be shielded from the financial consequences of theirs...a paranoid-schizoid social system...being one in which blame is clearly attached to 'them', the other side, and one has to live in fear of what 'they' are up to. Hence 'them' and 'us', (splitting, hence schizoid) and fear of what they're up to and planning against us (paranoid). (Obholzer, 1993, p. 279)

He fears that the result of this and other processes of

> projective identification... is a process of conducting oneself according to a state of mind in which 'keeping one's nose clean' is the central concept. This refers firstly to an undermining of the process of conducting oneself as an adult within one's own organization: a state of mind of passive acceptance of change with a minimum of resistance. Secondly, and at the same time, there is a disturbing reduction in creativity and thought, with innovation the main casualty. (*Ibid.*, p. 278)

But if the RCN Leadership Programme enables nurses, in psychoanalytic terms, to maintain or regain their adult status, to challenge, to be creative and innovate in the face of infantalizing forces, and if there is good pre/post-test evidence that this is the case (Cunningham and Kitson, 2000), then the nursing profession *as a whole* is attaining a position of leadership – and adulthood – within the UK health care system.

Notes

1   In retrospect, this notion of equality seems consistent with Warren's (1996) 'egalitarian outlook' upon personal constructs and 'group realities', in which the subject rather than the analyst determines the problem.
2   Leading an Empowered Organization (LEO) workshops offered by the School of Healthcare Studies, Leeds University, Britain.
3   'This labour requires one to induce or suppress feeling in order to sustain the outward countenance that produces the proper state of mind in others – in this case the sense of being cared for in a convivial and safe place. This kind of labour calls for co-ordination of mind and feeling, and sometimes it draws on a sense of self that we honour as deep and integral to our individuality' A. R. Hoschild (*The Managed Heart*, 1983, p. 7).
4   'Good Breast' refers to the capacity of the carer to convey to the child/ client or other subject, that s/he recognizes and acknowledges their anxiety in full.
5   In Kelly's (1991) personal-construct psychology, psychological space consists of 'individual and shared construing' of verbal and pre-verbal, and conscious and pre-conscious emotion action and thought.
6   This has a wider membership than the focus group.

References

Bion, W. R. (1967) *Second Thoughts* (New York: Jason Aronson).
Cohen, M. D. and Sproul, L. S. (eds) (1996) *Organizational Learning* (Thousand Oaks: Sage).

Cunningham, G. and Kitson, A. (2000) 'An Evaluation of the RCN Clinical Leadership Development Programme: Part 1', *The Nursing Standard*, 15: 12 (6 December), pp. 34–7.

Dartington, A. (1993) 'Where Angels Fear to Tread: Idealism, Despondency and Inhibition of Thought in Hospital Nursing', in *Winnicott Studies*, 7 (Spring), pp. 21–41.

Easterby-Smith, M., Burgoyne, J. and Araujo, L. (eds) (1999) *Organisational Learning and the Learning Organisation: Developments in Theory and Practice* (London: Sage).

Fabricus, J. (1999) 'The Crisis in Nursing', *Psychoanalytic Psychotherapy*, 13: 3, pp. 203–6.

Goodwin, N. (2000) 'Leadership and the UK Health Service', *Health Policy*, 51, pp. 49–60.

Holt, J. (1995) *How Children Fail* (Massachusetts: Perseus Books).

Hoschild, A. R. (1983) *The Managed Heart: The Commercialisation of Human Feeling* (California: University of California Press).

Kelly, G. A. (1991) *A Theory of Personality: The Psychology of Personal Constructs* (London: Routledge).

Menzies-Lyth, I. E. P. (1970/1959) *The Functioning of Social Systems as a Defence Against Anxiety: A Report on the Study of Nursing Service of a General Hospital.* Tavistock Pamphlet no. 3, The Centre for Applied Social Research (London: The Tavistock Institute). Also published in 1959 in *Containing Anxiety in Institutions* (London: Free Association Books).

Menzies-Lyth, I. E. P. (1999) 'Facing the Crisis', *Psychoanalytic Psychotherapy*, 13: 3, pp. 207–12.

Miller, J. (2001) 'Space and Time in Natural Language: Some Parallels between Spatial and Temporal Expressions in English and Russian', in M. Stroinska (ed.), *Relative Points of View; Linguistic Representations of Culture* (New York and Oxford: Berghahn Books).

Morgan, G. (1986) *Images of Organization* (Bristol: Sage).

Obholzer, A. (1993) 'Institutional Forces', *Therapeutic Communities*, 14: 4, pp. 275–82.

Sims, D. and Doyle, J. R. (1993) 'Cognitive Sculpting as a Means of Working with Managers' Metaphors', *Omega*, 23: 2, pp. 117–24.

Sims, D. and Doyle, J. R. (2001) 'Enabling Strategic Metaphor in Conversation: A Technique of Cognitive Sculpting for Explicating Knowledge', in A. Sigismund Huff and M. Jenkins (eds), *Mapping Strategic Knowledge* (London: Sage).

Titchen, A. (1998) *A Conceptual Framework for Facilitating Learning in Clinical Practice* (Lidcombe, Australia: Centre for Professional Educational Advancement).

Warren, W. (1996) 'The Egalitarian Outlook as the Underpinning of the Theory of Personal Constructs', in D. Kalekin-Fishman and B. Walker (eds), *The Construction of Group Realities: Culture, Society and Personal Construct Theory* (Malabar, Fla: Krieger).

3

Identifying Leadership on the Front Lines: Demography and Integration within US Psychiatric Treatment Teams

Rebecca Wells, Jeffrey Alexander, Richard Lichtenstein and Fiona Lee

Interdisciplinary teams as a form of dispersed leadership

As in many other industries, health care organizations are seeking to provide complex services with increasing efficiency (*Crossing the Quality Chasm*, 2001). Within mental health care, the care of the seriously mentally-ill, defined by the presence of schizophrenia or other major mood disorders (Rosenheck and Horvath, 1998), remains particularly challenging because of both the chronic nature of their diseases and the frequent presence of physical and social problems. Nowhere is this more true than in Veterans Administration (VA) facilities, the setting of the current study, where patients are sicker, older and poorer than the general population (Wilson and Kizer, 1997). VA psychiatric facilities therefore face a particular imperative to draw on all their disciplines effectively.

One strategy for involving all relevant disciplines in care is the interdisciplinary treatment team (ITT). ITTs can enhance care by systematically coordinating complementary services, including pharmacology, social work, psychotherapy, and social and vocational rehabilitation (Dill and Rochford, 1989). Coordination across functions minimizes gaps in care and enables staff members to adjust more quickly based on better feedback (Perl, 1997). Finally, team members can offer each other social support, and thus sustain motivation and mitigate stress (Toseland *et al.*, 1986).

Although leadership has typically been treated as an individual characteristic, in organizations such as the VA this function is in fact dispersed across the members of treatment teams (Vanderslice, 1988). In order for these teams to achieve their potential, members must be actively engaged in their shared work, ideally contributing according to their specific areas of expertise. However, sharing decision-making has been problematic because of the hierarchical tradition of medical care. In principle leadership should rotate according to members' issue-specific competencies, but in reality power often resides among a few, with functionally vital members relegated to marginal roles (Cott, 1997).

The issue of who engages in cross-functional teams and at what level is linked to the demographics of their members. Previous analyses found that staff members tended to view those teams as less integrated when their membership was more demographically diverse (Lichtenstein *et al.*, 1997). However, the exact way in which demographics affect individual staff-member integration within cross-functional teams is unclear. The purpose of this chapter is to probe how individual staff-member demographics affect integration within interdisciplinary teams, with integration defined as a multidimensional construct including participation, clarity about one's role within the team, use of skills by the team, influence on decisions, and social integration.

Theoretical context

Two theories offer distinct perspectives on the effects of demographics on member integration within teams. Social identity and self-categorization theory have been applied to posit the effects of proximate comparisons. Status characteristics theory has been used to show how the societal prestige of one's attributes affects behaviour within work groups. Their potentially complementary contributions are explored below.

The relevance of social identity theory to integration within teams

Social identity theory posits that people favour others whom they see as similar to themselves, regardless of whether or not there is a history of previous interaction (Tajfel and Forgas, 2000). The motivation behind such behaviour is a desire to maintain a positive self-image, because individual esteem rises along with group esteem (Wagner *et al.*, 1986). One way to do this is to ascribe desirable qualities to groups to which one sees oneself as belonging. Such attitudes then lead people to invest preferentially in similar others and to ascribe negative qualities to those seen as different. This is a zero-sum game, with favour towards one group coming at the expense of other groups (Tajfel, 1970).

Research has found that individuals who differ demographically from colleagues tend to be less attracted to those colleagues (Tsui and O'Reilly, 1989) and communicate less with them (Chatman *et al.*, 1998; Zenger and Lawrence, 1989), feel more stress (Fiedler *et al.*, 1961; Triandis *et al.*, 1965), and perceive greater levels of conflict within their work groups (Pelled, 1996). Given these findings, it is not surprising that dissimilar individuals have exhibited lower levels of organizational attachment (Tsui *et al.*, 1992) and left groups at higher rates (Jackson *et al.*, 1991; O'Reilly *et al.*, 1989; Wagner *et al.*, 1984). The more an individual differs from the rest of the team, the more he or she may disengage, although reviewers of this field have expressed reservations about the strength and consistency of empirical results (Lawrence, 1997).

The relevance of status characteristics theory to integration within teams

In contrast to the proximate comparisons of social identity theory, status characteristics theory focuses on how societal valuations of individuals' demographic categories affect individuals' roles within work groups. Status characteristics theory's fundamental proposition is that work-group hierarchies replicate those of society at large.

According to status characteristics theory, any time people differ in a respect that has status connotations they develop differential expectations. These expectations apply to themselves and others based on those attributes. Those with status advantages then play privileged roles within groups. They talk more, are listened to more attentively, and have greater influence over group decisions than others (Wagner and Berger, 1993). Moreover, these patterns of deference to higher-status members exceed those that might be explained on the basis of competence. For instance, status characteristics theory predicts that members of higher-status occupations will enjoy more input and feedback benefits than their training would justify. Unrelated demographic characteristics such as sex, race and age also affect how much people invest in and receive from teams (Berger *et al.*, 1972).

Applied to interdisciplinary treatment teams, status characteristics theory implies that individuals whose demographic status is low will have reduced opportunities to participate in team discussions and will receive less validation when they do. Their consequent psychological and behavioural withdrawal from the team will manifest in lower integration within the team. Studies have revealed hierarchies within medical care organizations that parallel those of medicine as a whole (Bloom, 1980). Despite efforts to broaden participation in clinical decision-making, there is evidence that higher-status disciplines (that is, physicians and registered nurses) continue to retain most of the authority in such matters (Cott, 1997).

Social identity theory and status characteristics theory have been employed separately in the past. However, both speak to individual integration within teams. To the extent that social identity theory holds, individual integration within teams will vary according to how much members differ from each other demographically. To the extent that status characteristics theory applies, individuals with lower status attributes will be less engaged.

Social identity theory hypotheses

One salient demographic attribute within a cross-functional team is occupation because the team's purpose is to foster collaboration across complementary areas of expertise. In medicine, a history of occupational stratification further focuses attention on discipline (Toseland *et al.*, 1986). Because different disciplines have distinct areas of expertise and authority (for example, physicians make final treatment decisions, whereas pharmacists tend to have the most recent pharmacological knowledge), staff members are likely to see themselves and respond to others in terms of their disciplinary identities. There are also attitudinal differences, such as the greater emphasis on autonomy among physicians and psychologists relative to other team members (Rubin and Beckhard, 1972). In addition, there are racial, class and gender tensions between disciplines (Feiger and Schmitt, 1979; Gomez *et al.*, 1980), with physicians being typically high socioeconomic status white males and other team members more likely to be women from less privileged backgrounds, with the lowest paid staff members being the most likely to be non-white (Rosella *et al.*, 1994). Previous literature has cited the poor relationships nurses and other personnel have with physicians as a key source of dissatisfaction (Stamps *et al.*, 1978).

Discipline is a critical source of social identity within treatment teams. As a consequence, if the degree of social difference from other team members affects integration, then individuals should react to greater disciplinary difference from other team members with reduced integration within the team.

Hypothesis 1a. Individual staff members will be less integrated within treatment teams to the extent that their discipline is a numerical minority within the team, *ceteris paribus*.

Another salient source of social identity within teams is age (Zenger and Lawrence, 1989). Age is a visible attribute that also connotes differences in historical and cultural referent points. Such common experiences tend to foster values and perspectives that differ from those of other cohorts (Rhodes, 1983). Social identity theory implies that people in any given age range will tend to make positive attributions towards their chronological peers at the expense of other age groups (Tajfel and Forgas, 2000). If this is true, and if the degree of social difference affects individual integration within teams, then:

> *Hypothesis 1b.* Individual staff members will be less integrated within treatment teams to the extent that they differ from other team members in age, *ceteris paribus.*

Sex is another demographic attribute that is immediately visible in social interactions (Stangor *et al.*, 1992) and salient within organizations (Ely, 1995). In health care, there has been an historical tendency for women to be overrepresented in subordinate groups such as nurses and underrepresented in dominant groups such as physicians and psychologists (Freidson, 1970). Gender thus signals differences in task-related power. Previous research has also found that men and women tend to approach group work differently, with men tending to focus more on task outcomes and women emphasizing interpersonal relationships more (Eagly, 1987; Matthews *et al.*, 1982; Steckler and Rosenthal, 1985). Given the salience of gender, social identity theory implies that being a gender minority within a team would negatively affect an individual's integration within the team. Note that this implies that being the lone male has the same consequences as being the lone female: the issue is difference, not status.

> *Hypothesis 1c.* Individual staff members will be less integrated within treatment teams to the extent that they are in a minority in terms of gender, *ceteris paribus.*

Another visible demographic attribute is race. One indication of this attribute's salience is the heavy concentration of racial groups within specific disciplines, such that, for instance, 33 per cent of nurse aides, attendants and orderlies are black, while only 8 per cent of RNs are black. Another indication is a general tendency for staff to cluster by race during social times such as lunch (Dreachslin *et al.*, 2000). While results sometimes appear to vary across groups, there is evidence that being in a racial minority can sometimes be negatively associated with perceptions of group functioning (DiTomaso *et al.*, 1996). Thus, we would expect that being in a racial minority within a team might also be negatively related to individual integration within the team.

Hypothesis 1d. Individual staff members will be less integrated within treatment teams to the extent that they are in a minority in terms of race, *ceteris paribus*.

A final relevant demographic attribute included in this study is tenure, in this context measured as the length of the individual's service within the team. Individuals who enter a group at similar times compose a cohort within that team, regardless of other differences (Ryder, 1965). Conversely, individuals who are not close to any other team members in tenure may lack identification with the group (McCain *et al.*, 1983; Pfeffer, 1983), and may also find that they do not share common bases for communicating (Zenger and Lawrence, 1989). Previous research has found that individuals who are most different from their colleagues in tenure were most likely to leave their organizations (Pfeffer and O'Reilly, 1987). This is prima facie evidence that tenure difference has a socially alienating effect on members of organizations.

Hypothesis 1e. Individual staff members will be less integrated within treatment teams to the extent that they differ from other team members in tenure, *ceteris paribus*.

Status characteristics theory hypotheses

Similar to social identity theory, status characteristics theory assumes social comparisons relative to other work group members. However, unlike work based on social identity theory, status characteristics theory does not base its predictions on the degree of difference. Instead, demographic attributes are assumed to become relevant to social comparisons whenever there is any diversity with respect to those attributes. Individuals with relatively low demographic status are assumed to have less prestige within the treatment team because of the relative positions of their disciplines in the broader medical system. They are therefore expected to experience fewer opportunities to contribute to teams as well as less validation for the contributions they make. As a result, they are expected to identify less than other members with their ITT, and consequently experience lower integration within the team.

The opposite effect is expected for individuals with relatively high demographic status, who are expected to have more positive experiences in ITTs by virtue of their privileged status. Therefore, such individuals are expected to identify and consequently invest more in the team. This builds on the premise that people do more of whatever makes them feel good about themselves (Sherif and Cantril, 1947). Higher-status individuals generally receive more positive feedback than other team members, are evaluated as more competent, and enjoy more influence over team processes than do lower status members (Berger *et al.*, 1977; Cohen, 1982; Lockheed, 1985). Such dynamics in turn encourage greater engagement in the group.

Within medical care, two of the lowest status disciplines are licensed practical nurses (LPNs) and nurse aides, both of whom provide a variety of tasks under registered nurse (RN) supervision (Stevens and Featherman, 1981). LPNs, for instance, may check patient blood pressure, and nurse aides may escort patients to appointments. Both disciplines are characterized by low pay and low autonomy. Status characteristics theory would predict that LPNs and nurse aides would have reduced social status because of their discipline, and hence, lower integration within ITTs. In contrast, psychiatrists, psychologists and social workers, belonging to the three highest paid and highest status disciplines in ITTs, should enjoy privileged interactions because of their disciplinary status.

> *Hypothesis 2a.* The lower the discipline's status, the lower its members' integration will be within treatment teams, *ceteris paribus.*

Individuals between their late 30s and late 50s enjoy a dominant status in the United States (Alderfer, 1987). Because only a small number of team members in this study were over 60 years of age, the following assumes a linear relationship between age and social status in this study of work groups. Building on this assumption about the status implications of age is the prediction that:

> *Hypothesis 2b.* Younger staff members will be less integrated within treatment teams than older staff members, *ceteris paribus.*

Although mental health workers are predominantly female, this majority status has not necessarily conferred social equality upon women within treatment settings. Women have traditionally had less power in organizations than men have enjoyed (Kanter, 1977; Epstein,

1988). Although the results were not uniform, a review of 64 datasets from 29 studies found women have generally lower status in mixed-sex groups (Lockheed, 1985). To the extent that lower status in the broader organizational context translates into lower status within treatment teams, female staff members may react by identifying less with these teams, and consequently become less integrated within them.

Hypothesis 2c. Female staff members will be less integrated within treatment teams than men, *ceteris paribus.*

Another permanent and visible source of status is race, with non-white races being accorded generally lower status in society. When these status distinctions are imported into treatment teams, we might therefore expect that non-whites would react to their reduced status through reduced integration.

Hypothesis 2d. Non-white staff members will be less integrated within treatment teams than white staff members, *ceteris paribus.*

In addition, some aspects of team structure may affect individual integration within treatment teams. Therefore this model controls for both the size of the team and team tenure, as discussed further below. These relationships are shown in Figure 3.1.

Methods

Data sources

The data are from a study conducted as part of the US Department of Veterans' Affairs Long-Term Mental Health Enhancement Program (LTMHEP). The criteria for inclusion in the study were: (1) that a substantial number of the unit's patients have a psychotic diagnosis (such as schizophrenia, major mood disorder, or dementia), and (2) a total stay in VA medical centres of at least 150 days in the previous year or five or more admissions to a VA medical centre within the last year. One hundred and seven units meeting these criteria were selected at random from among 29 hospitals, and 14 additional units were non-randomly selected participants in inpatient or outpatient demonstration programmes.

Analyses incorporated data from the 1995 wave of a job-satisfaction survey based on previous work by Lichtenstein (1984a,b), Price and Mueller (1989), Davis-Sacks (1991) and Hackman (1987) administered

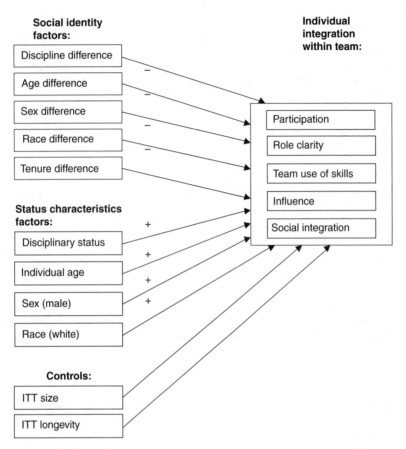

Figure 3.1   Theorised effects of demographic differences and simple demographics on staff member integration within interdisciplinary treatment teams

in 1992, 1994 and 1995. Participation in the job-satisfaction survey was voluntary and confidential, and follow-up yielded an individual staff-member response rate above 95 per cent. There were a total of 2129 respondents to the job-satisfaction survey in 1995, 1225 of whom in 134 units belonged to treatment teams with three or more members and were thus included in these analyses.

Field study

In order to learn more about the nature of integration within treatment teams, one member of the research team conducted informal field observations on four treatment teams (three inpatient and one outpatient) in two facilities. The researcher observed each team over periods of two to five meetings. After completing observations for each team, members were interviewed separately (total $n = 22$). The meeting observations provided insights into dynamics within treatment teams. A sorting exercise completed during the interviews served as the basis for a rank-ordering of disciplines. In common with published sources (Stevens and Featherman, 1981) this ranking indicated that psychiatrists, psychologists and social workers had consistently higher status than did LPNs and nurse aides.

Data analysis

Measurement of independent variables: simple demographics and distance scores

For simple demographics, age was measured as the focal individual's age in years, sex was dichotomous, race was measured through a dummy variable for non-white (with the referent group being white) and position tenure was indicated in number of months.

In order to measure demographic difference, a Euclidean distance score was calculated, equal to the square root of the summed squared distances between an individual's (S_i) value on each demographic variable and the value of each other team member (S_j) on the same demographic variable, divided by the total number of respondents (n) on the team. This is the most common measure used in relational demography studies (see for sample (Jackson *et al.*, 1991; Tsui *et al.*, 1992). For categorical variables, belonging to a different category than another individual was entered as a difference of $S_i - S_j = '1'$. For racial difference, individuals were compared on the basis of six available response categories (white, black/African-American, Asian/Pacific Islander, American Indian/Alaskan Native, Hispanic/Latino, and other).

Measurement of dependent variables: the multidimensional nature of integration

This study examined five elements of integration in order to capture both its functional and affective aspects and both investment and return: participation in team meetings; individual clarity about one's role within the team; the team's use of a member's professional skills; influence on team decisions relative to deserved ('How much influence do you think you actually have on treatment planning?' minus 'How much influence do you think you should have with treatment planning?'); and social integration (for example, 'The people I work with take a personal interest in me'). Items are available from the corresponding author.

Controls

There is substantial evidence that members of larger groups experience decreased satisfaction (Mullen *et al.*, 1989) and cohesiveness (Thomas and Fink, 1963), therefore analyses controlled for the size of the team itself, measured as the number of staff members within each individual's team. The second group-level factor controlled for was the longevity of each individual's team. Previous research has found that individual demographics have more effect when people have not worked together long (Berger *et al.*, 1972). Teams of greater longevity may also be more socially cohesive, thus facilitating integration for any given individual. Team longevity was measured through the median of the members' tenures in their current positions.

Modelling

The nested nature of the data (individuals within teams) made multilevel modelling appropriate, which was conducted using Hierarchical Linear Modelling. Multilevel modelling enables the analyst to control appropriately for team-level effects when predicting individual outcomes (Hamilton, 1992). The results of the random coefficients models revealed that there was not sufficient variation in slopes across teams to model slopes as outcomes. The slopes were therefore fixed for subsequent analyses, with only the intercept allowed to vary (Bryk and Raudenbush, 1992).

Findings

There were a number of statistically significant bivariate correlations (Table 3.1) between simple demographic attributes in the sample, although tolerance statistics indicated that collinearity was not severe for these data (Hamilton, 1992). Physicians, psychologists, social workers, ancillary personnel and nurse aides were more likely than other respondents to be male. Physicians tended to be older than other respondents, whereas ancillary personnel and aides tended to be younger. Aides also tended to have longer position tenure than other staff members in the sample. The correlation between respondent sex and sex difference from other team members was -0.57 ($p < .001$) and the correlation between position tenure and difference from other team members in tenure was 0.62 ($p < .001$).

Table 3.1 Pearson correlations of level-1 (individual-level) variables (*n* = 1225)

	Mean	S.D.	1	2	3	4	5	6	7	8	9	10	11	12	13	14	15	16	17	18	19
1 Psychiatrist	.07	.26	—																		
2 Psychologist	.04	.20	-.06*	—																	
3 Social work	.14	.34	-.11***	-.08**	—																
4 Ancillary	.17	.37	-.13***	-.09**	-.18***	—															
5 LPN	.06	.24	-.07*	-.05	-.10***	-.11***	—														
6 Aide	.13	.34	-.11***	-.08*	-.15***	-.17***	-.10***	—													
7 Age	46.64	9.85	.15***	.07*	.02	-.14***	-.05	-.07*	—												
8 Sex	1.65	.48	-.19***	-.20***	-.12***	-.10***	.11***	-.08**	-.15***	—											
9 Race	1.42	.91	.20***	-.04	-.04	-.06*	-.00	.12***	-.01	-.06	—										
10 Tenure	82.18	82.20	-.02	.01	-.10	.02	.04	.22***	.34***	-.12**	.05**	—									
11 Disc. diff.	.81	.16	.14***	.14***	-.11***	.27***	.18***	.14***	-.00	-.14***	.09**	.05	—								
12 Age diff.	12.08	4.69	.05	-.00	-.04	.04	-.01	.04	.02	.01	.04	.03	.11***	—							
13 Sex diff.	.60	.19	.11***	.09*	.01	.08**	-.06	.08**	.09**	-.57***	.07*	.09**	.23***	.06*	—						
14 Race diff.	.48	.30	.16***	-.01	-.04	-.1**	.03	.14***	.05	-.01	.58***	.05	.18***	.12***	.04	—					
15 Ten. diff.	7.69	4.35	-.01	-.01	-.05	-.04	.04	.15***	.21***	-.05	.04	.62***	.00	.16***	.11***	.11***	—				
16 Participat.	6.59	1.01	.17***	.09**	.14***	-.11***	-.14***	-.24***	.07*	-.01	.06	-.03	-.03	-.03	.01	.02	-.05	—			
17 Clarity	4.83	1.09	.07*	.05	.08**	.00	-.11***	-.10***	.10*	-.03	-.03	.01	.01	-.04	-.02	-.07*	-.04	.44***	—		
18 Skills	5.22	1.33	.09**	.01	.10***	-.01	-.09**	-.09**	.12***	-.01	.07*	.03	.06*	-.04	-.03	.05	.00	.49***	.53***	—	
19 Influence	-.50	.85	.05	.05	.10*	.02	-.07*	-.09**	.07*	-.1**	.05	.02	.03	-.02	.03	.03	-.03	.35***	.33***	.48***	—
20 Social	5.35	1.14	.04	.03	.05	.02	-.01	.04	.05	-.08**	.01	.01	.08**	.01	.01	.01	-.01	.27***	.39***	.45***	.32***

***p* < .001; ***p* < .01; *p* < .05

Table 3.2   Pearson correlations of level-2 (team level) variables ($n = 134$)

Variable	Mean	S.D.	Team size	Median position tenure
1 Team size	8.38	5.18	–	−0.09
2 Median position tenure	4.38	3.14	–	–

$^{***}p < .001$; $^{**}p < .01$; $^{*}p < .05$

Overall, the social-identity prediction that demographic difference from other staff members would cause lower levels of integration within the treatment team was not supported. Being different from other team members in age was negatively associated with perceived use of skills. However, the effects of difference in discipline were, contrary to predictions, positive. Differences in sex, race and tenure had no effects on staff-member integration within treatment teams.

Relative to discipline and age, there was fairly consistent support for the status characteristics prediction that individuals with higher-status demographics would be more integrated within treatment teams. Compared to the baseline group of RNs, physicians reported more participation in team meetings and greater clarity about roles. Social workers reported more participation, better use of skills, more appropriate levels of influence on team decisions, and higher social integration. Psychologists, contrary to prediction, experienced neither enhanced nor decreased integration because of discipline.

As predicted, LPNs and nurse aides reported lower integration in all task-related areas (participation, role clarity, use of skills, and influence) than RNs. Only in social integration did nurse aide reports contradict predictions, with higher perceived interpersonal support than RNs enjoyed. Consistent with predictions, older team members reported greater role clarity, use of skills, and social integration than younger team members perceived. There was no statistically significant support for predictions about the effects of either sex or race on integration (Table 3.3).

Discussion

Relational demography speaks to how social comparisons affect organizational dynamics. Previous relational studies of organizational behavior have employed a similarity-attraction framework (Byrne, 1971; Schneider *et al.*, 1995) or, more recently, social identity

Table 3.3 Effects of demographic differences and simple demographics on staff-member integration within interdisciplinary treatment teams

Predictor	Dependent variables				
	Participation	Role clarity	Use of skills	Influence	Social integration
Group level:					
Team tenure			0.035+		−0.038*
			0.019		0.018
Team Size	−0.0138+				
	0.007				
Individual:					
MD	0.432**	.294*			
	0.132	0.146			
Psychologist					
Social work	0.203*		0.266*	0.189*	0.263*
	0.098		0.133	0.087	0.118
Ancillary	−0.491***				
	0.100				
LPN	−0.871***	−0.676***	−0.836***	−0.350**	
	0.136	0.150	0.182	0.126	
Nurse aide	−0.967***	−0.293**	−0.523***	−0.368***	0.305*
	0.107	0.118	0.143	0.101	0.125
Age		0.008*	0.010*		0.009*
	0.004	0.004	0.004		0.004
Sex				−0.135+	
				0.074	
Race (non-white)					
Position tenure	0.01*				
	0.000				
Disc. difference	0.681**	0.586*	1.184***	0.462*	
	0.238	0.264	0.323	0.211	
Age difference			−0.019*		
			0.009		
Sex difference					
Race difference					
Tenure difference					

***$p < .001$, **$p < .01$, *$p < .05$ +$p < .10$ (non-significant associations with $p > .10$ are blank). Standard error terms italicized below coefficients.

and self-categorization theory to speak to the effects of proximate comparisons on organizing. In other words, what matters is who else is in the room.

This study has broadened relational demography by incorporating the predictions of status characteristics theory. Status characteristics theory differs in two ways from social identity theory as it has been applied to organizations. First, status characteristics theory explicitly incorporates social status, arguing that people engage more in groups when they enjoy more prestige. Second, status characteristics theory speaks to broader societal referents rather than to proximate comparisons to coworkers.

This study has provided further evidence for relational demography's premise that social category membership affects how individuals relate to groups. However, for the most part, contrary to predictions based here on social identity theory, staff members did not react to demographic difference from other team members, and, when they did, they generally did so positively. Analyses of the 1994 responses to the same items by members of the same teams yielded no significant effects of disciplinary difference on integration; cumulatively, these findings provide little support for social identity theory predictions that individuals will respond to demographic differences by disengaging from teams. Closer examination of the most closely related previous work offers some insight into why the findings of this study did not support social identity predictions.

One of the most applicable previous studies (O'Reilly, Caldwell and Barnett, 1989) examined how both group and individual-level demographic factors affected social integration within work groups as well as how integration then affected turnover. Those authors found support for their predictions at the group level, but did not find that individual demographic difference affected social integration within groups or that individual integration affected turnover.

O'Reilly *et al.*'s results suggest that demography may affect individual integration within work groups through patterns occurring at the team and/or organizational level rather than through the individual's difference from immediate coworkers. Similarly, Lichtenstein, Alexander, Jinnett and Ullman (1997) found that individuals who were in more demographically diverse treatment teams tended to see those teams as less integrated. Together, these two studies imply that the effects of diversity on integration may occur at the group rather than individual level.

An emphasis on the broader context within which groups form is central to status characteristics theory, with its predictions that work group hierarchies will replicate those of society. The current findings provide stronger support for status characteristics theory than for social identity, as the latter has been applied to organizations. However, a more historical perspective on social identity theory reveals a profound interest in the societal context of group identity, as well as the status implications of these processes.

Social identity theory was developed after the Second World War to explain how group identities led to intergroup rivalries (Turner, 1996). Status was integral to early work in this theory. Researchers, for instance, noted that when asked to respond repeatedly to the question 'Who am I?', women tended to mention their sex more often than men, blacks referred to race more often than whites, and Jews cited religion more frequently than Christians (Deschamps, 1982). Similarly, studies found that higher-status teenagers were less likely than lower-status students to mention social categories and more able to see themselves as distinct individuals (Doise *et al.*, 1976). Two more recent studies also found that responses to difference varied depending on their status implications (Brewer *et al.*, 1993; Tsui *et al.*, 1992). However, subsequent research has not built on these findings to explain how and why status may affect interactions within work groups.

Thus, the relative neglect of social status is not inherent in social identity theory, but rather a feature of its recent application to organizations in studies of relational demography. Results from the current study suggest a reincorporation of social status into relational demography, drawing on the predictions of status characteristics theory.

For integration within teams, what matters most may be who you are, relative to others, in society at large.

Conclusion

The need to engage people across functional and hierarchical boundaries to solve complex problems remains vital both in health care and other sectors. This study has found that demographic status affects individual integration within treatment teams. This is important for organizations that seek to share leadership functions across their members, for such inclusivity may exist in name only unless people feel truly validated for sharing according to competence rather than social rank. Teams will only fulfil their potential when all members engage appropriately.

The good news from this study is that sex and race do not appear to matter. The bad news is that discipline does matter, as do age and position tenure, beyond the extent that could be explained functionally. Certainly, the role requirements of different psychiatric disciplines played a role in the findings relative to simple demographics. Attending physicians, for example, tend to run team meetings; this would account for the positive effect of being a physician on participation.

These arguments become less convincing, however, relative to other elements of integration. Is there any functional reason why physicians should enjoy more role clarity than LPNs and nurse aides? Why should physicians see their skills as being better utilized than those of either LPNs or aides? Even the influence gap measure is not obviously accounted for by the differential training or roles across occupations, because this measure included perceived actual influence relative to how much the respondent thought he or she ought to have, and LPNs and aides already thought they should have substantially less influence than either physicians or social workers felt they deserved. LPNs and nurse aides still had less positive reports than higher status social workers.

One interesting anomaly was psychologists, for whom, contrary to status characteristics predictions, discipline was not associated with integration. This might be due to their relatively low apparent esteem within the Veterans Administration. Field work for this study yielded the impression that psychologists and psychiatrists had competed for influence within the VA, and psychiatrists had won. In terms of status, psychologists may thus not have enjoyed dominance as a group.

These findings imply that managers wishing to encourage dispersed leadership should focus on teams' lower-status members first. One possible intervention would be to train psychiatrists, who most frequently lead team meetings, to both elicit and validate participation by LPNs and nurse aides directly in some team discussions. This would need to be handled with care in order to avoid undermining the authority of the RNs who supervise the rest of the nursing staff. The payoff could include insights that RNs are not bringing to team discussions and a better understanding by the LPNs and aides of the team's rationale behind treatment decisions. Similar interventions might be targeted at other disciplines if leaders identify communication problems with their members. For example, during the field study some occupational therapists mentioned that they did not feel that other team members listened to them during meetings. If there are treatment problems stemming from poor communication with any specific discipline, then team leaders may focus specifically on this group.

Theoretically, this study implies that we need to broaden relational demography to include status explicitly and to consider societal as well as proximate social comparisons. Recent applications of relational demography have invoked concepts of social identity (Tajfel, 1970; Tajfel *et al.*, 1971; Turner, 1985) to predict that people will withdraw from different others, a proposition for which this sample provided only sparse support. This chapter, however, has demonstrated the relevance of broader social categories such as discipline and age, and shown that these are inextricably intertwined with status. Individuals engage in teams in part according to their demographic groups' societal prestige. In psychiatric teams, at least, what matters appears to be primarily who one is, regardless of who else is in one's team. Managers who want to encourage dispersed leadership will need to overcome this barrier in order to make full use of everyone's talents.

References

Alderfer, C. P. (1987) 'An Intergroup Perspective on Group Dynamics', in J. W. Lorsch (ed.), *Handbook of Organizational Behavior* (Englewood Cliffs, NJ: Prentice Hall), pp. 190–222.

Berger, J., Cohen, B. P. and Zelditch, M. (1972) 'Status Characteristics and Social Interaction', *American Sociological Review*, 37: 3, pp. 241–55.

Berger, J., Fisek, M. H., Norman, R. Z. and Zelditch, M. (1977) *Status Characteristics and Social Interaction: An Expectation-States Approach* (New York: Elsevier).

Bloom, J. R. (1980) 'Status Characteristics, Leadership Consensus and Decision-Making among Nurses', *Social Science and Medicine*, 14A, pp. 15–22.

Brewer, M. B., Manzi, J. M. and Shaw, J. S. (1993) 'In-group Identification as a Function of Depersonalization, Distinctiveness, and Status', *Psychological Science*, 4: 2, pp. 88–92.

Bryk, A. S. and Raudenbush, S. W. (1992) *Hierarchical Linear Models* (Newbury Park: Sage).

Byrne, D. E. (1971) *The Attraction Paradigm* (New York: Academic Press).

Chatman, J. A., Polzer, J. T., Barsade, S. G. and Neale, M. A. (1998) 'Being Different Yet Feeling Similar: The Influence of Demographic Composition and Organizational Culture on Work Processes and Outcomes', *Administrative Science Quarterly*, 43: 4, pp. 749–80.

Cohen, E. G. (1982) 'Expectation States and Interracial Interaction in School Settings', *Annual Review of Sociology*, 8, pp. 209–35.

Cott, C. (1997) '"We decide, you carry it out": A Social Network Analysis of Multidisciplinary Long-term Care Teams', *Social Science and Medicine*, 45: 9, pp. 1411–21.

Crossing the Quality Chasm: A New Health System for the 21st Century (1998) Occupational outlook handbook, 1998–99 edition. Bureau of Labor Statistics, Superintendent of Documents, US Government Printing Office, Washington, DC.

Crossing the Quality Chasm: A New Health System for the 21st Century (2001) (Washington, DC: Institute of Medicine).

Davis-Sacks, M. L. (1991) *Final Report: Evaluation of Collaborative Program in Psychiatry*. VA Great Lakes Region Health Services Research and Development Program (Ann Arbor, MI).

Deschamps, J.-C. (1982) 'Social Identity and Relations of Power Between Groups', in H. Tajfel (ed.), *Social Identity and Intergroup Relations* (New York: Cambridge University Press), pp. 85–98.

Dill, A. E. and Rochford, D. A. (1989) 'Coordination, Continuity, and Centralized Control: A Policy Perspective on Service Strategies for the Chronic Mentally Ill', *Journal of Social Issues*, 45, pp. 145–59.

DiTomaso, N., Cordero, R. and Farris, G. F. (1996) 'Effects of Group Diversity on Perceptions of Group and Self Among Scientists and Engineers', in M. N. Ruderman, M. W. Hughes-James, and S. E. Jackson, (eds), *Selected Research on Work Team Diversity* (Greensboro, NC: American Psychological Association), pp. 99–119.

Doise, W., Meyer, G. and Perret-Clermont, A.-N. (1976) *Etude Psycho-Sociologique des Representations d'eleves en fin de Scolarite Obligatoire. Pratique et Theorie.* Cahiers de la Section des Sciences de l'Education de l'Université de Geneve, Vol. 2, pp. 15–27.

Dreachslin, J. L., Hunt, P. L. and Sprainer, E. (2000) 'Workforce Diversity: Implications for the Effectiveness of Health Care Delivery Teams', *Social Science and Medicine*, 50, pp. 1403–14.

Eagly, A. H. (1987) *Sex Differences in Social Behavior: A Social Role Interpretation* (Hillsdale, NJ: Lawrence Erlbaum).

Ely, R. J. (1995) 'The Power of Demography: Women's Social Constructions of Gender Identity at Work', *Academy of Management Journal*, 38: 3, pp. 589–634.

Epstein, C. F. (1988) *Deceptive Distinctions: Sex, Gender, and the Social Order* (New Haven: Yale University Press).

Feiger, S. M. and Schmitt, M. H. (1979) 'Collegiality in Interdisciplinary Health Teams: Its Measurements and Effects', *Social Science and Medicine*, 13A, pp. 217–29.

Fiedler, F. E., Meuwese, W. and Oonk, S. (1961) 'An Exploratory Study of Group Creativity in Laboratory Tasks', *Acta Psychologica*, 18, pp. 100–19.

Freidson, E. (1970) *Professional Dominance: The Social Structure of Medical Care* (New York: Atherton Press).

Gomez, E., Ruiz, P. and Langrod, J. (1980) 'Multidisciplinary Team Malfunctioning on a State Hospital Unit: A Case Study', *Hospital and Community Psychiatry*, 31, pp. 38–40.

Hackman, J. R. (1987) 'The Design of Work Teams', in J. W. Lorsch (ed.), *Handbook of Organizational Behavior* (Englewood Cliffs, NJ: Prentice-Hall), pp. 315–42.

Hamilton, L. C. (1992) *Regression with Graphics: A Second Applied Course in Statistics* (Belmont, California: Duxbury Press).

Jackson, S. E., Brett, J. F., Sessa, V. I., Cooper, D. M., Julin, J. A. and Peyronnin, K. (1991) 'Some Differences Make a Difference: Individual Dissimilarity and Group Heterogeneity as Correlates of Recruitment, Promotions, and Turnover', *Journal of Applied Psychology*, 765, pp. 675–89.

Kanter, R. M. (1977) *Men and Women of the Corporation* (New York: Basic Books).

Lawrence, B. S. (1997) 'The Black Box of Organizational Demography', *Organization Science*, 8: 1, pp. 1–22.

Lichtenstein, R. (1984a) 'The Job Satisfaction and Retention of Physicians in Organized Settings: A Literature Review', *Medical Care Review*, 41, pp. 139–79.

Lichtenstein, R. (1984b) 'Measuring the Job Satisfaction of Physicians in Organized Settings', *Medical Care*, 22: 1, pp. 56–68.

Lichtenstein, R., Alexander, J. A., Jinnett, K. and Ullman, E. (1997) 'Embedded Intergroup Relations in Interdisciplinary Teams: Effects of Perceptions of Level of Team Integration', *Journal of Applied Behavioral Science*, 33: 4, pp. 413–34.

Lockheed, M. E. (1985) 'Sex and Social Influence: A Meta-analysis Guided by Theory', in J. Berger and M. Zelditch (eds) *Status, Rewards, and Influence: How Expectations Organize Behavior* (San Francisco, CA: Jossey-Bass), pp. 406–29.

Matthews, R. C., Lane, I. M., Reber, R. A., Buco, S. M., Chaney, C. M. and Erffmeyer, R. C. (1982) 'Toward Designing Optimal Problem-solving Procedures: Comparisons of Male and Female Interacting Groups' *Group and Organization Studies*, 7, pp. 497–507.

McCain, B. R., O'Reilly, C. O. and Pfeffer, J. 'The Effects of Departmental Demography on Turnover: The Case of a University', *Academy of Management Journal*, 26, pp. 626–41.

Mullen, B., Symons, C., Hu, L.-T. and Salas, E. (1989) 'Group Size, Leadership Behavior, and Subordinate Satisfaction', *Journal of General Psychology*, 116: 2, pp. 155–69.

O'Reilly, C. A., Caldwell, D. F. and Barnett, W. P. (1989) 'Work Group Demography, Social Integration, and Turnover', *Administrative Science Quarterly*, 34, pp. 21–37.

Pelled, L. H. (1996) 'Relational Demography and Perceptions of Group Conflict and Performance: A Field Investigation', *The International Journal of Conflict Management*, 7: 3, pp. 230–46.

Perl, E. (1997) 'Treatment Team in Conflict: The Wishes for and Risks of Consensus', *Psychiatry*, 60, pp. 182–95.

Pfeffer, J. (1983) 'Organizational Demography', in L. L. Cummings and B. M. Staw (eds), *Research in Organizational Behavior* (Greenwich, CT: JAI Press), pp. 299–357.

Pfeffer, J. and O'Reilly, C. (1987) 'Hospital Demography and Turnover Among Nurses', *Industrial Relations*, 36, pp. 158–73.

Price, J. L. and Mueller, C. W. (1989) 'Some Consequences of Turnover: A Work Unit Analysis', *Human Relations*, 42, pp. 389–402.

Rhodes, S. (1983) 'Age-related Differences in Work Attitudes and Behavior: A Review and Conceptual Analysis', *Psychological Bulletin*, 93, pp. 328–67.

Rosella, J. D., Regan-Kubinski, M. J. and Albrecht, S. A. (1994) 'The Need for Multicultural Diversity Among Health Professionals', *Nursing and Health Care*, 15: 5, pp. 242–6.

Rosenheck, R. and Horvath, T. (1998) 'The Impact of Reorganization on Patterns of Mental Health Care', *Psychiatric Services*, 49: 1, p. 53.

Rubin, I. M. and Beckhard, R. (1972) 'Factors Influencing the Effectiveness of Health Teams', *Milbank Memorial Fund Quarterly*, 50, pp. 317–35.

Ryder, N. B. (1965) 'The Cohort as a Concept in the Study of Social Change', *American Sociological Review*, 30, pp. 843–61.

Schneider, B., Kristof, A. L., Goldstein, H. W. and Smith, D. B. (1995) 'What is This Thing Called Fit?' *Handbook of Selection and Appraisal*, 2nd edn (London: John Wiley & Sons).

Sherif, M. and Cantril, H. (1947) *The Psychology of Ego-involvements: Social Attitudes and Identifications* (New York: John Wiley & Sons).

Stamps, P. L., Piedmonte, E. B., Haase, A. B. and Slavitt, D. B. (1978) 'Measurement of Work Satisfaction Among Health Professionals', *Medical Care*, 16, pp. 337–52.

Stangor, C., Lynch, L., Duan, C. and Glass, B. (1992) 'Categorization of Individuals on the Basis of Multiple Social Features', *Journal of Personality and Social Psychology*, 62, pp. 207–18.

Steckler, N. A. and Rosenthal, R. (1985) 'Sex Differences in Nonverbal and Verbal Communication with Bosses, Peers, and Subordinates', *Journal of Applied Psychology*, 70, pp. 157–63.

Stevens, G. and Featherman, D. L. (1981) 'A Revised Socio-economic Index of Occupational Status', *Social Science Research*, 10, pp. 364–95.

Tajfel, H. (1970) 'Experiments in Intergroup Discrimination', *Scientific American*, 223: 5, pp. 96–102.

Tajfel, H., Flement, C., Billig, M. G. and Bundy, R. F. (1971) 'Social Categorization and Intergroup Behavior', *European Journal of Social Psychology*, 1, pp. 149–77.

Tajfel, H. and Forgas, J. P. (2000) 'Social Categorization: Cognitions, Values and Groups', in C. E. Stangor, (ed.), *Stereotypes and Prejudice: Essential Readings* (Philadelphia: Psychology Press), pp. 49–53.

Thomas, E. J. and Fink, C. F. (1963) 'Effects of Group Size', *Psychological Bulletin*, 60: 4, pp. 371–84.

Toseland, R. W., Palmer-Ganeles, J. and Chapman, D. (1986) 'Teamwork in Psychiatric Settings', *Social Work* (Jan.–Feb.) pp. 46–52.

Triandis, H. C., Hall, E. R. and Ewen, R. B. (1965) 'Member Heterogeneity and Dyadic Creativity', *Human Relations*, 18, pp. 33–55.

Tsui, A. S., Egan, T. D. and O Reilly, C. A., III. (1992) 'Being Different: Relational Demography and Organizational Attachment', *Administrative Science Quarterly*, 37: 4, pp. 549–79.

Tsui, A. S. and O'Reilly, C. A., III. (1989) 'Beyond Simple Demographic Effects: The Importance of Relational Demography in Superior–Subordinate Dyads', *Academy of Management Journal*, 32: 2, pp. 402–23.

Turner, J. C. (1985) 'Social Categorization and the Self-concept: A Social Cognitive Theory of Group Behavior', in E. J. Lawler (ed.), *Advances in Group Processes* (Greenwich, CT: JAI Press), pp. 77–122.

Turner, J. C. and Tajfel H. (1996) 'An Introduction', in W. P. Robinson (ed.), *Social Groups and Identities: Developing the Legacy of Henri Tajfel* (Boston: Butterworth Heinemann), pp. 1–23.

Vanderslice, V. J. (1988) 'Separating Leadership from Leaders: An Assessment of the Effect of Leader and Follower Roles in Organizations', *Human Relations*, 41: 9, pp. 677–96.

Wagner, D. G. and Berger, J. (1993) 'Status Characteristics Theory: The Growth of a Program', in J. Berger and J. Morris Zelditch, (eds), *Theoretical Research Programs: Studies in the Growth of Theory* (Stanford, CA: Stanford University Press), pp. 23–63.

Wagner, U., Lampen, L. and Syllwasschy, J. (1986) 'In-Group Inferiority, Social Identity and Out-Group Devaluation in a Modified Devaluation in a Modified Minimal Group Study', *British Journal of Social Psychology*, 25, pp. 15–23.

Wagner, W. G., Pfeffer, J. and O'Reilly, C. A. (1984) 'Organizational Demography and Turnover in Top-Management Groups', *Administrative Science Quarterly*, 29, pp. 74–92.

Wilson, N. J. and Kizer, K. W. (1997) 'The VA Health Care System: An Unrecognized National Safety Net', *Health Affairs*, 16: 4, pp. 200–4.

Zenger, T. R. and Lawrence, B. S. (1989) 'Organizational Demography: The Differential Effects of Age and Tenure Distributions on Technical Communications', *Academy of Management Journal*, 32: 2, pp. 353–76.

4

Pursuing Clinical Governance through Effective Leadership

Peter Spurgeon and Linda Latham

Introduction

This chapter considers the operationalization of leadership in two National Health Service (NHS) Trusts as part of the wider programme of the implementation of clinical governance in the UK health services. It is part of a larger study on the development of clinical governance in the UK NHS.

Background context to clinical governance

In a series of initiatives the UK government has sought to tackle deficiencies in the quality of care provided by the National Health Service. Many of these processes depend on a clear definition of standards of care and associated processes of delivery, and it is in this aspect that clinical governance is crucial. Clinical governance was defined by the consultation document as:

> A framework through which NHS organizations are accountable for continuously improving the quality of their services and safeguarding high standards of care by creating an environment in which excellence in clinical care will flourish. (Department of Health, 1998)

Clinical governance is, in many ways, the centrepiece of the NHS quality reforms, without which other components are unlikely to be able to bring about improvement. Government guidance has described clinical governance as the 'linchpin' of the quality strategy (NHS Executive, 1999a), and has begun to outline what it might consist of and what the first steps in its implementation should be. Key components of clinical governance should include:

- clear lines of responsibility and accountability for the overall quality of clinical care;
- a comprehensive programme of quality improvement activity;
- clear policies aimed at managing risks; and
- procedures for all professional groups to identify and remedy poor performance. (Department of Health, 1998)

Four key actions in the implementation of clinical governance are to:

- establish leadership, accountability and working arrangements;
- carry out a baseline assessment of capacity and capability;
- formulate and agree a development plan in the light of this assessment; and
- clarify reporting arrangements for clinical governance within board and annual reports. (NHS Executive, 1999a)

However, defining clinical governance in terms which support its implementation is difficult. While a clear vision of its aims has been articulated (Scally and Donaldson, 1998), some commentators have argued that the rhetoric obscures a lack of real and concrete ideas about how to turn the vision into reality (Goodman, 1998, 2000). Making quality improvements work in health care organizations is more complex and difficult than at first appears, as others have observed internationally (Blumenthal and Kilo, 1998). The whole systems thinking implicit in many of the changes presents some particular challenges for the NHS.

The definition of clinical governance combines elements of external quality assurance with internal quality improvement: the former for the purpose of upward-vertical accountability, in part to assuage public demand for action, and the latter for continuous internal service development. There may well be some tensions in promoting both goals simultaneously. The somewhat heavy-handed external assurance requirements with the use of a range of performance indicators could well conflict with the conditions of trust, honesty and innovation necessary for internal quality improvement (Davies and Mannion, 1998). The tension has been described by some as bridging the gap between managerial and clinical approaches to quality (Buetow and Roland, 1999). There is growing unease that the long-term cultural change agenda of clinical governance will lose out to an overzealous pursuit of performance management (Freeman *et al.*, 2001).

The NHS does not have a history of strong corporate culture and leadership – on the contrary, NHS organizations often have complex formal and informal systems of clinical and managerial leadership, and have less cultural coherence or fewer shared cultural values (Degeling, Kennedy and Hill, 2001). In the NHS, functional and professional boundaries have been very important, and systems for improvement have often worked within those boundaries rather than crossed them. Getting cross-functional multiprofessional improvement teams to work has been very difficult. The NHS is not well-recognized for its customer orientation, and professional or provider perspectives on quality and performance have predominated. Systems and processes of care in the NHS have been very poorly understood, and only quite recently has attention been focused on studying and improving processes. Finally, though the NHS has undoubtedly been capable of improvement, the context of continuing resource constraint and cost improvement has done much to create a culture of learned helplessness in which no improvement seems possible without an investment of more resources.

From the research programmes initial baseline survey and follow-up interviews, six clear themes emerged as perceived outcomes of implementing clinical governance, and these are summarized in Table 4.1.

Table 4.1 Interviewees' views of the objectives of clinical governance

Consistency and reduced variation	• [Clinical governance is] a useful overarching approach to delivering the best quality care we can…pulling together different elements under a single framework • Greater uniformity and equality of service delivery • [It would mean] standards Trust-wide [with] directorates not going their own way
Whole system approach	• A more comprehensive and systematic approach to quality. Much of it is stuff we've been doing for years but it's uncoordinated and isolated. You can end up with lots of good work but great variation. It's about knitting all that together • Organizationally everyone should be doing it – the whole organization • [It's] about everything from clinical quality to [the] quality of interactions. Mustn't be a bolt on – needs to be integral to what people do when they come to work here, whatever you do • It gives the opportunity to integrate the various activities and to draw the clinicians in more to the process

Table 4.1   continued

Evolutionary approach to development	• I see it as not new, but developing what we have already – evidence-based practice, audit and so on [they] need to be spread wide and integrated • [Clinical governance is] not about doing anything new but bringing [audit, risk management] into a new framework
Raising the status of quality	• [Making] Trusts responsible for the quality of clinical care in the same way as they are for financial • I'd like to see this organization turned round to focus on healthcare, not on the business end. The Trust board in the past has been dominated by the finance, business cases, and so on • Locally it is about coordinating and pulling together quality and linking it to how we govern the Trust. We have been exceedingly financially focused and plainly it is important we shift that to a clinical focus, that is being recognized
Organizational development	• Get the organization in a better position to deliver [the] best possible care to patients • When staff see that something is wrong or could be improved should be able to feel that they can raise this with management • Need [a] culture where people can ask questions
Poor performance	• Backlash from Bristol and other incidents of clinical arrogance • To put it bluntly, we're trying to prevent a 'Bristol' • [An] attempt by the government to stop another Bristol, Kent and Canterbury from occurring

The role of leadership in clinical governance

It has been suggested that the implementation of clinical governance represents a long-term cultural transition for the NHS. Many clinicians have pointed out that they were already conducting clinical audits on their clinical service and therefore the change is less great than it appears. Whilst critical reflection may have been practiced by many clinicians, to suggest that audit equals clinical governance is to over-simplify and to misunderstand the nature of clinical governance.

There are two particular strands of clinical governance that underpin the description of it as a significant cultural change. The first revolves around the externality, the visibility of accreditation processes that go beyond individual clinician behaviour. For example, the introduction of consultant appraisal places clinical performance within the performance management framework of the whole organization. The second key feature is the assignment of accountability for clinical governance to the chief executive, irrespective of his/her clinical background. This not only reinforces the organization-wide focus of governance, but places a demand on the chief executive as an individual to create, influence and sustain the process of clinical governance – to exercise leadership. This is not to imply a single-handed conception of leadership residing solely within the chief executive. Clearly there is a key role for clinical leadership whether expressed through the medical director or clinical director. Emphasizing again the externality of governance and the public's concern to ensure safe practice there is an important leadership contribution, potentially, from the non-executive director or directors within each NHS trust, especially where they have been given an identified lead role for clinical governance.

Much has been written over the past two decades about the critical contribution of managers in supporting and delivering a range of NHS reforms and initiatives (Paton, 1996; Stewart, 1996). Much of the language used in policy documents about the need for and the process of establishing clinical governance has emphasized the need for leadership – both from the chief executive as the accountable officer and also from within the clinical profession. It is, however, couched in generic and rhetorical terms, with statements about leadership as if it was a universal process. The literature on leadership is enormous. Much of it consists of describing the processes by which leaders exercise power or the characteristics that seem to distinguish leaders from others (Du Brin, 1994) but this material is often contradictory in content and somewhat bewildering in terms of concrete action.

From transactional to transformational leadership

There has been in the NHS a gradual movement along a dimension of leadership. This began in the 1980s with the movement from administrator to manager, through the 1990s with the shift from manager to leader, and perhaps now at its most sophisticated with the notion that transactional leadership needs to be replaced by transformational leadership. A simplistic distinction would suggest that transactional leadership places great emphasis upon organizing and planning the use of resources, fixing problems that emerge and monitoring the outcomes and predetermined objectives.

In contrast, transformational leadership goes beyond the management processes and is about creating new scenarios and visions, challenging the status quo, initiating new approaches and exciting the creative and emotional drive in individuals to strive beyond the ordinary to deliver the exceptional (Bass and Avolio, 1995). Further support for the notion of a linkage between transformational leadership and the demands of clinical governance may be found in Conger's (1989) adumbration of the characteristics of transformational leaders. He suggests such leaders will:

- have vision,
- be excellent communicators,
- inspire trust in others,
- help individuals to feel capable, and
- have energy and be action-oriented.

In line with thinking of clinical governance as a team-based activity, so modern concepts of leadership emphasize the role of leaders to develop teams by encouraging, supporting and indeed being a member of such teams.

The notion of leadership as requiring ownership of a shared vision and the widest participation of the workforce is explored further by Hackett and Spurgeon (1996). They point to the evidence that the NHS requires new forms of leadership and that 'the initial steps that managers can adopt perhaps are to develop the "culture" of the vision through the promotion of core values and actions which are needed to deliver the strategic goals', as above. Typically, transformational change will involve a clear vision of the future following baseline assessment or external benchmarking to underline the need for change. In respect to clinical governance it is rather more a centrally imposed change without the preparatory phases, and as a consequence a potential difficulty is in galvanizing staff to the desired end-goal.

Empowerment is a central theme of transformational leadership, that the role of the leader is essentially to lead people to lead themselves. It is suggested here that the cultural transition proposed and the behavioural change sought in clinicians and others is most likely to be effected by use of these transformational leadership processes. In terms of actors within the clinical governance domain, perhaps the key individuals are the chief executive (who is formally accountable) and the clinical governance lead within NHS Trusts.

The role of the chief executive in clinical governance

The transformational/transactional leadership dichotomy appears to be a powerful structure with which to examine the leadership contribution of the chief executive (at least as represented by their response to our interviews). The results, though, are rather disappointing, especially if one leans to the view that the implementation of clinical governance is a major cultural transition. If this is the case then one would expect or hope to see a majority of activities coded in the transformational area. The opposite appears to be the case. The majority of respondents see their role in terms of statutory accountability, the establishment of appropriate systems and structures, and trying to ensure resources are in place to support implementation. These would all be seen as typical transactional leadership activities. Some responses to illustrate this point are:

> It's my job to make sure there is a process there and that it works. The accountability is different in one sense, there is a national focus and expectation that is helpful though it hasn't changed the way I see my role.

> To ensure that those who have responsibility for doing things are doing so.

> Ultimate accountability rests with the CEO. Personally I find it difficult to be accountable for something [I'm] not directly associated with and able to influence.

> I have the responsibility to ensure that the structures are there to enable MD to deliver clinical governance systems.

In contrast, relatively few of the respondents saw their role in transformational terms – for example:

> Trying to create a culture, environment in which clinical governance can flourish.

> It's a huge challenge – unrecognizable. As a result of the White Paper the responsibility for quality rests with me. There's a legitimate interest of the Board in clinical practice. If people think that they have been doing clinical governance for years they're fooling themselves.

> My role is to encourage, influence and inspire – not to order them to do it.

The majority of responses from interviewees fall into these two categories. The remaining responses, although few in number, fall into some related categories of (a) giving priority and emphasis to clinical governance, (b) communicating as much as possible about the meaning and implication of governance and (c) legitimizing the role for the chief executive to challenge clinicians. The full set of responses is represented in Table 4.2.

Where does the current discussion lead us in terms of our understanding of leadership and its role in clinical governance? In terms of the model adopted, transactional and transformational leadership, there is an apparent emphasis upon transactional activities. However, there are two important caveats to this as a negative conclusion.

Firstly, it may be because of the early stage at which the interviews were conducted that they may have identified the structural elements required both nationally and regionally in setting up appropriate committees and infrastructures. This would, of course, be coded as largely transactional leadership activities. Second, the interview schedule was initially designed to assess how the roles of chief executive, clinical lead and non-executive director were seen by incumbents and those closely related to them. This prompted largely descriptive accounts and hence, once again, a tendency to focus upon task-based, transactional leadership. The instances of transformational leadership emerged more as a byproduct of the interview and may, therefore, be underrepresented compared to reality.

Table 4.2   The role of the chief executive in clinical governance

Role areas	Number	Examples
Transformational leadership (vision, empowerment)	6	'The chief executive has to foster an opening up in the culture and style of culture, management.'
Transactional leadership (formal accountability, processes, resources)	18	'Needs a formal process for clinical qual ity – I am formally accountable and I am willing to take action. It can formalize what I would have done.'
Communication	8	'To ensure people are clear about what it is
Prioritize clinical governance	6	'To make sure it gets a high enough priority. Make sure it is at the top of the agenda.'
Legitimize challenge to clinicians	4	'Clinical governance has strengthened my hand. I've not seen a change from my point of view but the clinicians have. Whereas before this guy was impertinently asking questions, now they see he's got a right to do so.'

Perhaps one of the key issues contributing to the relative absence of evidence of transformational leadership is that, in most of the cultural transition models available, great emphasis is placed upon developing and communicating a vision of what the future will look like. If we consider the origin of clinical governance, it seems largely to have acquired impetus from serious clinical problems. Apart from the avoidance of such issues it is rather less easy to develop a coherent model of what a fully implemented clinical governance system looks like within a specific Trust.

Change in response to crises tends to be transactional; that is, the establishment of new procedures to avoid a further crisis. The challenge is to 'transform' this reactive change to one that becomes the norm. It is in this challenge that transformational leadership is critical. It may be, therefore, that this is the next phase. Perhaps this is best summarized by Kotter (1995):

> In the final analysis, change sticks when it becomes 'the way we do things around here', when it seeps into the bloodstream of the corporate body. Until new behaviours are rooted in social norms and shared values, they are subject to degradation as soon as the pressure for change is removed.

Implementing clinical governance: two case studies

The purpose of the case studies described below, within the whole research programme, was to trace the process of implementation and to determine the merits of organizational initiatives, whether individual or collective, to support implementation. A more specific purpose was to assess how far the concepts of leadership were useful in understanding the behaviour observed, or indeed whether they are meaningful when confronted with real behaviour.

The two case study Trusts were both relatively large although very different in type and location. One was an acute Trust based in a large urban conurbation, whilst the other was a significantly dispersed community Trust with a rural and semi-rural setting. Each case study was conducted over a period of 18 months and involved regular interviews with sets of key stakeholders, participation and observation of relevant committees and meetings as well as analysis of appropriate documents. The very abstracted material utilized here attempts to characterize what was observed concerning the leadership style, and more specifically the approach, of the chief executives in each organization.

Using a dichotomized approach to leadership style always runs the risk of simplistic stereotyping. However, as Hackett and Spurgeon (1996) describe, the transformational leader emphasizes the formulation of a future vision, builds commitment to achieve it and seeks to empower other key stakeholders to take the organization forward to attain its goal. Whether stereotypic or not one chief executive fulfilled his role in regard to clinical governance in exactly this way. Very erudite and abstracted papers were produced providing a description of what clinical governance in its implemented state might look like. These were supported by similarly styled briefing meetings for clinical staff in particular. However, despite the creation of relevantly titled committees and groups, the evidence from our case study observation was that the message stopped at an extremely limited role set attached to the chief executive. Interviews with other staff who might have been expected to have been involved in the process of implementation suggested that they did not really understand the vision described and were even less clear about what exactly they were meant to do.

Transformational leadership as evidenced in this way seems to make assumptions that communication equals understanding, and that both clarity of role expectation and the competence to fulfill any such expectations exist. Virtually all of these assumptions were false to a greater or lesser degree. The attraction of transformational style to both leader and followers should perhaps be recognized as appropriate when certain conditions of capacity, competence and motivation exist. It also perhaps serves to underline the dangers inherent in the apparent fad of seeing transformational leadership as a preferred style. Interestingly, as our action research-based feedback began to percolate through regarding the lack of real implementation, so a much more transactional style was adopted to ensure that things happened.

The second case study site also revealed the difficulty of creating cultural change such that the approach of clinical governance becomes embedded in the working practice of front-line staff. However, the style of leadership observed was different. Although formal documents were issued and committees were set up there was no real sense of communication of a vision. The culture of this Trust is one of empowered staff able to enact decisions and operate with considerable autonomy at a very local level. This empowerment, although real in the context of clinical governance, seemed somewhat remote, at a distance and to some degree hopeful. It was as if by general discussion and awareness staff would come to recognize the implications for them and thereby change their own behaviour to the required situation. It felt a little like a process of osmosis where one assumes motivated staff will come to accept and internalize the necessary changes. This belief, whilst enlightened and far from authoritarian, also lacked the classic transactional components of monitoring, checking and controlling, and as a consequence the lack of progress was not really recognized until our case study feedback. Once again the response has been to focus on rather more traditional, perhaps transactional, behaviours to ensure that there is greater clarity of definition and expectation and associated monitoring of progress.

What does this mean for our understanding of leadership?

At a superficial level at least, the concepts of transformational and transactional leadership provide a useful *post hoc* explanatory framework with which to describe observed behaviours. However, other frameworks might well have been equally useful, and perhaps importantly the use of any existing leadership concepts are no more than explanatory after the event. The current NHS interest (obsession) with leadership is rather more with leadership as a predictive concept such that if the appropriate model is adopted it will lead to the desired successful outcome. The reality is that the concern with leadership as solution is essentially naive and simplistic, politically motivated and lacking intellectual rigour. Moreover the nature of how we understand science (social science) is to seek control, prediction and thereby solution to complex, multifaceted problems.

It is suggested instead that the ways in which we seek the holy grail of leadership, and indeed much that is written about leadership, actually take us no further forward at all. The semantic space associated with leadership is overfull and we need some new innovative thinking and concepts in this area. A recent very helpful paper by Alimo-Metcalfe and Lawler (2001) after surveying private-sector organizations suggests that 'leadership is a "woolly" concept. The term "leader" is widely used but ill defined, so that it becomes in practice a nebulous concept.' Perhaps the writings of Wheatley (1993) can suggest where we might go for new thinking. She is of the school that sees concepts such as leadership as emergent. Her work is frequently expressed as analogy and indeed in dramatic format. It takes a largely individual perspective and is quite complex, but the key idea seems to be that the set of variables operating within an organization are too complex, too chaotic to be predictable and controllable. She argues that there is continual multilayered change occurring between the individuals within the organization, and that what will evolve is what works, not what is right. Wheatley is pointing to the reality that our world is inherently dynamic and therefore not susceptible to prediction or control, certainly not with the static concepts we currently have available within the domain of leadership.

References

Alimo-Metcalfe, B. and Lawler, J. (2001) 'Leadership Development in UK Companies at the Beginning of the Twenty-first Century: Lessons for the NHS', *Journal of Management in Medicine*, 15: 5, pp. 387–404.

Bass, B. M. and Avolio, B. J. (eds), (1995) *Improving Organisational Effectiveness through Transformational Leadership* (London: Sage).

Blumenthal, D. and Kilo, C. (1998) 'A Report Card on Continuous Quality Improvement', *Milbank Quarterly*, 76: 4, pp. 625–48.

Buetow, S. A. and Roland, M. (1999) 'Clinical Governance: Bridging the Gap Between Managerial and Clinical Approaches to Quality of Care', *Quality and Safety in Health Care*, 8, pp. 184–90.

Conger, J. (1989) *Transformational Leadership* (Chicago: San Francisco: Jossey Bass).

Davies, H. T. O. and Mannion, R (1998) *Clinical Governance: Striking A Balance Between Checking and Trusting* (York: Centre for Health Economics, University of York).

Degeling, P., Kennedy, J. and Hill, M. (2001) 'Mediating the Cultural Boundaries between Medicine, Nursing and Management – the Central Challenge in Hospital Reform', *Health Services Management Research*, 14, pp. 36–48.

Department of Health (1998) *A First Class Service: Quality in the New NHS* (London: Department of Health).

Du Brin, A. J. (1994) *Applying Psychology: Individual and Organisational Effectiveness*, 4th edn (New Jersey: Prentice Hall, 1994).

Freeman, T., Latham, L., Walshe, K., Wallace, L. and Spurgeon, P. (2001) 'How do Trusts intend to Measure Progress in Clinical Governance?', *Journal of Clinical Governance*, 9: 1, pp. 37–43.

Goodman, N. W. (1998) 'Clinical Governance', *British Medical Journal*, 317: 7174, pp. 1725–7.

Goodman, N. W. (2000) 'Accountability, Clinical Governance and the Acceptance of Imperfection', *Journal of the Royal Society of Medicine*, 93: 2, pp. 56–8.

Hackett, M. and Spurgeon, P. (1996) 'Leadership and Vision in the NHS: How do we Create the "Vision Thing"', *Health Manpower Management*, 22: 1, pp. 5–9.

Kotter, J. (1995) 'Leading Change: Why Transformation Efforts Fail', *Harvard Business Review*, 73: 2, pp. 59–67.

NHS Executive (1999a) *HSC 1999/065. Clinical Governance in the New NHS* (Leeds: NHS Executive).

Paton, C. (1996) *Health Policy and Management: The Healthcare Agenda in a British Political Context* (London: Chapman & Hall).

Scally, G. and Donaldson, L. J. (1998) 'Clinical Governance and the Drive for Quality Improvement in the New NHS in England', *British Medical Journal*, 317, pp. 61–5.

Stewart, R. (1996) *Leading in the NHS: A Practical Guide*, 2nd edn (Basingstoke: Macmillan – now Palgrave Macmillan).

Wheatley, M. (1993) *Leadership and the New Science* (Chicago: Berrett-Koehler).

5

Clinical Leadership in the Intensive Care Unit*

Simon Carmel

This chapter presents an ethnographic analysis of intensive care, explicitly connecting the concepts of uncertainty, interprofessional working and clinical leadership for this particular setting. The focus is on clinical working relationships in the intensive care unit (ICU) – that is, the work of doctors and nurses.

Earlier organizational studies of ICUs, undertaken mainly in North America and Europe, have adopted quantitative approaches and attempted to relate 'organizational factors' to patient outcome. Few results are definitive; briefly, though, several sets of results are relevant to this chapter. Medical leadership by a doctor trained in intensive care and resident senior medical staff have been persistently associated with improved patient outcome. On the other hand, the nursing skill mix has not had a demonstrable impact on patient outcome adjusted for case mix, whilst attempts to measure teamwork or collaboration have found a marginal impact on patient outcomes.[1] This suggests that it is the consultant doctor's actual presence on the unit which has a measurable effect. Some of the mechanisms whereby this occurs are suggested in this chapter.

Given the equivocality of these quantitative studies, which have tended to focus on measurable factors through survey methods, this

*Portions of this chapter's analysis were first presented at the British Sociological Association Medical Sociology Group Conference, 2001. A fuller account of this research will be found in my doctoral thesis. I would like to thank: the managers and staff at the ICUs who kindly allowed ethnographic work to take place; my PhD supervisor Dr Judy Green; and the NHS Research and Development Directorate for its financial support.

study by contrast aims to identify other salient but difficult-to-measure factors which may have more theoretical power or practical use in explaining some of the associations found (for example, that it is the consultant doctor's actual presence on the unit which has a measurable effect). Two such factors which have been found are the concept of 'uncertainty' in medical work, and the working relationships between doctors and nurses in intensive care. Close examination of these factors suggests that clinical leadership in the ICU is provided by consultant clinicians' ability to 'manage' organizational and clinical uncertainty, and to encourage and train other staff in such 'management'.

Background

The topics of uncertainty in medical work, organizational uncertainty, the division of labour in healthcare and leadership have all received considerable theoretical and empirical attention. In this section I highlight some of the main arguments as background to the results.

The first major exponent of uncertainty in medical work was Renee Fox, who drew on her studies of students undertaking medical training in the 1950s (Fox, 1979 [1957]); she later reviewed and charted the progress of the concept (Fox, 1980). In her earlier work, Fox identified two sources of uncertainty for medical students: the 'incomplete or imperfect mastery of available knowledge... [and] the limitations of current medical knowledge' (Fox, 1979, p. 20). According to Fox, the difficulty of distinguishing between these two sources of uncertainty is a third source of uncertainty.

However these analyses were critiqued by Paul Atkinson (1995). His main concern was that a kind of reductionism was occurring, whereby a 'number of different issues are collected together and glossed under this single heading....[which] may obscure as much as it illuminates' (Atkinson, 1995, p. 113). Analysing in detail the situated talk of haematologists, he demonstrated the complexity of clinical culture and talk and argued that '[n]either uncertainty, nor over-confidence, nor dogmatism are all-encompassing features of medical knowledge' (*ibid.*, p. 150). Atkinson did not dismiss the concept of uncertainty altogether, but was rather concerned to accurately interpret its effects in clinical practice.

The concept of uncertainty also appears as a recurring theme in organizational studies, notably related to the perspective of 'Structural Contingency' (Donaldson, 1999). This perspective gained currency when 'uncertainty' appeared in some landmark organizational analyses, for example Crozier (1964) relating uncertainty to the control of power by technical staff in bureaucratic organizations and Thompson (1967) arguing that organizations have a technical core which must be protected against uncertainty. The 'Structural Contingency' perspective seems to have been adopted by van Rossum and colleagues in a large organizational and management study of intensive care:

> The starting point... is the assumption that ICUs can, from the point of view of organizational analysis, be considered as uncertainty-decreasing units. Uncertainty refers, in this case, to various aspects of the input of critically ill patients. [We assume] that uncertainty has to be reduced not only by medical but also management and organizational means. (Van Rossum *et al.*, 1998, p. 153)

In response to this, however, a point Atkinson made (with regard to the sociological theme of uncertainty in medical work) can be appropriately transferred to the theme of uncertainty in organizational research:

> it is necessary to pay rather close attention to *how* uncertainty or certainty are actually conveyed in the course of everyday medical work. It is not enough to account for these things in terms of generic and pervasive features. (Atkinson, 1995, p. 117)

This is not to say that van Rossum and colleagues' approach is necessarily wrong, just that it is in danger of being unidimensional. It is necessary to ascertain empirically the types and kinds of uncertainty in the ICU; only then can we consider what may be the consequences for the accomplishment of organization.

The second theme I address is the nature of interprofessional work. ICUs are formally organized into two professional hierarchies as (Reis Miranda *et al.*, 1998). As I discuss shortly, these two hierarchies overlap they are criss-crossing working relationships within and between the professional groups as they accomplish work in the ICU. Several researchers have demonstrated in other contexts that nurses' work encroaches onto areas that are purportedly the exclusive domain of doctors (Stein, 1967; Hughes, 1980, 1988; Stein *et al.*, 1990; Svensson, 1996; Allen, 1997). These studies indicate that the grounded reality of clinical work contains flexible professional boundaries – not just that the hierarchies overlap but that they are effectively intertwined in work processes. Allen, for example, identified ways that nurses organized activities (for example, the prescription of drugs) which were officially medical, whilst formally asserting a separate jurisdiction (*'de facto* boundary-blurring' – Allen, 1997, p. 511). She also noted that while negotiation of 'blurred boundaries' was claimed by interviewees, it was less observable in practice – perhaps indicating that ultimately it is medical responsibility which has the strongest influence on clinical practice.

In this analysis I assume that consultant clinicians are formally clinical 'leaders' of the ICU, having ultimate responsibility for patient treatment; but I also examine how leadership is achieved in practice. Many of the interactions between consultants and junior doctors (and senior nurses and junior doctors) are demonstrated in my discussion on aspects of uncertainty in the ICU, so I concentrate the second part of the analysis on the interactions between consultant doctors and staff nurses. These data, and in particular the links between uncertainty and interprofessional work, suggest aspects of the nature of leadership in the ICU. Alimo-Metcalfe (1999) has commented that 'transformational leadership', which empowers staff and allows them autonomy and discretion, is best combined – at least in the NHS context – with aspects of 'transactional leadership' which sets clear objectives. In ICU the clinical objectives are generally quite clear, given the acute patient conditions which are presented, but within that there is scope for autonomy for staff to determine aspects of their work. I also want to suggest from the following empirical evidence that the relationship with uncertainty needs to be considered in this regard.

Methods

The methods employed were ethnographic; that is, observational techniques and informal interviews. The particular advantages of this approach are that the workplace is studied *in situ*, directly observing and recording the work as it happens. In addition, by using these methods primacy may be accorded to examining the 'taken-for-granted...practices that influence the way lives are lived, and constructed, in organizational contexts' (Schwartzman, 1993, p. 4).

The data derive from observations of the work and activity of two ICUs for a total of about 200 hours observation. Following ethical approval from university and local research ethics committees, observation was carried out at different times of the week, including nights and weekends; contemporaneous notes were reviewed daily and later transcribed for data analysis.[2]

Uncertainty in the ICU

I identified three broad categories of uncertainty in the ICU, related to medical knowledge, patient treatment and organizational issues. Examples of these three kinds of uncertainty, and the responses to them, are presented below.

First, then, there is the uncertainty in medical knowledge. Following Fox, 'uncertainty in knowledge' can be divided into two parts – uncertainty in the knowledge base of medicine as a whole, and uncertainty in an individual's knowledge. But, at least for the case of the ICU, the response to both these sources of uncertainty is basically the same: practical solutions are what matter.

> During the ward round, Consultant K: 'No-one understands the physics of high-frequency ventilation [all we know for sure is that it's something to do with] the increased surface area...that was one of the few things I learnt at Bart's.' (Extract 1, ICU_1)

Apparently the physical effects of this technology on the human lung are not understood. But this lack of biophysical understanding is irrelevant to all intents and purposes – all that matters is that the 'black box' works and that the treatment of the patient is clinically effective.

The uncertainty in an individual's knowledge, which Fox found was pertinent to medical students' perceptions, is much less important for an 'experienced practitioner', who seems to have a better-developed understanding of particular clinical situations in comparison with junior doctors and nurses. For example, uncertainty about whether intensive care treatment is appropriate is rendered less salient by a consultant's greater experience:

> A new admission has been called a 'crumbly' [patient inappropriate for intensive care] by junior doctors and nurses, who say that 'the patient is self-ventilating, so why is she being admitted?' Some time after this patient comes in, and he's discussed it with the consultant, G [specialist registrar] explains to me that she might be in renal failure (but they don't know that for certain – and the patient needs to be in ICU for the time being). (Extract 2, ICU_1)

Note here also that another source of uncertainty – whether the patient has kidney failure – is dealt with by keeping the patient for observation in the ICU. The attitude of ICU consultants to the clinical problems they are presented with in intensive care was nicely summed up by consultant M:

> 'I think medicine is quite simple really, so long as you do the simple things well...It doesn't matter what's wrong with the patient, whether they've got some rare disease....intensive care is not rocket science. ICU doctors believe we can spot a problem – ABC [Airway, Breathing, Circulation].' (Extract 3, ICU_2)

Even where biomedical and technical knowledge is widely accepted and well-known, there are still sources of 'uncertainty' in patient treatment. These tend to be managed by risk assessments, for example 'nursing risk assessment' for moving patients, and routine clinical audit. For example, lines are regularly changed as part of infection control and are routinely sent to labs for detection of infectious agents. The response to detection of infectious agents combines routine work and clinical judgement informed by other, non-biomedical, evidence:

> B [junior doctor] told me about a worry regarding the patient in bed 2 – the tip of the epidural had grown an antibiotic-resistant bug. Also, as she was waking up she had been saying she didn't like the light (and now had a mask over her eyes) – an indication for meningitis...So B is going to take bloods and send them off to the lab, as well as change the antibiotics they had been giving. But the consultant had not been too bothered as the patient's daughter had said that the patient normally doesn't like the light – has curtains drawn at home etc. (Extract 4, ICU_2)

The point is that the consultant uses and interprets a very different kind of knowledge (biographical knowledge from the patient's relatives) to deal with what had been a 'worry' (from a purely biomedical viewpoint) for the junior doctor.

Similarly, some treatments and procedures have inherent risks, but these can be managed by obtaining specialist advice; in the following example advice was obtained from both doctors in the infectious diseases department (regarding the probable diagnosis and consequential treatment), and subsequently neurologists (regarding the safety of a particular investigation):

One of the patients has suspected meningitis – this necessitates a lumbar puncture (LP) to obtain the cerebral spinal fluid. This is potentially a risky procedure as consultant A tells me that the 'brain can come out through the skull'; he is happy to pass on to the infectious disease doctors... [Later that day] They didn't rush to do the LP, wanted to see the scan formally reported. As there is no asymmetry in the scan they'll go ahead: 'Neurology are happy.' (Extract 5, ICU_2)

Medical investigations carried out in series can entail long periods of waiting for results or the effects of earlier treatment. This can make treatment difficult to plan, but planning is still seen as important by ICU consultants:

[During a ward round] Consultant M: 'What's the motivation with this patient? Is it to get her out of ICU to die or is it to get her out of ICU to be a long-term respiratory patient? Neither [respiratory physician] would be happy with that.' The long-term objective is unclear even though they had discussed this patient at the 'grand round'...M seemed disappointed that there wasn't an objective, a rationale. (Extract 6, ICU_2)

So far I have identified uncertainty at two broad levels: knowledge and patient treatment. A third kind of uncertainty can be called organizational contingency. Approximately 75 per cent of admissions to intensive care in the UK are unplanned[3]; for much of the time ICU staff do not know what kind of patient will be admitted next. These unplanned admissions necessitate liaison between the ICU and other parts of the hospital. In the following two examples, liaison with the operating theatre would be required; the first example is for a patient awaiting surgery:

At the bedside of patient number one, consultant B asked: 'Do we know what time he's on?' Junior doctor: 'No, we know he's on the list, we just don't know what time.' Consultant W makes a joke about it being like airlines – 'they overbook by 10%.' To which one of the nurses replied 'It's OK, we'll be here all night!' (Extract 7, ICU_1)

Hence a confidence about dealing with contingencies is clearly expressed by the nurse. In the following example liaison is required with the operating theatre regarding a patient admitted to the hospital in an emergency. It can be seen how practical organizational contingencies are planned for by junior doctors and senior nurses working closely together:

> (9:25pm) Phone call, V [staff nurse] answers, she passes on to B [junior doctor]: 'B, there's an anaesthetist on the phone, it sounded bad.' B comes round and takes the call, spends a while listening: '...Right...Oh God...Hmmm...Right...Cool. That's fine. What's he got?' J (charge nurse) wanders up to the workstation, leans over and says quietly (while B is still on the phone) '[There] aren't any beds to transfer to.' As soon as B finishes on the phone J says 'Only contingency we could think of the other night, as [HDU (high dependency unit)] was full, was theatre and recovery...not ideal – on HDU they've got five on ventilators.' B: 'Trouble is these two' (he indicates beds 3 and 4) 'are quite high maintenance aren't they?' B phones the regional bed monitor – there are no available ICU beds in the region. B: 'Triple A in theatre, lots of medical problems...'. J: 'See if HDU can transfer out...[because] if in theatre and recovery, you'll need two nurses down there'. [which will leave them very short-staffed on ICU]. (Extract 8, ICU_2)

The junior doctor in this example successfully negotiated a transfer of one of the patients in intensive care to the HDU by discussing with the HDU nurses which of their patients could be discharged to a general ward – this freed up a bed without having to keep the emergency patient in Recovery. Later on that night there were two more referrals to the ICU, which necessitated the doctors visiting a surgical ward and Accident and Emergency to assess patients. For one of these it was decided that they 'won't survive ICU' (I later learnt that this patient subsequently died); the other was transferred, after much negotiation, to another ICU nearby. So although the 'contingency planning' by the charge nurse and junior doctor was not actually utilized that night, it is clear that it forms a part of the accomplishment of organization in the ICU.

Finally, patterns and routines can mitigate against the feeling of chaos and uncertainty:

> T [junior doctor] talks me through admission. 'You have about an hour on bits and pieces, get patient settled, take bloods, do admin. Then you start to assess the O_2 levels. Stabilizing takes about an

hour.' Then about an hour assessing 'the direction they're going in.' All in all about 2–3 hours 'at least.' (Extract 9, ICU_2)

So work in the ICU is often uncertain and contingent on organizational and knowledge-based factors. ICU workers demonstrate a variety of responses to these sources of uncertainty, including the adoption of routines (which may or may not be codified in protocols); the continual planning of patient treatment and organizational activities; and focusing on the practicalities of patient treatment rather than worrying unduly about abstract knowledge. These are the ways in which uncertainty is effectively dealt with.

'Overlapping hierarchies' in the ICU

The 'overlapping [clinical] hierarchies' in ICU (Reis Miranda *et al.*, 1998) are easily distinguished. For example, doctors sometimes did not know who senior nursing staff were: in one instance a junior doctor, on answering the phone, had to ask a nurse 'who's G?' – G was in fact the nurse manager for the ICU. Another telling example, in one of the ICUs, was in the different rooms for medical and nursing staff to take their breaks. The 'staff room' was for the nurses, used for their hand-over meetings and breaks, and notices advertising meetings for nurses were put up in here. The 'seminar room' was for the doctors, used for their hand-over meetings and breaks, and medical journals were kept in this room. Having said this, there was some overlap in the use of these rooms, especially at weekends and at times when the unit was less busy – this finding is similar to Hughes' (1980, p. 69): at night, in contrast to daytime, casualty doctors and nurses would congregate around tea and coffee-making facilities.

To give a flavour of the generality of the interaction between the two professions, consider the following from a junior doctor:

T [junior doctor] says she tries not to call out consultants unless absolutely necessary (and sometimes it is necessary). In turn, she says, the 'nurses here are very good, they try not to disturb you [i.e. if asleep] unless absolutely necessary...that isn't always the best thing, as sometimes you wish you could have been disturbed earlier.' (Extract 10, ICU_2)

Thus at night particularly, although the junior doctor doesn't put it in these terms, there is considerable symmetry in the junior doctor's work.

The nurses try not to wake up the junior doctors, who in turn try not to wake up consultants. There is thus a close interaction between the two formally 'distinct' hierarchies.

The work of junior doctors and 'middle-manager' nurses (sisters or charge nurses, who lead a shift) requires particularly close coordination. In one unit I studied this appeared to be a result of the way that work is distributed by the consultants at the ward round: both junior doctors and nurses are given things to do by the consultant(s) at this time. Whilst the sister or charge nurse must take responsibility for the activities of the nurse at the patient's bedside, the junior doctors are given work to do directly. In particular, close working between these two groups is required around the period of a new admission, and in liaison with other parts of the hospital (Extract 8). Perhaps inevitably, this close working relationship can result in problems arising:

> While the doctors are away from the unit, J [charge nurse] says to me: 'one of these times is when it's difficult.' Why? Basically the doctors are all away and he has responsibility for the patient just admitted, and he has had to make decisions which he feels are not effectively nurse's to make (e.g. deciding which drugs to give etc.). (Extract 11, ICU_2)

These tensions are not always conspicuous, and on other occasions I observed these two sets of workers interacting over several different issues. For example, the senior nurse might explain monitoring equipment to a junior doctor; might need authorization for a course of action or clinical advice (for example, possible side-effects of a drug), or may even just need to encourage the junior doctors to go back to the main ward when they have been too long on a hand-over.

The responsibilities and work of senior nurses and junior doctors overlap to a great extent, partly a function of how consultants give instructions. An additional factor might be that senior nurses are permanent members of staff whereas junior doctors are temporary and trainees. We have seen examples of how consultants treat uncertainty with respect to junior doctors (Extracts 2, 4, 6) – I now come to consider interactions with nursing staff.

There were noticeable differences in medical consultant 'styles', and not all consultants were approachable on any matter:

> E [staff nurse] came up to the workstation, where the consultant [Dr F] was; she showed him some blood gas readings. He said 'Who's

this?' When she indicated bed 4, he said 'that's the SHO's job: "Dr F [i.e. me] is on call today"'. (Extract 12, ICU_2)

Other consultants were on first name terms with all staff, and behaved informally, for example 'mucking in' with many aspects of ICU work:

Y [charge nurse] came back from his break, needed help with lifting a heavy patient...he asked three nurses, who were at the workstation, to help. 'I need to roll him, change his sheet, put his cream on'...He sees consultant M at the workstation and says 'Come on M!' M goes behind the curtain to assist the four nurses. (Extract 13, ICU_2)

This consultant explained to me that he tried in general to be sensitive to the nursing perception of either the organizational or clinical situation:

Consultant M explained to me his normal routine. He comes in a few minutes early and sits at the workstation... [partly to assess whether] there are enough staff. 'Eventually someone talks to me'; the nursing view is very different from the medical view: 'Medically, you might need something doing...[but] there's no use in planning, say, a tracheostomy if you're short of staff'...(The consultant previously on call had telephoned to suggest a tracheostomy for patient 5, but as they're short staffed today 'that never crossed my mind'). (Extract 14, ICU_2)

In another example, a consultant demonstrates his awareness of (and respect for) the nurse's viewpoint:

[During doctor's hand-over] Consultant A said 'It's interesting, you know, I was with E [staff nurse] in cubicle B and she said "where are we going with [name of patient in bed 2]? I've not actually nursed him, but..."'...It's interesting if that's the prevailing view of the nursing staff.' (Extract 15, ICU_2)

It may be that the consultant here is 'enrolling' the nurse to strengthen his case to his colleagues that they *should* be 'going somewhere' with this patient, but this still shows an awareness of nursing staffs' viewpoints.

One aspect of intensive care is the habitual presence on the unit of consultants, which facilitates the close working relationship between them and nurses over periods of time. An example of this was the

setting up of a 'follow-up' clinic: one of the nurses talked very enthusi-
astically about working closely with one of the consultants on this
clinic. In addition, consultants can sometimes use their authority in the
hospital hierarchy to act on behalf of the ICU and the nurses within it.
For example, one staff nurse told me of an occasion when they had been
trying to discharge a patient for several days, but the bed manager had
repeatedly said 'there are no beds' while still admitting new patients
from outside the hospital. The nurse mentioned this to a consultant
who apparently took the issue up directly with the bed-manager's supervisor.

There are more direct ways in which the consultants' presence on the
ICU is useful to nurses. Firstly, in 'emergency' clinical situations they
can be on hand to administer treatment. On two occasions I witnessed
ward rounds being interrupted when a particular course of treatment
had precipitated an adverse patient response. On these occasions the
consultants (and junior doctors) were called over to the bed in question,
and when there implemented treatment directly. A second way in
which the presence of consultants is useful for the nurses might be
termed non-clinical reasons:

> When consultant A returned from lunch, R [staff nurse] said 'I need
> you in cubicle B' – the relatives were trying to take the body, but A's
> view is that a coroner's report would be required. (Extract 16,
> ICU_2)

So the consultant's authority enables him to intervene directly in a
potentially tricky situation with a patient's relatives.

Another aspect of the interaction between medical consultants and
staff nurses is the way that staff nurses may interrupt meetings between
doctors on behalf of patients and relatives:

> At bed 2, E [staff nurse] is explaining something to relatives, but
> they had not really understood – they came up to the workstation
> asking to speak to a doctor...E reappeared, took them back to bed 2
> to try again. They still weren't satisfied...[Later:] On the way to her
> early evening break, E pops in to the seminar room where consult-
> ant N had been explaining something to B [SHO], a kind of *ad hoc*
> teaching session. E: 'You won't forget "my relatives" will you?'
> N. says 'No', and a minute or so later he says to B, 'Who wants to
> talk to bed 2's relatives?' B agrees to, and they discuss the 'plan'.
> (Extract 17, ICU_2)

So the medical and nursing hierarchies do more than just overlap; there are particular points of intersection and close working between them. Consultants, at the top of one particular hierarchy but also clinical leaders for the ICU, could be seen to participate in all aspects of patient care, and sometimes demonstrated a sensitivity to the nursing viewpoint. Additionally, they were on hand to assist with difficult situations in treatment or with patients' relatives.

Clinical leadership in the ICU

In considering the data I have presented thus far, I would like to make a few comments pertaining to the leadership by medical consultants in the ICU. Leadership is principally provided by ICU consultants in being present on the unit while major interventions (and concomitant possible difficulties) are occurring and discussions with patients' relatives. But importantly, in addition to this there are ways in which consultants attempt to rhetorically reduce the effects of uncertainty in order to provide their leadership. For example, they may indicate that intensive care medicine is not that difficult:

> [Consultant A:] 'Medical decisions in intensive care are not that difficult, especially once the patient has been admitted, because at that stage you can just wait and see (more difficult decision is when to admit, what to say to relatives, etc.)...medicine is 75% auto-pilot, 25% thinking on feet. You don't have to be that clever.' (Extract 18, ICU_2)

This portrayal of intensive care as 'not that difficult' can be contrasted with the earlier examples about how treatments in intensive care can be uncertain (for example, Extract 5). The combined effect is to provide an organizational context in which discussions about patient treatment may be held with nursing staff, on a trial and error basis:

> Consultant M told me that when nurses come up with an idea he tends to be relaxed and say 'OK, let's go with it for now – after all, half of what I try doesn't work...We all feel like we get our own way.' Just as we were speaking, N [staff nurse] came up and asked about a feed, tidal volumes. M said 'try it for a little while'. (Extract 19, ICU_2)

This openness to nursing suggestions was also mentioned by another nurse, who told me a story of when he had gone to ask a consultant's opinion about treatment of a patient. The consultant interrupted him, saying 'I don't want to know what you think should be done, I want to know what you have done.' In this way the consultant is clearly stretching responsibilities and acting in a transformational way.

ICU consultants I interviewed also emphasized the importance of planning, for example:

> [What is the purpose of the morning ward round?] Consultant S: 'There are several things. Firstly there is the changeover of staff...a communication exercise in terms of what *has* happened...who the patients are, what has gone on over the previous night. The second place is to plan what we're going to do with that patient or what the plans are in terms of: are we moving forward; are we going backwards; what interventions do we need to do; are they going to need surgery. Are we getting to the point where they should be leaving for the ward. So really it's a business round to sort out what has happened.' (Interview, Consultant, ICU_1)

So at the patient level consultants provide leadership by planning; at the organizational level consultants provide leadership by acting on behalf of the nurses in their unit. They may also cultivate an atmosphere of being open to suggestions which is facilitated by representing intensive care as 'not that difficult' *and* uncertain. Regarding their interactions with junior doctors, they seem to just dismiss the issues and emphasize that practical solutions are what matters.

Conclusion

This research has suggested ways that consultants demonstrate their leadership of the ICU, in both transactional and transformational ways. By being present and accessible on the ICU, they not only foster good relationships with the nursing staff but are able to assist with difficulties experienced by the nurses as they arise. These difficulties may be acute clinical situations, issues with relatives, or broader organizational matters. In addition, by instilling the virtues of 'planning' (especially in patient treatment) they help to give more junior staff a sense of purpose in their work. Furthermore, by being open to suggestions from nursing staff the consultants can foster a sense of collaboration within the ICU.

ICU is a particular clinical context, and some of these findings may not be readily generalizable to other contexts. In particular, the ICU is an organizational entity with a concentration of both medical and nursing staff, and provided many examples of interprofessional work which may either be more difficult to observe on other wards with fewer staff, or the interactions on other wards may be of a substantively different quality. Perhaps more generalizable were the examples found of particular consultants – clinical leaders – being sensitive to the situations of more junior staff, being prepared to take on board alternative viewpoints, and encouraging the development of the staff who reported to them.

Notes

1 The major quantitative studies of organizational factors and intensive care have been: Shortell and colleagues, 1994 (USA); Reis Miranda and colleagues, 1998 (Europe); and the Audit Commission, 1999 (UK). The results of these and other studies are summarized in Carmel and Rowan (2001).
2 Field notes, where presented, have been grammatically and cosmetically improved to aid legibility. Quotation marks indicate verbatim or near-verbatim recording.
3 *Source*: Intensive Care National Audit and Research Centre's Case Mix Programme Database, accessed August 2000; data from 46,587 admissions to 93 ICUs in England, Wales and Northern Ireland.

References

Alimo-Metcalfe, B. (1999) 'Leadership in the NHS: What are the Competencies and Qualities Needed and How Can They Be Developed?' in A. L. Mark and S. Dopson (eds), *Organisation Behaviour in Health Care: The Research Agenda* (Basingstoke: Macmillan – now Palgrave Macmillan).

Allen, D. (1997) 'The Nursing–Medical Boundary: A Negotiated Order?' *Sociology of Health and Illness*, 19: 4, pp. 498–520.

Atkinson, P. (1995) *Medical Talk and Medical Work* (London: Sage).

Audit Commission (1999) *Critical to Success: The Place of Efficient and Effective Critical Care Services Within the Acute Hospital* (London: The Audit Commission).

Carmel, S. and Rowan, K. (2001) 'Variation in Intensive Care Unit Outcomes: A Search for the Evidence on Organizational Factors', *Current Opinion in Critical Care*, 7: 4, pp. 284–96.

Crozier, M. (1964) *The Bureaucratic Phenomenon* (Chicago: University of Chicago Press).

Donaldson, L. (1999) 'The Normal Science of Structural Contingency Theory', in S. R. Clegg and C. Hardy (eds), *Studying Organization: Theory and Method* (London: Sage).

Fox, R. C. (1957) 'Training for Uncertainty', in *Essays in Medical Sociology: Journeys into the Field* (Chichester: John Wiley & Sons), 2nd edn, 1979.

Fox, R. C. (1980) 'The Evolution of Medical Uncertainty', *Milbank Memorial Fund Quarterly*, 59: 1, pp. 1–49.

Hughes, D. (1980) '*Lay Assessment of Clinical Seriousness: Practical Decision-Making by Non-Medical Staff in a Hospital Casualty Department*', unpublished PhD thesis, University College of Swansea.

Hughes, D. (1988) 'When Nurse Knows Best: Some Aspects of Nurse/Doctor Interaction in a Casualty Department', *Sociology of Health and Illness*, 10: 1, pp. 1–22.

Reis Miranda, D., Ryan, D. W., Schaufeli, W. B. and Fidler, V. (eds) (1998) *Organisation and Management of Intensive Care: A Prospective Study in 12 European Countries* (Berlin: Springer).

Rossum, W. van (c. 1997) *The Implementation of Technologies in Intensive Care Units: Ambiguity, Uncertainty and Organizational Reactions*. http://www.ub.rug.nl/eldoc/som/97B51/97b51.pdf (accessed 21 Sept 2001).

Rossum, W. van (1998) 'Organization', in D. Reis Miranda, D. W. Ryan, W. B. Schaufeli and V. Fidler (eds), *Organisation and Management of Intensive Care: A Prospective Study in 12 European Countries* (Berlin: Springer), pp. 151–69.

Schwartzman, H. B. (1993) *Ethnography in Organizations* (London: Sage).

Sexton, J. B., Thomas, E. J. and Helmreich, R. L. (2000) 'Error, Stress, and Teamwork in Medicine and Aviation: Cross Sectional Surveys', *British Medical Journal*, 320, 745–9.

Shortell, S. M., Zimmerman, J. E., Rousseau, D. M., Gillies, R. R., Wagner, D. P., Draper, E. A., Knaus, W. A. and Duffy, J. (1994) 'The Performance of Intensive Care Units: Does Good Management Make A Difference?', *Medical Care*, 32: 5, pp. 508–25.

Stein, L. (1967) 'The Doctor-Nurse Game', *Archives of General Psychiatry*, 16, pp. 699–703.

Stein, L., Watts, D. and Howell, T. (1990) 'The Doctor–Nurse Game Revisited', *The New England Journal of Medicine*, 322: 8, pp. 546–49.

Svensson, R. (1996) 'The Interplay Between Doctors and Nurses – A Negotiated Order Perspective', *Sociology of Health and Illness*, 18: 3, pp. 379–98.

Thompson, J. D. (1967) *Organizations in Action* (London: McGraw-Hill).

Part II

Leading Health Care Organizations

6

Knowledge Management and Communities of Practice in the Private Sector: Lessons for Leading the 'Quality Revolution' in Health Care*

Paul Bate and Glenn Robert

Introduction

Following publication of the National Health Service (NHS) Plan (Department of Health, 2000a), the health service in England and Wales has embarked upon a radical and far-reaching programme of change and reform. Leading the implementation of the Plan is the Modernisation Agency which has been charged with providing the NHS 'with a centre of excellence as to how knowledge and 'know-how' about best practice can be spread' (Department of Health, 2000b). The Agency also incorporates the NHS Leadership Centre which aims to produce a 'step change in the development of leadership within the NHS' and, with it, 'a revolution in health care'.

*We are grateful to colleagues who have assisted with our research into the Cancer Services (Hugh McLeod and Chris Ham), Mental Health (Jeanne Hardacre and Louise Locock) and Orthopaedic Services (Hugh McLeod) Collaboratives. Our research into the Orthopaedic Services Collaborative was funded by the Eastern, South-East, South & West and Trent regional offices of the NHS Executive. Our research into the Mental Health Collaborative was funded by the Northern & Yorkshire and Trent regional offices. GR's research into the Cancer Services Collaborative was funded by the Department of Health. The views expressed here are those of the authors and do not necessarily represent the views of the respective funding agencies. Some of the material in this chapter first appeared in an article in the journal *Public Administration*. We are grateful to Blackwell Publishing for granting us permission to use this material here.

The Plan explicitly commits the NHS to an approach to service redesign that 'mirrors the change management approach taken in much of the private sector'. Following others who have sought to interpret business approaches for public-service contexts (Alimo-Metcalfe and Lawler, 2001; Pollitt, 1996), in this chapter we investigate the knowledge management (KM) practices of leading private-sector organizations and assess their likely relevance to those leading NHS reform, the particular focus in this instance being quality improvement.

Within the broader context described above, the ten-year NHS Plan singled out one particular methodology for bringing about the necessary step change in the quality of care. 'Breakthrough Collaboratives' would provide a 'new system of devolved responsibility' and 'help local clinicians and managers redesign local services around the needs and convenience of patients' (Department of Health, 2000a). The result is that numerous national or multi-regional Collaboratives are now to be found operating within the NHS, involving thousands of improvement teams and hundreds of Trusts, and said to be affecting millions of patients (Department of Health, 2002). There are also a great number of Collaboratives taking place in other parts of the world, making it one of the leading contemporary methodologies in health care improvement. Two years on from the Plan, the first progress report by the NHS Modernization Board (Department of Health, 2002) recently reaffirmed this earlier commitment, describing the Collaboratives as 'playing a major role in spreading best practice' and 'helping to improve patients' experiences of the NHS'.

The real innovation (and distinguishing feature) of Collaboratives lies in the creation of horizontal networks which cut across the hierarchical and relatively isolated organizations that make up the NHS. Such clinician-driven networks enable a wide range of professionals in a large number of organizations to come together to learn and 'harvest' good practice from each other, and to go back and apply this to their own services. They also empower relatively junior staff to take ownership for solving local problems by working with clinicians who have taken change leadership roles. Through such mechanisms Collaboratives aim to implement an incremental bottom-up improvement process (a learning-based approach to change) rather than simply applying an 'off the shelf' top-down methodology.

This chapter draws on our extensive qualitative and quantitative research into three Collaboratives in the NHS during the period April 2000 to January 2002 (Robert *et al.*, 2002, 2003; Bate *et al.*, 2002) and an exploration of contemporary private-sector practices with regard to

KM and (as one specific part of that) communities of practice. In so doing the chapter examines how private-sector KM concepts and practices might further assist organizations already at the forefront of quality improvement in health care and in other public sectors.

Improving quality in the NHS

Notwithstanding the difficulties of researching total quality management (TQM) and continuous quality improvement (CQI) strategies (Maguerez *et al.*, 2001), past attempts at securing big improvements in both public and private-sector service quality appear to have proved difficult, with anticipated gains often failing to materialize or to be sustained in the longer term. This is broadly consistent with the findings of our research into NHS Collaboratives which, whilst showing positive and by no means insignificant outcomes, suggest something more modest than originally hoped for or claimed (Bate *et al.*, 2002; Robert *et al.*, 2003).

This profile of outcomes and levels of success that are less – sometimes considerably less – than originally planned or predicted has been widely documented in the organization development and strategy literatures, and often referred to as the 'implementation gap' (Centre for the Evaluation of Public Policy and Practice, 1994; Shortell *et al.*, 1995; Ovretveit, 2000; Coyle-Shapiro and Morrow, 2001; Iles and Sutherland, 2001; Counte and Meurer, 2001). Consequently, there is a danger that the Collaborative approach may not lead to any significant or sustained improvements in service and that the quality revolution fails to materialize.

Finding ways of increasing the impact and effectiveness of Collaboratives begins with a recognition that the method involves the creation of a network organization for the sharing of knowledge, experience and good practice, the knowledge network being the 'lifeblood' of the approach. Collaboratives thereby represent one approach among many to attempt to build learning and knowledge networks between participating health care organizations. The basis of KM is that individual knowledge is largely unknown to others and therefore wasted (Quintas, 2002), and in this context the whole point of a Collaborative is to liberate that knowledge and enable others to benefit from it.

As we examine the wider literature on networks and KM and explore contemporary private-sector practices, we shall question the extent to which Collaboratives, as they are presently constituted, are effective mechanisms for knowledge transfer and joint learning, and what potential they might have of becoming so. We ask if there is something we can learn from the private sector, especially service organizations, about KM that can lead the NHS Modernization Agency to realize more from this methodology. Might there be, for example, better ways of bringing people together and of interactively developing and sharing their knowledge? And a broader question, to what extent does the KM perspective help us to develop new concepts and vocabularies for interrogating, and ultimately improving, existing approaches to health care quality?

Knowledge management and communities of practice

Knowledge management

The purpose of KM as a field of research and practice is how to better utilize the knowledge or 'intellectual capital' contained in an organization's network (Cummings, 2001; Stewart, 1997; Teece, 2000). KM may therefore be defined as any process or practice of creating, acquiring, capturing, aggregating, sharing and using knowledge, wherever it resides, to enhance organizational learning and performance (Scarbrough *et al.*, 1999). KM recognizes that knowledge, and not simply information, is the primary source of an organization's innovative potential (Castells, 1996; Marshall, 1997). What KM does is make knowledge a problematic: it says that the mere possession of potentially valuable knowledge somewhere within an organization does not mean that other parts of the organization benefit from this knowledge (Szulanski, 2000). And further to this it says that just because a knowledge network (such as a Collaborative) exists does not necessarily mean that the desired knowledge flows are actually occurring.

Academic interest in KM has increased rapidly since the mid-1990s as reflected in the burgeoning literature and attempts at identifying the key success factors for implementing a KM strategy (Davenport and Prusak, 1998). Such interest is mirrored in, indeed probably derivative of, practice, as the majority of leading companies now have a KM strategy and related policies and practices for building knowledge highways across traditional structures (Allee, 2000; Murray and Myers, 1997). Quintas (2002) suggests that for most firms the priorities are the 'capture' of employees' knowledge, exploitation of existing knowledge resources or assets, and improved access to expertise. Amongst others he cites Ernst and Young's sharing knowledge and best-practice initiative, Dow Chemical's leveraging intellectual assets project, and Skandia's efforts to measure and audit the value of knowledge and intangible assets. It is the first part of KM, the *storage* of information, that is most often described (Martensson, 2000) and most work relates to practice-based descriptions of information systems and information technology – the 'hardware' of KM. In contrast, there is a relative scarcity of empirical, especially in-depth case-study-based work on the 'people issues' – the 'software' – and almost no reference to KM in the public sector.

Our research on NHS Collaboratives offers support for such an alternative 'social constructivist' model of knowledge: knowledge is not objective but exists subjectively and intersubjectively through people's interactions, through working together, sharing knowledge, respect and trust:

> Our view is that [Collaboratives] should retain the basics of what they are doing but avoid overemphasising the 'rules, regulations and reporting relationships' and develop a parallel OD programme to deal with all the important (but missing) 'people' processes. This calls for a very different perspective on the task at hand, one that puts less weight on mechanics, programme rules and regulations ('Collaborative as a machine') and more on the idea of nurturing a social and community process ('Collaborative as an organic entity'). (Bate *et al.*, 2002)

In such models, interest in the second aspect of KM (more pertinent to NHS modernization) – the *transfer* of knowledge – builds on the work of Polanyi (1958, 1966) and others who make an important distinction between different types of knowledge: *explicit* knowledge consists of facts, rules, relationships and policies that can be faithfully codified in paper or electronic form and shared without the need for discussion (Wyatt, 2001), whereas *tacit* knowledge is engrained in the analytical and conceptual understandings of individuals ('know what') and also embodied in their practical skills and expertise ('know how') (Kogut and Zander, 1992; Nonaka, 1994). The value of such tacit knowledge has long been recognized by private-sector companies (Hauschild *et al.*, 2001; Grant, 2001).

However, individually-held tacit knowledge is a 'precarious way of storing, maintaining and transferring knowledge' (Argote, 1999) as, although individuals can improve their performance as they gain experience with a task, they may not be able to articulate what strategies they used to achieve this improvement (the notion 'we know more than we can tell'). Consequently, tacit knowledge is 'sticky' and often travels poorly between organizations (Zander, 1991; Szulanski, 1996; Schulz, 2001), which has important implications for NHS modernization.

One way of overcoming such difficulties is to convert tacit knowledge to explicit knowledge – codifiability holding the key to spread – a process that Collaboratives seek to facilitate through discussion of locally designated 'best' practice and the subjective experiences of participants, and using these to inform shared guidelines and protocols. Fundamental to knowledge creation, therefore, is the blending of tacit and explicit knowledge and the need to convert and codify tacit knowledge in order to improve its 'fluidity' or 'transferability' across organizational boundaries.

Given the emphasis attached to the importance of tacit knowledge in the KM literature, the informal processes for knowledge generation and transfer in the three Collaboratives we studied seem very limited. The Collaborative method affords ample opportunity for providing evidence, facts, rules, information and data (explicit knowledge), but relatively little scope for sharing know-how, experience and wisdom (tacit knowledge): a product of the rational scientific paradigm underpinning it. However, an illustration of the potential of facilitating better opportunities to transfer tacit knowledge and to convert tacit to explicit knowledge was the very positive reaction of participants in the Collaboratives to the involvement of patients in their quality improvement work. It seemed that the views of patients – and junior staff – were in the event as or more powerful than expert 'evidence', mirroring the dichotomy between 'folk' and 'expert' knowledge found in cognitive anthropology (D'Andrade, 1995; Holland and Quinn, 1987).

Extensive research carried out in this area has shown that most everyday thinking and practice, even of scientists themselves, is driven by 'folk,' 'naïve' or 'commonsense' theories rather than 'expert' or 'academic' theories. If it is indeed the case that folk knowledge is more powerful, dominant and motivating than expert knowledge, then it follows that the NHS needs to find ways of recognizing, and subsequently accommodating and harnessing, this particular variety of cultural knowledge within its quality improvements methods and processes.

Theoretically, networks are superior to hierarchies in terms of facilitating knowledge generation and transfer, and studies within large organizations – and, to a lesser extent, in health care (Go *et al.*, 2000) – have consistently pointed to the importance of informal networks and professional communities for bringing about major change. Therefore on the face of it the general thrust of a Collaborative seems absolutely right, for central to the approach is the concept of the network organization which is 'infinitely flat' and much more open to knowledge exchange (cf. Hirschorn *et al.*, 1992; Jones *et al.*, 1997; Bate, 2000). The importance of this concept is based on studies of the ways in which innovations and changes diffuse within large organizations, which have consistently pointed to the importance of informal networks and professional communities as the main drivers for change (McDermott and O'Dell, 2001).

Communities of practice

Communities of practice sit within this wider KM context. The term 'community of practice' was first coined by Etienne Wenger and Jean Lave in their 1991 book *Situated Learning*. The theory and philosophy shaping this view of social learning have been progressively elaborated in later publications by them (cf. Wenger, 1998; Wenger *et al.*, 2002) and numerous others, especially Brown and Duguid (1991, 1998, 2000). Wenger and Snyder (2000) define a community of practice as one where people share their experiences and knowledge in free-flowing creative ways so as to foster new approaches to problem solving and improvement, help drive strategy, transfer best practice, develop professional skills and help companies recruit and retain staff.

Companies such as Xerox have chosen to base almost their entire change process upon 'communities of practice' rather than any kind of formal change programme, which they claim rarely delivers anything of lasting significance. Such networks or 'communities of practice', much more than formal management structures, are vital to how people share experiences, learn about new ideas, coach one another in trying them out, and share practical tips and lessons over time. So Xerox began by commissioning a $1 million ethnographic study to search out emerging patterns, and found that 'cascaded' formal information was not very useful to people in getting their work done; the valuable information was that which moved from one field office to another, despite the fact that there were no formal lateral channels of communication. These networks of people who rely on one another in the execution of their work came to be regarded as the 'critical building blocks of a knowledge-based company' (Turner, 1999).

Such informal networks and 'thought communities' have been studied by anthropologists for as long as their subject has existed but, as part of the growing interest in KM, private-sector companies have also come to acknowledge the importance of such networks or communities for learning and change:

> The subject of communities in the business environment has recently taken on heightened interest among some of the world's

largest companies. Organizations such as BP Amoco, Royal Dutch Shell, IBM, Xerox, The World Bank and British Telecom have all undertaken significant community development efforts in an attempt to leverage the collective knowledge of their employees. (Lesser *et al.*, 2000)

Argote's (1999) finding that organizations embedded in a superordinate relationship are able to increase their capacities for learning and knowledge transfer suggests that being embedded in a network improves organizational performance (Fischer *et al.*, 2001) and that leaders can help:

> Rather than building new networks for sharing knowledge, the companies built on already existing ones. In some cases they formalized them into official knowledge sharing networks. In other cases they lightly authorized them by giving them a budget, information systems, space, library support, time for network coordinators to manage network affairs, and recognition of their contribution. They did not dictate who should be part of a network, assign them major projects, and direct them to focus on specific issues, or dictate the way they should work. (McDermott and O'Dell, 2001)

This raises many questions about what the NHS must do to encourage the growth and development of communities of practice and to ignite the spontaneous informal processes that create the energy for a successful change effort:

> Ultimately, we know of no company that has generated significant momentum in profound change efforts without evolving spirited, active, internal networks of practitioners, people sharing progress and helping one another. (Senge *et al.*, 1999)

Table 6.1 illustrates the differences between these 'communities' and other structural forms that may be found in organizations, including the NHS (Wenger and Snyder, 2000).

The KM literature suggests that knowledge dissemination and transferability only occur when there is a collective identity and the existence of a wider social network, neither of which seemed to be fully present in the NHS Collaboratives we have studied. Overall the Collaboratives have formed time-limited project teams but not linked and active communities of practice – which puts something of a question mark over the

Table 6.1 'Communities of practice'

	Purpose?	Who?	Held together by?	How long?
Communities of practice	To develop members' capabilities: to build and exchange knowledge	Members who select themselves	Passion, commitment and identification with the group's expertise	As long as there is interest in maintaining the group
Formal work group	To deliver a product or service	Everyone who reports to the group's manager	Job requirements and common goals	Until the next reorganization
Project team	To accomplish a specific task	Employees assigned by senior management	The project's milestones and goals	Until the project has been completed
Informal network	To collect and pass on business information	Friends and business acquaintances	Mutual needs	As long as there is a reason to connect

Source: Wenger and Snyder (2000).

likely sustainability of the changes and quality improvements that have been made. This suggests the need for a more interactive model than has been observed in the NHS to date, a joint problem-solving approach, and more of a social network with greater joint working across and between Trusts. Newell *et al.* talk about a community of practice engaging in a *process* of constructing meaning:

> Within such communities shared means for interpreting complex activity are thus constructed, often out of conflicting and confusing data. It is this *process* of constructing meaning, which provides organizational members with identity and cohesiveness. (Newell *et al.*, 2001)

Unfortunately, the process of knowledge transfer *between* and *amongst* organizations in general is still not well-understood (Argote, 1999). While evidence suggests that firms embedded in networks often demonstrate a greater propensity to transfer information among and between its network partners, the underlying mechanisms have not yet been widely explored. Nonetheless, networks are aiming at realizing 'collaborative advantage' (Kanter, 1997), and this is why more and more companies are using business anthropologists to identify such naturally occurring cultural communities: those which hold tacit, yet unvoiced, and therefore unused, knowledge. However, a *community* has to exist before knowledge and learning will begin to spread and this may require specific managerial efforts to develop them and to integrate them into the organizations so that their full power can be leveraged: this is the role that Collaboratives should seek to fulfill. The remainder of this chapter looks at quality improvement in health care in this context. We believe that the answers have broader lessons for the modernization agenda currently being addressed in the NHS and in many other countries.

Discussion

As indicated above, the vast majority of experience with KM resides in the private sector and has tended to focus on the development and provision of IT solutions to challenges around knowledge storage and access. 'Softer' KM issues – such as the functioning and value of communities of practice – have received much less attention and the literature around implementing and evaluating KM in the public sector is negligible. Whilst numerous company-specific case studies of a host of KM interventions are available – and Scarbrough and Swan (2001) have reviewed the literature in order to examine the implications of KM for the practice of people management – no systematic reviews of the effectiveness of KM in a public (or private) sector context currently exist.

Recent work by the NHS Modernization Agency demonstrates, however, that the potentially beneficial impact of KM has now been acknowledged, at least in some quarters of the NHS. There are significant knowledge-related pilot projects and local initiatives underway. This being said, KM thinking and practice in the NHS, in contrast to the private sector, are still in their infancy, an aspiration (of the few) rather than a reality (for the majority). However, the issue in this case may not be of growing something afresh but of looking for existing practices that might act as organizational surrogates for KM concepts.

Many of the lessons from our research into NHS Collaboratives – the need for senior management support, incentives, clinical 'buy in' and so on – are the same or similar as those from earlier change-management and/or quality-improvement approaches in general

(Powell and Davies, 2001). These lessons are likely to apply equally to other elements of the work of the Modernization Agency. However, adopting a KM perspective and building on the evidence from the private sector provides a different way of examining reasons for the patchy or disappointing results from quality-improvement strategies as they have been applied in the NHS to date. From this perspective the Collaborative method itself is good in concept – and certainly addresses the methodology and somewhat neglected 'how' of KM – but our analysis suggests there have been a number of problems and challenges in practice, not least a considerable naiveté around the issue of knowledge transfer and 'knowledge into practice' within organizations. Most pertinent is the observation:

> Organizations vary dramatically in the rate at which they learn: some organizations show remarkable productivity gains with experience, whereas others evidence little or no learning. (Argote, 1999)

Such variations have been clearly reflected in the outcomes from our research and highlight the need for local customization of quality improvement approaches (so-called 'localization') with the overall aim of increasing the absorptive capacity or receptivity within health care organizations and in turn facilitating the internalization, embeddedness and retention of knowledge. Most of the issues revolve around improving the *process* of a Collaborative, which from a KM perspective involves finding better ways of encoding knowledge in forms suitable for transmission, and ensuring that local knowledge is transformed into organization-level knowledge (Schulz, 2001).

We therefore conclude this chapter with some pointers from our examination of the KM literature and private sector practice as to how the NHS – and other health care systems – might get more from Collaboratives and other service improvement initiatives, and what their future direction of travel might usefully be. Table 6.2 suggests four broad areas for possible development.

Table 6.2 Possible future directions for Collaboratives

'Now'	'Next'
Information	Knowledge
Knowledge application	Knowledge generation
Explicit (evidence)	Tacit (experience)
Contrived network	Community of practice

From 'information' to 'knowledge'

On the spectrum of data – information – knowledge – wisdom, Collaboratives are currently more about data and information than knowledge or wisdom. So much of what people know and feel – and what experience tells them – about how to improve quality remains locked up in their heads, and Collaboratives do little to liberate this. This prompts us to ask, is one of the present weaknesses of Collaboratives that they are information-rich but knowledge-poor, and is there a need to begin to shift the current emphasis from 'best practice' to 'best knowledge,' from 'information communication' to 'knowledge elicitation,' and from 'data dumping' to 'knowledge generation'? Knowledge is the step beyond information; it is 'the capacity to act' (Sveiby, 1997). In the context of a Collaborative, it is knowing what to do with the best practice you hear about at one of the Learning Events that make up the process, and how to apply it in your local situation – know-how not just know-what (Kogut and Zander, 1992). Information about how one organization has reduced length of stay for hip-replacement patients is not knowledge about how one is going to achieve this in one's own organization. It does not necessarily provide the capacity to act. No wonder, then, that information about good practice may be failing to *become* good practice. In Collaboratives, there needs to be a greater emphasis on spreading knowledge as opposed to merely information about best practice – know-how in other words, the ability to put knowledge into practice; knowledge that is actionable and operational.

From 'knowledge application' to 'knowledge creation'

A fundamental distinction in KM is between those activities that involve the application of existing knowledge and those that generate new knowledge. Most management principles deal with the organization of existing knowledge. The Collaboratives are no exception in this regard. As already stated, they rely solely upon the adaptation of *existing* knowledge to multiple settings. They work on the simple transmit–receive model of: I give you information about how we have improved our services and you, having received it, either discount it or choose to try and do something with it. Knowledge capture as distinct from knowledge creation. There is communication but almost no interaction or exchange between those involved.

Following recent private-sector practice in companies like Xerox and 3M, we are prompted to ask whether Collaboratives should be moving, or at least widening out, from 'knowledge application' (recipients) to 'knowledge generation' or creation (partners), the emphasis thereby shifting from the *communication* to the *co-creation* of knowledge. As opposed to the present model, which assumes someone has the 'answer' (which may be true for them but not necessarily for others), co-creation takes place when neither party has the 'answer' but by working together they are more likely to generate the knowledge to find it. In this process, the Collaborative becomes less of a listening experience and more of a joint venture, a search for creative solutions, and a sharing of knowledge and wisdom; a creative as opposed to replicative or reproductive act.

From the 'explicit' (evidence) to the 'tacit' (experience)

While the NHS has been vigorously promoting evidence-based medicine and the use of explicit, expert knowledge in clinical practice, the private sector has been moving in the opposite direction, stressing the value of intuitive, tacit knowledge in its quest for quality excellence. This again prompts us to ask, is tacit knowledge – the knowledge inside the heads of hundreds of thousands of NHS employees – an untapped source of knowledge and wisdom about good clinical practice in the NHS, and could the contribution of Collaboratives be to find better ways of making tacit knowledge about quality available to participant NHS organizations? Certainly this will mean change to the process itself, and generally speaking less formality and science and more informality and art. For example, the UK Post Office has explored how stories and storytelling may be used to communicate tacit knowledge and experience (Quintas, 2002) – an approach that could easily be accommodated within Collaborative learning sessions alongside the more formal communication processes. The broader challenge in KM terms is to increase the 'bandwidth' of communications within Collaboratives (for example, by using more channels and media: stories, pictures, telephone, email, videoconferencing) and the degree of 'interactivity' or two-wayness between participants.

The issue for future health care quality improvement initiatives is to find a way of encoding tacit knowledge in forms suitable for transmission between organizations. Such 'conversion' implies beginning by taking the evidence base and adapting and reconstructing it in a local context. As Wyatt (2001) points out – whilst strategies for codifying and transferring tacit knowledge do need to be developed – this does not mean that explicit knowledge is without value. However, the Collaborative method as currently practiced talks solely about 'replication' of best practice but not conversion. None of this should mean abandoning evidence-based notions, merely recognizing that the 'chariot' of quality might be pulled by two horses not one, and making Collaboratives as reliant upon tacit knowledge as explicit knowledge.

From 'temporary network' to 'community of practice'

Tacit knowledge can only be 'passed' from one person or place to another if a social network exists. Indeed, the ease of transfer depends entirely on the *quality* of the source-recipient relationship and the *strength* and denseness of that relationship (Szulanski, 1996). Therefore, for knowledge exchange of this kind there needs to be strong personal connections, a high degree of cognitive interdependence among participants (Yoo and Kanawattanachai, 2001) and a shared sense of identity and belongingness with one's colleagues and the existence of cooperative relationships (Bresman *et al.*, 1999). In short, a community of practice. If, as the KM writers are suggesting (cf. Brown and Duguid, 1998), organizational knowledge is heavily social in character, much greater attention will need to be paid to the social dimension of Collaboratives – creating a social network and providing the necessary informal knowledge exchange mechanisms for tacit knowledge flows to occur. Virtual networking may help but there is no substitute for real face-to-face working and extended social contact (Iacono and Weisband, 1997; Baughn *et al.*, 1997; Davenport and Prusak, 1998).

This may mean more joint-learning sessions and regional or special-interest groups within the Collaborative network, although we suspect new mechanisms may also need to be found for supporting the social and the informal interactions. One innovative example from Dixon (2000) based on the private sector is 'serial transfer,' where the team that is the source of the idea works with the team implementing the idea, repeating the 'practice' in the new context – a cooperative relationship that closes the gap between source and recipient and different locales. Another example is the use of 'translators' and 'knowledge brokers' (Hargadon and Sutton, 1997) to spread knowledge, capture good ideas, and act as go-betweens for participating organizations (Brown and Duguid, 1998). Individual Collaboratives and the Collaborative programme overall might have their own Chief Knowledge Officer, Directors of Knowledge Networks, Knowledge Leader or Facilitator of Knowledge Communities, these roles being widespread in the private sector and a more formal expression of the knowledge broker idea. Following Szulanski (1996), one role that future research might play in this regard is to begin by identifying the organizational impediments to the transfer of good practice within the NHS, and the mechanisms that will be required to allow the necessary knowledge conversions and boundary crossings to occur.

This all implies that Collaboratives, or rather the process of collaborating, needs to change, to become more equal, spontaneous, naturalistic and improvisatory, and less routine, hierarchical, structured and orchestrated than it has been. The consequence of taking away the controls and allowing Collaboratives to become more self-managing and self-organizing – 'capturing knowledge without killing it' (Brown and Duguid, 2000) – is that the resulting communities of practice (in contrast to the rather 'damp,' half-activated networks we observed) become explosive, fostering invention and allowing new ideas to spark and ignite. As an aim for future Collaboratives, Hedstrom's (1994) phrase 'contagious collectivities' is a good one. Unfortunately, it is also a reminder of how far they still have to go, and how they will need to let go of the prevailing 'knowledge is power' mindset (that is, holding not sharing knowledge) and the underlying culture of rationality, verticality and control.

Concluding remarks

The 'new organization forms' writings in the management sciences (cf. Daft and Lewin, 1993) are unanimous in advocating a shift away from the 'stability-orientation' of the traditional professional bureaucracy such as the NHS, to the strong 'change-orientation' of the contemporary 'transformational' or 'innovating' organization (Pettigrew and Fenton, 2000). Whilst the debate continues as to the precise shape and form this will take, there is already broad agreement that it will almost certainly be a 'knowledge-based,' 'networked community' organization (Bartlett and Ghoshal, 1989; Nohria and Eccles, 1992; Blackler, 1995; Nonaka and Takeuchi, 1995; Castells, 1996; Hastings, 1996).

In the context of public-sector transformation, what makes the 'Collaboratives' so promising and exciting in this regard is that they bring together – or at least have the potential for bringing together – both of these elements in a single organizational archetype for the NHS. With their strong emphasis upon building clinically led interorganizational networks between participating Trusts, and an information-sharing process that could so easily become a knowledge-sharing/KM process, Collaboratives seem ideally placed for translating these new organization design principles into practice and in so doing playing a major role in bringing about the 'quality revolution' in health care. Unfortunately, they remain some way off this point at the moment. Our aim in this chapter has been to map out some of the directions in which they will need to develop if this is to happen. The journey must surely be worth making.

References

Alimo-Metcalfe, B. and Lawler, J. (2001) 'Leadership Development in UK Companies at the Beginning of the Twenty-First Century. Lessons for the NHS?', *Journal of Management in Medicine*, 15: 5, pp. 387–404.

Allee, V. (2000) 'Knowledge Networks and Communities of Practice', *OD Practitioner Online*, 32: 4, 13pp. www.odnetwork.org/odponline.

Argote, L. (1999) *Organisational Learning: Creating, Retaining and Transferring Knowledge* (New York: Kluwer Academic).

Bartlett, C. A. and Ghoshal, S. (1989) *Managing Across Boundaries: The Transnational Solution* (Boston, MA: Harvard Business School Press).

Bate, S. P. (2000) 'Changing the Culture of a Hospital: From Hierarchy to Network Community', *Public Administration*, 78: 3, pp. 485–512.

Bate, S. P., Robert, G. and McLeod, H. (2002) *Report on the 'Breakthrough' Collaborative Approach to Quality and Service Improvement Within Four Regions of the NHS. A Research Based Investigation of the Orthopaedic Services Collaborative Within the Eastern, South & West, South East and Trent Regions* (Birmingham: HSMC, University of Birmingham, 2002).

Baughn, C., Denekamp, J., Stevens, J. and Osborn, R. (1997) 'Protecting Intellectual Capital in International Alliances', *Journal of World Business*, 32: 2, pp. 103–17.

Blackler, F. (1995) 'Knowledge, Knowledge Work and Organizations: An Overview and Interpretation', *Organisation Studies*, 16: 6, pp. 1021–46.

Bresman, H., Birkenshaw, J. and Nobel, R. (1999) 'Knowledge Transfer in International Acquisitions', *Journal of International Business Studies*, 30: 3, pp. 439–62.

Brown, J. S. and Duguid, P. (1991) 'Organisational Learning and Communities-of-Practice: Toward A Unified View of Working, Learning and Innovation', *Organisation Science*, 2: 1, pp. 40–57.

Brown, J. S. and Duguid, P. (1998) 'Organising Knowledge', *California Management Review*, 40: 3 (Spring), pp. 90–112.

Brown, J. S. and Duguid, P. (2000) 'Balancing Act: How to Capture Knowledge Without Killing It', *Harvard Business Review*, May–June, p. 73.

Castells, M. (1996) *The Rise of the Network Society* (Oxford: Blackwell).

Centre for the Evaluation of Public Policy and Practice (CEPPP) (1994) *Total Quality Management in the National Health Service: Final Report of an Evaluation* (Uxbridge; CEPPP, Brunel University).

Counte, M. A. and Meurer, S. (2001) 'Issues in the Assessment of Continuous Quality Improvement Implementation in Health Care Organisations', *International Journal for Quality in Health Care*, 13: 3, pp. 197–207.

Coyle-Shapiro, J. A.-M. and Morrow, P. C. (2001) 'Individual and Organisational Antecedents of TQM: A Comparison of Relative Effects and Implications for Organisational Change', Paper presented at the Annual Meeting of the Academy of Management, Washington DC.

Cummings, J. L. (2001) 'Key Factors Affecting Knowledge Transfer: An Organizing Framework', Paper presented at the Annual Meeting of the Academy of Management, Washington, DC (2001).

D'Andrade, R. (1995) *The Development of Cognitive Anthropology* (Cambridge: Cambridge University Press).

Daft, R. L. and Lewin, A. Y. (1993) 'Where are the Theories for the "New" Organizational Forms? An Editorial Essay', *Organisation Science*, 4: 4, pp. i–iv.

Davenport, T. H. and Prusak, L. (1998) *Working Knowledge: How Organisations Manage What They Know* (Boston, MA: Harvard Business School Press).

Department of Health (2000a) *The NHS Plan: A Plan for Investment, A Plan for Reform* (London: HMSO).

Department of Health (2000b) *The NHS Plan – Implementing the Performance Improvement Agenda. A Policy Position Statement and Consultation Document* (London: HMSO).

Department of Health (2002) 'The NHS Plan – a Report', *The NHS Modernisation Board's Annual Report 2000–2001* (London: HMSO).

Dixon, N. M. (2000) *Common Knowledge: How Companies Thrive by Sharing What They Know* (Boston, MA: Harvard Business School Press).

Fischer, H. M., Brown, J., Porac, J. F. *et al.* (2001) 'Mobilizing Knowledge in Interorganisational Alliances', in C. W. Choo and N. Bontis (eds), *The Strategic Management of Intellectual Capital and Organisational Knowledge: A Collection of Readings* (New York: Oxford University Press).

Go, A. S., Rao, R. K., Dautermen, K. W. *et al.* (2000) 'A Systematic Review of the Effects of Physician Specialty on the Treatment of Coronary Artery Disease and Heart Failure in the United States', *American Medical Journal*, 108, pp. 216–26.

Grant, R. (2001) 'Knowledge and Organisation', in I. Nonaka and D. Teece (eds), *Managing Industrial Knowledge Creation Transfer and Utilisation* (London: Sage).

Hargadon, A. and Sutton, R. I. (1997) 'Technology Brokering and Innovation in a Product Development Firm', *Administrative Science Quarterly*, 42, pp. 716–49.

Hastings, C. (1996) *The New Organisation. Growing the Culture of Organizational Networking* (London: McGraw-Hill).

Hauschild, S., Licht, T. and Stein, W. (2001) 'Creating a Knowledge Culture', *The McKinsey Quarterly*, no. 1.

Hedstrom, P. (1994) 'Contagious Collectivities: On the Spatial Diffusion of Swedish Trade Unions', *American Journal of Sociology*, 99, pp. 1157–79.

Hirschorn, L. and Gilmore, T. (1992) 'The New Boundaries of the 'Boundaryless Company', *Harvard Business Review* (May–June), pp. 104–15.

Holland, D. and Quinn, N. (eds) (1987) *Cultural Models in Language and Thought* (New York: Cambridge University Press).

Iacono, C. S. and Weisband, S. (1997) 'Developing Trust in Virtual Teams', Paper presented to HICSS-30 Conference, Hawaii.

Iles, V. and Sutherland, K. (2001) *Managing Change in the NHS. Organisational Change. A Review for Health Care Managers, Professionals and Researchers* (London: National Centre For Community of Service, Delivery and Organization Research).

Jones, C., Hesterly, W. S., Borgatti, W. S. and Borgatti, S. P. (1997) 'A General Theory of Network Governance: Exchange Conditions and Social Mechanisms', *Academy of Management Review*, 22: 4, pp. 911–45.

Kanter, R. M. (1997) *Frontiers of Management* (Harvard, MA: Harvard Business Press).

Kogut, B. and Zander, U. (1992) 'Knowledge of the Firm, Combinative Capabilities, and the Replication of Technology', *Organisation Science*, 3, pp. 383–97.

Lesser, E. L., Fontaine, M. A. and Slusher, J. A. (2000) *Knowledge and Communities* (Oxford: Butterworth-Heinemann).

Maguerez, G., Erbault, M., Terra, J. L., Maisonneuve, H. and Matillon, Y. (2001) 'Evaluation of 60 Continuous Quality Improvement Projects in French Hospitals', *International Journal for Quality in Health Care*, 13: 2, pp. 89–97.

Marshall, L. (1997) 'Facilitating Knowledge Management and Knowledge Sharing: New Opportunities for Information Professionals', *Online*, 21: 5, pp. 92–8.

Martensson, M. (2000) 'A Critical Review of Knowledge Management as a Management Tool', *Journal of Knowledge Management*, 4: 3, pp. 204–16.

McDermott, R. and O'Dell, C. (2001) 'Overcoming Cultural Barriers to Sharing Knowledge', *Journal of Knowledge Management*, 5: 1, pp. 76–85.

Murray, P. and Myers, A. (1997) 'The Facts About Knowledge', *Information Strategy* (September), pp. 31–3.

Newell, S., Edelman, L. and Bresnaen, M. *et al.* (2001) 'The inevitability of rein-vertion in project-based learning', The Odyssey of organising, 17th EGOS colloquium, Lyan, 5–7 July.

Nohria, N. and Eccles, R. G. (eds) (1992) *Networks and Organisations: Structure, Form and Action* (Boston, MA: Harvard Business School Press).

Nonaka, I. (1994) 'A Dynamic Theory of Organisational Knowledge Creation', *Organisation Science*, 5: 1, pp. 14–37.

Nonaka, I. and Takeuchi, H. (1995) *The Knowledge-Creating Company: How Japanese Companies Create the Dynamics of Innovation* (Oxford: Oxford University Press).

Ovretveit, J. (2000) 'Total Quality Management in European Healthcare', *International Journal of Health Care Quality Assurance*, 13: 2, pp. 74–80.

Pettigrew, A. M. and Fenton, E. M. (eds) (2000) *The Innovating Organization* (London: Sage).

Polanyi, M. (1958) *Personal Knowledge. Towards a Post-critical Philosophy* (Chicago: Chicago University Press).

Polanyi, M. (1966) *The Tacit Dimension* (London: Routledge & Kegan Paul).

Pollitt, C. (1996) 'Business Approaches to Quality Improvement: Why They are Hard for the NHS to Swallow', *Quality in Health Care*, 5, pp. 104–10.

Powell, A. E. and Davies, H. T. O. (2001) 'Business Process Re-engineering: Lost Hope or Learning Opportunity?', *British Journal of Healthcare Management*, 7: 11, pp. 446–9.

Quintas, P. (2002) 'Managing Knowledge in a New Century', in S. Little, P. Quintas and T. Ray (eds), *Managing Knowledge. An Essential Reader* (London: Sage), pp. 1–14.

Robert, G., McLeod, H. and Ham, C. (2003) Modernising and Cancer Services: an evaluation of phase I of the Cancer Services Collaborative (Birmingham: Health Services Management Centre, University of Birmingham).

Robert, G., Hardacre, J., Locock, L., Bate, S. P. (2002) *Evaluating the Effectiveness of the Mental Health Collaborative as an Approach to Bringing About Improvements to Admission, Stay and Discharge on Acute Wards in the Trent and Northern & Yorkshire Regions. An Action Research Project* (Birmingham: Health Services Management Centre, University of Birmingham).

Scarbrough, H., Swan, J. and Preston, J. (1994) *Knowledge Management: A Literature Review* (London: Institute of Personal and Development).

Scarbrough, H. and Swan, J. (2001) 'Explaining the Diffusion of Knowledge Management: The Role of Fashion', *British Journal of Management*, 12, pp. 3–12.

Schulz, M. (2001) 'The Uncertain Relevance of Newness: Organisational Learning and Knowledge Flows', *Academy of Management Journal*, 44: 4, pp. 661–81.

Senge, P. and associates (eds) (1999) *The Dance of Change. A Fifth Discipline Resource* (London: Nicolas Brealey), pp. 477–80.

Shortell, S. M., O'Brien, J. L. and Carmen, J. M. (1995) 'Assessing the Impact of Continuous Quality Improvement/Total Quality Management: Concept Versus Implementation', *Health Services Research*, 30: 2, pp. 377–401.

Stewart, T. A. (1997) *Intellectual Capital: The New Wealth of Nations* (New York: Doubleday).

Sveiby, K.-E. (1997) *The New Organisational Wealth: Managing and Measuring Knowledge-Based Assets* (San Francisco: Berrett-Koehler).

Szulanksi, G. (1996) 'Exploring Internal Stickiness: Impediments to the Transfer of Best Practices within the Firm', *Strategic Management Journal*, 17 (Winter special issue), pp. 27–43.

Szulanski, G. (2000) 'The Process of Knowledge Transfer: A Diachronic Analysis of Stickiness', *Organisational Behaviour and Human Decision Processes*, 82: 1, pp. 9–27.

Teece, D. J. (2000) 'Strategies for Managing Knowledge Assets: The Role of Firm Structure and Industrial Context', *Long Range Planning*, 33, pp. 35–54.

Turner, C. (1999) 'What are Communities of Practice?', in P. Senge and associates (eds), *The Dance of Change. A Fifth Discipline Resource* (London: Nicolas Brealey), pp. 477–80.

Wenger, E. (1998) *Communities of Practice* (Cambridge: Cambridge University Press).

Wenger, E. and Snyder, W. (2000) 'Communities of Practice: The Organisational Frontier', *Harvard Business Review* (Jan.–Feb.), pp. 139–53.

Wenger, E., McDermott, H. and Snyder, W. M. (2002) *A Guide to Managing Knowledge. Cultivating Communities of Practice* (Boston: Harvard Business School Press).

Wyatt, J. (2001) *Clinical Knowledge and Practice in the Information Age: A Handbook for Health Professionals* (London: Royal Society of Medicine).

Yoo, Y. and Kanawattanachai, P. (2001) 'Developments in Transactive Memory and Collective Mind in Virtual Teams', Paper presented to the Annual Meeting of the Academy of Management, Washington, DC.

Zander, U. (1991) *Exploiting a Technological Edge: Voluntary and Involuntary Dissemination of Technology* (Stockholm: Institute of International Business).

7

Coordination of Services: The Use of Multidisciplinary Interagency Teams

Sharon Topping, Tumutual Norton and Brenda Scafidi

Introduction

Health care organizations in the twenty-first century are faced with increasing demands to serve clients with concurrent health, mental health and substance abuse problems; therefore, it is impossible for one organization to deliver on its own. Furthermore, because of limited resources, managers of health care organizations must be able to develop alliances and partnerships with other agencies to coordinate services so as to eliminate costly duplication while effectively serving clients. In recent years, multidisciplinary teams have become an important strategy used to coordinate services, such as public health teams in the community, treatment teams in hospitals, and 'care teams' in managed care settings (Alexander, Lichtenstein, Jinnett, D'Aunno and Ullman, 1996; Cott, 1997; Lovelace, 2000; Schofield and Amodeo, 1999). This strategy has been particularly prevalent in the delivery of mental health services, and often involves not only multidisciplinary members but also persons from different agencies (Laditka and Jenkins, 2000; Vinokur-Kaplan, 1995; Weist, Lowie, Flaherty and Pruitt, 2001).

In general, the use of multidisciplinary interagency teams is based on the assumption that members will work together to coordinate and provide services needed by clients (Laditka and Jenkins, 2000). However, multidisciplinary teams, by definition, are composed of professionals from different occupational groups, who typically work independently and autonomously (Brown, Crawford and Darongkamas, 2000; Weist *et al.*, 2001). When interagency teams are used, members come from different organizations with different cultures, reward systems and goals (Toseland, Ivanoff and Rose, 1987). Even so, with the formation of such diverse teams, these same professionals are expected to work together providing care more effectively than the existing fragmented system. This, however, does not usually happen; what generally results is conflict and miscommunication (Coopman, 2001).

Despite such problems and the importance of multidisciplinary interagency teams in the delivery of care, very little is known about how these teams operate and what makes them effective (Alexander *et al.*, 1996; Cott, 1997; Toseland *et al.*, 1987). Following from this, our research focuses on Multidisciplinary Assessment and Planning (MAP) teams that are used to coordinate services to children and youth who are severely emotionally disturbed and/or severely mentally ill. The major objective of the chapter is to identify those factors that facilitate and hinder the operation of multidisciplinary, interagency teams, and in so doing, develop a conceptual model that is specific to these teams and can serve as a guide for future research.

Teams and the provision of care to children and youth

Over the past three decades, considerable effort has been made to improve services for children and youth with serious emotional or mental disorders and their families (Duchnowski, Kutash and Friedman, 2002). A number of national demonstration programmes in the United States have been initiated to develop comprehensive systems of care throughout the country. The philosophy and values that underlie the system of care approach include services that focus on the individual child and family, use a strengths-based orientation, and are culturally competent (Katz-Leavy, Lourie, Stroul and Zeigler-Dendy, 1992). The major emphasis is on community-based services with the objective of children remaining in the least restrictive, most normalized environment as possible.

Following from this, the interdisciplinary approach to providing services to children and families is essential in community-based systems of care (Pumariega, Nace, England *et al.*, 1997). Moreover, the process of implementing a system of care involves interagency coordination and integration of services that are generally accomplished through interagency multidisciplinary teams. One model that is used involves the wraparound process approach in which an array of individualized services are developed and coordinated by community-based teams that may include the biological parents, the youth, the case worker, and representatives from education, court system, mental health and other relevant areas (Burchard, Bruns and Burchard, 2002; VanDenBerg and Grealish, 1998). Non-traditional members are included as well, such as pastors, guidance counsellors, coaches and close relatives.

In a national survey of the different wraparound programmes, the interagency team was identified as an important factor contributing to the success of the programme (Faw, 1999). The team provided benefits that cannot be derived from individual fragmented services and if the group is effective, the creativity and energy of the team can be harnessed in planning for the youth. Although teams have been identified as a critical component in the success of wraparound and other community-based programmes, little is known about how they operate. For instance, Goldman (1999) in identifying the essentials of wraparound programmes states that it must be 'a team-driven process' with achieving consensus an important part, yet Goldman makes no reference to how consensus is accomplished. Thus, given that teams are critical in providing services, there is a need to know about the process of becoming a coordinated team and what makes it effective.

Methods

For purposes of this study, the terms 'group' and 'team' are used interchangeably. A group or team is defined as

> a collection of individuals who are interdependent in their tasks, who share responsibility for outcomes, who see themselves and who are seen by others as an intact social entity embedded in one or more larger social systems and who manage their relationships across organizational boundaries. (Cohen and Bailey, 1997, p. 241)

The study site

This study focuses on Multidisciplinary Assessment and Planning (MAP) teams in Mississippi, a rural southern state with a population of approximately 2.8 million. There are currently 24 MAP teams in the state with others continually being established. The MAP teams are established by county and, therefore, serve children and youth in that locale who have serious emotional disorders and are at imminent risk of being placed inappropriately in 24-hour care for lack of special supports and/or services in the community. Case managers refer cases to their local MAP teams. The teams, in turn, review the cases and attempt, if needed, to develop treatment plans while also identifying and coordinating appropriate services in the community. In order to promote the development of wraparound throughout the state, MAP teams can apply for up to $35,000 for the development and support of a MAP team System of Care. This money is to be used to purchase services for children and youth that may include non-traditional services, such as tutoring, baseball equipment or gymnastic classes.

Data collection and analysis

Since little is known about the operation of these teams, it was necessary to build a conceptual framework by which to guide the research. This involved three stages. First, a literature review was conducted which involved a MEDLINE search covering a 20-year period ending 2001, and using the key words 'health care teams' and 'mental health teams'. To further identify the literature, the reference lists of all publications from the search were checked for additional citations as well. Second, a series of structured interviews were conducted with MAP team facilitators and members. The interviews focused on three areas: history of collaborative activity in the community, the formation of the team, and identification of factors that facilitated effective functioning of the team. Questions also addressed team size, team composition and team process. In the third step, data from the literature review and the interviews were integrated to develop a conceptual framework for the study of multidisciplinary interagency teams.

The data from the two sources were analysed according to two criteria. First, the integration involved only those factors that were identified in both the interviews and the literature review as affecting team performance. Second, based on the assumption that teams act as input–output systems (Arrow, McGrath and Berdahl, 2000; Gist, Locke and Taylor, 1987; McGrath, 1984), the factors had to fall into one of three categories–inputs, process or outputs. This allowed the development of a parsimonious model that is specific to multidisciplinary interagency teams used in mental health services, particularly in provision of care to youth and children.

Findings and discussion

Since the understanding of team behaviour and effectiveness is dependent on numerous factors, the model used in this chapter is multidimensional (see Figure 7.1).

The model is based on a common premise that teams act as input–output systems (Arrow *et al.*, 2000; Gist *et al.*, 1987; McGrath, 1984), and the following subsections consider the different factors that correspond to the model.

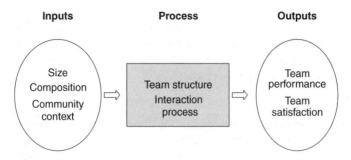

Figure 7.1   A multidisciplinary interagency team: an input–output model

In the model, team inputs – size, composition and community context – have a direct effect on outputs or a modifying effect through process. Schofield and Amodeo (1999), in their review of the literature on interdisciplinary teams, found that most authors fail to operationalize the team, assuming that it is a fixed entity. In actuality, teams vary greatly; therefore, each client can be exposed conceivably to a different kind of team. In order to minimize this 'black box' phenomenon, they advocate defining the team in future research. In this study, inputs are used to define the multidisciplinary interagency teams providing a baseline profile that can be monitored for changes.

Team composition

Team membership is an important factor in understanding group process and performance. Diversity or heterogeneity of membership is likely to affect the way individuals perceive each other in the group and how well they work together, and this in turn affects team effectiveness and performance (Fried, Topping and Rundall, 2000). Most research on group composition concludes that overall heterogeneity of group members is desirable when the task is complex requiring coordination and planning (Campion, Medsker and Higgs, 1993). Conversely, occupational diversity often leads to problems such as increased conflict and loss of cohesiveness (Arrow *et al.*, 2000; Alexander *et al.*, 1996). In multidisciplinary interagency health care teams, this is especially prevalent due to the differences between disciplines in basic philosophy and values, treatment modality, and terminology and jargon (Brown *et al.*, 2000; Weist *et al.*, 2001).

However, occupational diversity is an essential requirement for multidisciplinary interagency teams, since, to function, members must represent the varied organizations providing care in the community.

Because of this, a major issue confronting MAP teams concerns the identification of the organizational groups and the appropriate individual from each one. Although all organizations in the community serving children and youth are important, there are certain ones whose membership plays a significant factor. Given the experience of MAP teams, the presence of representatives from youth court, social services, the schools, mental health, health department, and families facilitate the decision–making process.

However, it is not always possible to have a representative cross-section of members. For instance, MAP teams often find social services participation problematic due to staff turnover, confidentiality restrictions and perceived turf issues. Moreover, family representatives on the teams present special problems since they may have to take off from work without reimbursement, or require respite services and transportation in order to attend. It is important to note that those MAP teams that are successful in recruiting family members are also those that encourage and support the development of family support groups in the community.

Tenure diversity

The length of time members have been on the team and status diversity can be detrimental to member relations and team performance as well (Owens, Mannic and Neale, 1998; Shaw, 1990). New members coming into an already functioning team have to be socialized by the remaining members, taking valuable time away from the task at hand. Thus, consistency in membership is extremely important. When various persons from the same agency rotate attendance, continuity and follow-up are threatened. Many MAP teams have solved this problem by using alternatives who are encouraged to attend all meetings.

In addition, research findings are fairly consistent in demonstrating that high-status members initiate communication more often, are provided more opportunities to participate, and have more influence over the decision-making process (Owens *et al.*, 1998). This situation is very likely in multidisciplinary interagency health care teams, where status differences among the professions are well-entrenched (Teram, 1991). As a result, MAP teams have found that selecting the appropriate individual from a certain agency is extremely important. Generally, this means that all members must have substantial influence in the community and within the organization they represent. They must be positioned so as to commit organizational resources if needed, while also still being involved in service delivery.

Team size

Another factor affecting team effectiveness is size. On one hand, size appears to have a U-shaped relationship with team effectiveness (Cohen and Bailey, 1997). As groups become larger, they tend to exhibit increased communication and coordination problems and less cohesiveness between members (McGarth, 1984); however, teams have to be large enough to accomplish the task assigned. On the other hand, there is some indication that the U-shaped relationship may not hold for all types of teams. In teams in which boundaries may be permeable – such as many multidisciplinary interagency mental health teams – performance may be negatively affected by size (Alexander *et al.*, 1996; Vinokur-Kaplan, 1995).

This factor is extremely important for multidisciplinary interagency teams since their effectiveness is a function of how representative the membership is of the community services available. Thus, team size is predetermined by the number of organizations providing services in the community and by their interest in participating. MAP teams generally range in size from eight to 25 members, meaning that from 8–25 agencies or sub-agencies are represented on the team. The range is necessary due to the diversity found in the MAP team communities; some are extremely rural with few resources, while others are more urban with numerous organizations serving children and youth. However, several MAP teams when approaching 25 members found that it was more effective to form smaller sub-teams when staffing very sensitive, complex cases.

Team context

Teams do not exist in a vacuum, but are constantly affected by influences from the external environment; therefore, it is important to understand how external factors influence team process and effectiveness (Arrow *et al.*, 2000). For many groups, the greater external environment exerts influence equal to or greater than the internal organizational environment (Fried *et al.*, 1999), and this is particularly true for multidisciplinary interagency groups, such as MAP teams, that interact with and depend on not only member organizations but also the community environment for critical resources and support. Since interagency multidisciplinary teams are often used in resource-deficient rural areas to extend services, it is critical to understand how these conditions affect the teams and if they develop strategies to override the effects.

One of the most influential contextual factors in MAP team effectiveness is the collaborative history of the community. Of those MAP teams whose members have a long history of service coordination, most report a remarkably easy process of forming and becoming a cohesive, effective group. In one community, an interagency team had been used previously to coordinate services in cases of child sexual abuse. Since the former team was led by a local social services agency, it made it easier not only for all organizations in the community to collaborate, but also for social services to be part of the new MAP team. Related to this, differences exist between urban and rural MAP teams. For instance, many of the rural sites report that, 'everyone knows each other and have worked together before because of the limited resources in the area'. Thus, a sense of 'teamness' is there from the beginning. In addition, the urban teams tend to include a larger proportion of professionals, while the rural site, having fewer service organizations, have many members from non-traditional groups such as the YMCA, churches, and Boys and Girls Clubs.

Team structure and the interaction process

Although individuals may be designated as members of a group, they may remain independent of one another and never truly become a functioning team. One critical challenge in building effective teams is the formation of the communication network, for this is the mechanism through which groups achieve goals (Shaw, 1981). For teams to be successful, activities must be structured and coordinated through the building of an adequate interaction system (Gist *et al.*, 1987; Lovelace, 2000). This system can be best described in terms of process behaviour and interaction strategies (Coopman, 2001). For instance, when task ends and means are clear and agreed upon, few interpersonal difficulties such as conflict and disagreements occur allowing teams to concentrate on the task at hand (Goodman, Ravlin and Schminke, 1987).

Specific to MAP teams in particular, and multidisciplinary interagency teams in general, are a number of structuring strategies that stand out. One involves an important leadership issue: determination of the lead agency and the MAP team facilitator. It is extremely important that the lead agency be one that has an outstanding reputation in the community – one of fairness and past collaborative behaviour. Although the community mental health centre (CMHC) is the most likely candidate for lead agency, this can be detrimental to the success of the MAP team when the CMHC is not a community player. In communities where the latter is true, social services agencies and religious-based mental health organizations have spearheaded successful MAP teams.

Just as important is the selection of the facilitator. Similar to the lead agency, this person must be well-known and respected in the community and have a long-history of collaborative activities. One MAP team, although successful today, took several years to develop into an effective team working together to serve children and youth. Many members attribute this long process to the newness of the facilitator in the particular community, and the consequent lack of experience working with the other local organizations. In addition, the facilitator should have other skills, some of which are identified by one of the MAP team members:

> Members need to know that this person is dedicated. The facilitator has to be someone who has a reputation for getting things done and taking the job seriously. Also, someone who sets the tune of respectfulness for each person's contribution to the team.

In addition to leadership, successful MAP teams pay particular attention to the structure of the team environment including role and mission clarity. Many of the newly formed MAP teams make this a priority during the initial stage of development. Many of the older MAP teams did not, and members were consequently confused as to the target population and goals of the team. Eventually, the team had to dedicate time to mission and goal clarification. A member commented that when 'mission and goals are agreed on and accepted by the team, it creates consistency which, in turn, engenders trust among the members'. A number of other mechanisms that are used by MAP teams to structure the interaction process are identified in Table 7.1. For example, one that has important ramifications is the need for follow-

Table 7.1 Mechanisms used to structure interaction in multidisciplinary interagency teams

---

- Interagency agreements specifying responsibilities
- Referral forms and procedures
- Follow-up procedures
- Meeting agenda
- Established meeting time and place
- Meeting-time management
- Ongoing training
- Agreed-upon mission and goals
- Definition of target population
- Confidentiality agreements
- Meeting reminders to all members

---

up. MAP team members have found that this has to be done at each meeting, and procedures should be followed in both assigning responsibilities and determining progress. One MAP Team member described the benefits of follow-up as:

> It is needed for the individual members of the MAP teams to feel good about what they are doing. With follow-up, they are able to see what good is being done, and feel part of the team.

Another significant factor, mentioned by almost everyone interviewed, is 'meeting-time management'. For example, although seemingly trite, MAP team members have found that it is essential to the well-being of the team to start and end meetings on time. Lastly, one of the most critical factors is the need for training, particularly since the MAP team members are being asked to perform in a manner consistent with a philosophy and values (that is, a system of care principles) that may be different from the clinical norm. Thus, training is needed not only in the initial stages but also on an ongoing basis.

Team performance

Team performance may be defined in a number of different ways depending on the purposes of the group (Cohen and Bailey, 1997). Examples from the health care and mental health literature include member satisfaction (Leiter, 1988), team functioning (Alexander *et al.*, 1996), goal clarity (Shaw, 1990), and standards met and cohesion (Vinokur-Kaplam, 1995). Another way of measuring group effectiveness is to think of interagency multidisciplinary teams as loosely coupled systems that are extremely flexible and adaptable to change (Orton and Weick, 1990). As such, these teams should not be assessed using the same criteria (for example, standards of efficiency) as tightly coupled systems, but through more appropriate criteria such as flexibility, adaptability and uniqueness of response to change (Orton and Weick, 1990).

This is particularly true of the MAP teams since one of their functions is the provision of non-traditional services. Many MAP teams find this difficult at first, particularly if funding is dedicated for this purpose. As a result, evaluation of team spending patterns may be necessary to encourage decisions to expend money on non-traditional services. Moreover, MAP teams become, if successful, a major source of resources in the community; therefore, they can be evaluated on networking outcomes and awareness of community resources. One veteran member reported that:

The MAP team has resulted in open avenues of communication between agencies. This has really increased the level of communication. Also it has resulted in increased awareness of services and how to pull together to integrate services on behalf of the family.

The process of evaluation is also an issue in determining team success, for it appears that legitimizing team accomplishments through an evaluation process may be necessary, particularly in the early life of the team. This creates a sense of pride in what is being accomplished and creates a more cohesive environment. A number of members identified a 'first success' as the event that finally brought the MAP team together.

Conclusions

Findings from this study are an initial step in understanding the 'black box' of process and structure in multidisciplinary interagency health care and mental health teams. Thus, this study is important for several reasons. Although much team and small-group research exists in the management and social psychology literature, it should be noted that health care and mental health teams might be very different from teams in other contexts. Therefore, it is not known whether the findings and models from the general group literature will apply to health care and mental health teams. As a result, research in this area is critical if we are to better understand the factors involved in effective functioning of these teams.

Interagency multidisciplinary teams are a form of interorganizational collaboration that has become critical in delivering services whether in mental health or health care in general. For one reason, resources are becoming more and more scarce especially in rural areas; therefore, these teams are a way of stretching resources among the various agencies, thereby increasing availability and accessibility of supportive services in the community. At the same time, the number of clients with multiple needs has increased, including those with substance abuse, serious mental illness and chronic health problems such as HIV/AIDS. Interorganizational collaboration is necessary to deliver care to multiple-need clients; interagency multidisciplinary teams are an effective means of accomplishing this integration.

Following from this, the MAP teams that are the focus of this study are leading the way in a major collaborative effort demonstrating how community-level coordination can be successful in delivering services. It is ironic that such leadership is occurring in a poor, rural state such as

Mississippi; however, the impetus for such change may very well come from such dire circumstances. Everyday, agencies in many of these communities face numerous clients needing services, but have few resources to comply. As a result, they realize that to meet future demands collaboration between providers is necessary, and they see the teams as a means of planning and coordinating care and treatment that is community-oriented. In so doing, they are providing valuable information to those managing *all* health care organizations in the twenty-first century on how to better use teams to coordinate services and provide effective care.

References

Alexander, J. A., Lichtenstein, R., Jinnett, K., D'Aunno, T. A. and Ullman, E. (1996) 'The Effects of Treatment Team Diversity and Sex on Assessments of Team Functioning', *Hospital and Health Services Administration*, 41: 1, pp. 37–53.

Arrow, H., McGrath, J. E. and Berdahl, J. L. (2000) *Small Groups as Complex Systems* (Thousand Oaks, CA: Sage).

Brown, B., Crawford, P. and Darongkamas, J. (2000) 'Blurred Roles and Permeable Boundaries: The Experience of Multidisciplinary Working in Community Mental Health', *Health and Social Care in the Community*, 8: 6, pp. 425–35.

Burchard, J. D., Burns, E. J. and Burchard, S. N. (2002) 'The Wraparound Approach', in E. J. Burns and K. Hoagwood (eds), *Community Treatment for Youth* (New York: Oxford University Press).

Campion, M. A., Medsker, J. G. and Higgs, A. C. (1993) 'Relations Between Work Group Characteristics and Effectiveness: Implications for Designing Effective Work Groups', *Personnel Psychology*, 46, pp. 823–50.

Cohen, S. G. and Bailey, D. E. (1994) 'What Makes Teams Work: Group Effectiveness Research from the Shop Floor to the Executive Suite', *Journal of Management*, 23: 3, pp. 239–90.

Coopman, S. J. (2001) 'Democracy, Performance, and Outcomes in Interdisciplinary Health Care Teams', *Journal of Business Communication*, 38: 3, pp. 261–81.

Cott, C. (1997) '"We Decide, You Carry It Out": A Social Network Analysis of Multidisciplinary Long-term Care Teams', *Social Science and Medicine*, 45: 9, pp. 1411–21.

Duchnowski, A. J., Kutash, K. and Friedman, R. M. (2002) 'Community-based Interventions in a System of Care and Outcomes Framework', in B. J. Burns and K. Hoagwood (eds), *Community Treatment for Youth* (New York: Oxford University Press).

Faw, L. (1999) 'The State Wraparound Survey', in B. J. Burns and S. K. Goldman (eds), *Promising Practices in Wraparound for Children and Families with Severe Emotional Disorders* (Washington DC: Georgetown University Child Development Center).

Fried, B., Topping, S. and Rundall, T. G. (1999) 'Groups and Teams in Health Services Organizations', in S. Shortell and A. Kaluzny (eds), *Health Care Management: Organization, Design, and Behavior*, 4th edn (Albany: Delmar Publishers).

Gist, M. E., Locke, E. A. and Taylor, M. S. (1987) 'Organizational Behavior: Group Structure, Process, and Effectiveness', *Journal of Management*, 13: 2, pp. 237–57.

Goldman, S. K. (1999) 'The Conceptual Framework for Wraparound: Definitions, Values, Essential Elements, and Requirements for Practice', in B. J. Burns and S. K. Goldman (eds) *Promising Practices in Wraparound for Children and Families with Severe Emotional Disorders* (Washington, DC: Georgetown University Child Development Center).

Goodman, P. S., Ravlin, E. and Schminke, M. (1987) 'Understanding Groups in Organizations', *Research in Organizational Behavior*, 9, pp. 121–73.

Katz-Leavy, J. W., Lourie, I. S., Stroul, B. A. and Zeigler-Dendy, C. (1997) *Individualized Services in a System of Care* (Washington, DC: CASSP Technical Assistance Center, Center for Child Health and Mental Health Policy, Georgetown University Child Development Center).

Laditka, S. B. and Jenkins, C. L. (2000) 'Enhancing Inter-Network Cooperation among Organizations Providing Mental Health Services to Older Persons', *Administration and Policy in Mental Health*, 28: 2, pp. 75–89.

Lovelace, K. (2000) 'External Collaboration and Performance: North Carolina Local Public Health Departments', *Public Health Reports*, 115: 4, pp. 350–65.

McGrath J. E. (1984) *Groups: Interaction and Performance* (Englewood Cliffs, NJ: Prentice Hall).

Orton, J. D. and Weick, D. E. (1990) 'Loosely Coupled Systems: A Reconceptualization', *Academy of Management Review*, 15: 2, pp. 203–23.

Owens, D. A., Mannic, E. A. and Neale, M. A. (1998) 'Strategic Formation of Groups: Issues in Task Performance and Team Member Selection', in D. H. Gruenfeld (ed.), *Research on Managing Groups and Teams* (Stanford, CN: MAI Press).

Pumariega, A. J., Nace, D., England, M. J. *et al.* (1997) 'Community-Based Systems Approach to Children's Managed Mental Health Services', *Journal of Child and Family Studies*, 6: 2, pp. 149–64.

Schofield, R. F. and Amodeo, M. (1999) 'Interdisciplinary Teams in Health Care and Human Services Settings: Are They Effective?', *Health and Social Work*, 24: 3, pp. 210–20.

Shaw, M. E. (1981) *Group Dynamic* (New York: McGraw-Hill).

Shaw, R. B. (1990) '*Mental Health Treatment Teams*', in J. Richard (ed.), *Groups That Work (and Those That Don't)* (San Francisco, CA: Jossey-Bass).

Teram, E. (1991) 'Interdisciplinary Teams and the Control of Clients: A Sociotechnical Perspective', *Human Relations*, 44: 4, pp. 343–56.

Toseland, R. W., Ivanoff, A. and Rose, S. R. (1987) 'Treatment Conferences: Task Groups in Action', *Social Work With Groups*, 2, pp. 79–93.

VanDenBerg, J. and Grealish, E. M. (1998) *The Wraparound Process: Training Manual* (Pittsburgh, PA: The Community Partnership Group).

Vinokur-Kaplan, D. (1995) 'Treatment Teams That Work (and Those That Don't): An Application of Hackman's Group Effectiveness Model to Interdisciplinary Teams in Psychiatric Hospitals', *Journal of Applied Behavioral Science*, 31: 3, pp. 303–27.

Weist, M. D., Lowie, J. A., Flaherty, L. T. and Pruitt, D. (2001) 'Collaboration Among the Education, Mental Health, and Public Health Systems to Promote Youth Mental Health', *Psychiatric Services*, 52: 10, pp. 1348–51.

8

Leadership in the Context of Health Reform: An Australian Case Study

Pieter Degeling, Rick Iedema, Mark Winters, Sharyn Maxwell, Barbara Coyle, John Kennedy and David Hunter

Introduction

Leadership is a concept in good standing with health policy-makers. This chapter questions the current faith in leadership on conceptual and practical grounds. We open with an examination of the leadership responsibilities placed on managers by the reform agenda, and against this background we examine the cultural composition of acute care settings in which Australian health managers are expected to discharge these responsibilities. The chapter concludes with an examination of how these two dimensions shape the context in which managers are meant to accomplish 'leadership'.

The agenda of reform

The promise of health care reform in Australia and England over the last 20 years is articulated in a procession of policy documents that envision a more efficient, effective, patient-centred, evidence-based and accountable health service. Policy foci have included the implementation of new funding systems (casemix, purchaser–provider split), harnessing of new information systems and, more recently, mobilizing discourses and associated technologies that are claimed to address issues of evidence, quality, effectiveness, safety and clinical accountability.

Implementation of the above initiatives in acute care settings has been attempted through a series of organizational redesign exercises (matrix structures, clinical directorates, streams of care). These arrangements presaged a reordering of relationships within hospitals both in terms of their substantive content and in the mechanisms of power used in directing and controlling work. The associated shift from 'administration' to 'management' foreshadowed current calls for better leadership.

The newly installed 'managers' were meant to be more proactive, directive and to have a specific concern for improving performance. Broad goals were supplanted by explicit targets, and subjective/intrinsic accountability arrangements (characteristic of profession) were complemented by extrinsic accountability to a change-oriented management élan. The benefits claimed to derive from these outcomes were seen to legitimate the associated shifts in power and authority embodied in the change.

The case literature strongly suggests that, as was the case in England (Harrison, 1998; Pollitt *et al.*, 1988; Pollitt, 1990), the foregoing reform initiatives in Australia have had very little impact (Braithwaite, 1995, 1999; Degeling, 1993, 1994). Viewed in terms of these implementation failures, current interest in leadership is little more than a further attempt to bridge the promise–performance gap. The hope is that where organization redesign and the search for proactive management have failed, leadership will prevail and succeed.

The conceptual foundations of current calls for leadership

Optimism about the capacity of leaders to achieve the desired order of change extends beyond policy circles. The last seven years have witnessed a flowering of educational offerings and textbooks on leadership; for example *Leading the Revolution in Health Care: Advancing Systems, Igniting Performance* (Wilson and Porter-O'Grady, 1999) and 'Transcendental Leadership' (Cardona, 2000). The rhetoric leaves little doubt about the faith that is invested in the extraordinary qualities and skills that leaders are meant to embody and put to good use. On examination, however, we find that many of these publications firstly tend to assume away the problems that leadership is meant to address, and second rely on modes of conceptualization that have been superceded in the mainstream literature.

An example of the former is evident in Wilson and Porter-O'Grady (1999). For these proponents, realizing improvements in the health care system depends on a physician–manager partnership in leadership and governance. As many front-line managers will attest, a proposition that assumes physicians as partners is equivalent to saying that the problem would be solved if it didn't exist.

An example of flawed conceptualization is found in Griffith, Sahney and Mohr (1995), who, positing that '...personal leadership...will start and sustain the process of developing tomorrow's lean and agile health care system', extol the virtues of successful leaders. These virtues are then distilled to lists such as the 'seven key abilities of successful leaders' and the 'ten key steps to create focus and produce results'. Within the resulting means-ends conception of leadership, leaders are depicted as people in positions of authority who harness organizational resources to achieve predetermined purposes and ends. The leader's capacity is evidenced by his/her ability to influence subordinates in setting and achieving goals.

This conception of leadership is open to question on a number of grounds. Among the most important is the presumption that leadership is restricted to persons who occupy senior management positions. Also important is the assumed functionality of leadership; that is, that its rationale is found in the way that its exercise furthers an organization's stated purposes. The first assumption conflates legal and social authority. Accordingly, much of the literature either ignores or denies the legitimacy of leaders whose authority is based not on their position (that is, legal authority) but in the 'following' they are able to command from people within and across organizational settings (that is, social authority). Alternatively, the tendency to restrict leadership to its exercise in enhancing organizational instrumentality means that, where the actions of leaders and their followings vary from what is deemed to be required for organizational purposes, such deviations provide grounds for denying the legitimacy of the actions or the presence of leadership.

The instrumental character of conventional depictions of leadership is also evident in the themes explored and in the way the resulting 'knowledge' is applied. Among others included here have been foci such as personality traits, behavioural styles and/or skills of 'good leadership' (Allport, 1937; White and Lippitt 1960). On traits, for example, leadership research focused on identifying a set of common characteristics (such as physical appearance, abilities and personality traits) innate to effective leaders, with the resulting trait profiles seen as providing criteria for selecting persons into leadership positions. This approach, however, is thrown into question by evidence about the multiplicity of traits displayed by leaders (Stogdill, 1948; Gibb, 1947; Bass, 1990). In response to these criticisms, attention focused on mapping and then teaching leadership behaviours and associated leadership styles, and two summary styles were identified. The first (a consideration style) emphasized the leader's trust in, and consideration for, subordinates. The second (a style which focused on structural initiatives) emphasized the leader's role in defining and monitoring subordinates' work (Stogdill, 1974).

Again, however, common patterns were not found (Korman, 1966; Lowin and Craig, 1968; Kerr *et al.*, 1974; Greene, 1975). These results led to an interest in what was deemed the contingent character of leadership (Fiedler, 1967, 1993 and Fiedler and Garcia, 1987). While generally regarded as emphasizing the context-dependent nature of style effectiveness, the contingency approach can equally be seen as marking a return to the earlier interest in traits (Bryman, 1996). In either case, there are questions about the generalizability and utility of the findings for instrumentalizing leadership.

Subsequent attempts to focus on the behaviour of leaders have emphasized their involvement in what is termed 'the management of meaning'. Within this frame, 'meaning' management is seen as taking place in a number of ways. In each case, however, the instrumental character of leadership is assumed. Hence, despite differences in emphasis, Burn's (1978) 'transactional leadership', Westley and Mintzberg's (1989) 'visionary leadership', Bass's (1985) transformational leadership and/or the charismatic leadership identified by House *et al.* (1991) are each viewed in terms of the way that efforts on 'managing meaning' are directed at defining organizational reality, articulating a vision and promoting practices, values and beliefs which reflect and support the leader's perception of the organization's mission.

There are, however, important differences between the 'exchange foundations' of transactional leadership and the 'value fusion' that is said to characterize the transformational and/or charismatic leadership currently being promoted within health circles. Indicators of transactional leadership are confined to senior managers' demonstrated capacity to exercise influence through control over rewards and punishments. Transformational leaders are said to be characterized by their capacity to develop a sense of mission, pride and trust among staff; their ability to mobilize symbols in motivating staff and lifting the performance staff expect of each other; and finally their capacity to challenge staff with new ideas and approaches.

To commentators such as Schein (1985), transformational leaders acquire these capacities by manipulating culture. The extent of cultural control exercised by transformational leaders was extended by Bass (1985) and Kotter and Heskitt (1992), who argued that the outcomes of transformational leadership are evidenced in the changed culture and *performance* of staff. These conceptions are open to question on two grounds. Firstly, there is an assumption that leaders can act independently of culture and hence are able to mould and change it almost at will. Equally, it is assumed that transformational leaders can act outside the constraints that are imposed by past events and/or are embodied in institutionalized agreements and commitments that continue to draw significant support from organized (and in that sense powerful) interests.

Second, and as a consequence of the first, culture is reduced to something that is primarily the product of senior managerial strategy and action and which provides a vehicle for senior management to 'colonize' the minds of staff (Willmot, 1993). This assumption denies the social and historical foundations of organizational culture; how its particularities are inscribed in the structures and practices that characterize individual organizations (DiMaggio and Powell, 1983) and how culture, via processes of structuration, is the product not simply of what leaders do, but also of what other players do or do not do (Giddens, 1984).

The following analysis proceeds from the view that these shortcomings can only be overcome by adopting a framework that (following Weber, 1990) conceives leadership as power that is seen to be legitimately exercised. Crucially, this formulation focuses attention on the significance of *followership* in constituting leadership.

Followership is central to realizing both the formal authority of a leader and/or his/her social authority. In other words, authority is not an immutable object; it is in constant need of being reconfirmed and enacted in the dynamics and performances of particular 'communities of practice' (Wenger, 1998). The following case study presents data that suggest that clinician managers as putative leaders (of professional groups such as medicine and nursing) recognize they cannot move too far from their following. Accordingly, the attitudes, values and beliefs of clinical staff become the starting point for understanding leadership in the context of health reform. It is that to which we now turn.

A case study of the implications of reform for leaders and followers

Viewed from a perspective that takes account of interconnections between leadership and *followership*, the reform programme in Australia signalled significant shifts in the value/rule basis of relations within clinical settings. With this in mind, the senior management of three hospitals invited the researchers to conduct a survey study of each staff's values. The study replicated previous studies in two Australian and four English hospitals (Degeling *et al.*, 1998, 2001).

The survey

The self-completion survey instrument elicited demographic informa-
tion on respondents' professional qualifications, sex, age, and clinical and managerial experience. Substantively, the questionnaire comprised sets of related items that elicited views on key health care issues; strate-
gies for dealing with hospital resource issues; interconnections between the clinical and resource dimensions of care; the causes of clinical practice variation; who should be involved in setting clinical standards; the forms of knowledge on which clinical standards should be based; management of clinical units; the accountability and autonomy of clinicians, and the organization of their hospital.

Respondents within each of the participating hospitals were ran-
domly selected to ensure representation from medical clinicians, medical managers, lay managers, nurse managers and nurse clinicians. The sample is reported in Table 8.1.

Principal component analysis of the highly correlated results in each set of questions resulted in a number of independent factors. Respondents' scores on these factors were taken to reflect patterns of values, meanings and beliefs that guided their assessments of the rele-
vant items. For each of the factors, two-way analysis of variance was used to examine the relationship between professional class and other variables such as hospital, gender, age and education. Consistent with findings from the earlier study of English and Australian hospitals and more recent studies of hospitals in New Zealand and Wales (Degeling, 1999, 2002), the results showed that *variation between respondents was most consistently explained by their professional backgrounds.*

Discriminant analysis was then used to examine the patterns of difference between professional groups on the mean scores for each

Table 8.1   Completed questionnaires by professional class and hospital

Hospital	Medical clinician	Medical manager	General manager	Nurse manager	Nurse clinician	Total
1	70	15	24	16	19	144
2	55	20	12	27	20	134
3	25	15	30	29	30	129
Total	150	50	66	72	69	407

of the factors. The results pointed to systemic differences in the values, attitudes and beliefs of nursing, medical and lay managerial staff on four dimensions, the first two of which (pictured in Figure 8.1) together accounted for 91.1 per cent of the variation between the professional groupings.

The factors that comprised the dimension represented on the vertical axis of Figure 8.1 are set out in Table 8.2. The data pointed to differences between medical and nurse clinicians' ascription to structures and methods which would engender *personalized/ opaque conceptions of clinical work organization and accountability*, as compared with lay managers' attachment to more *socially abstracted, transparent conceptions of clinical work organization and accountability*.

Across the sample as a whole, the *personalized/opaque conceptions of work organization and accountability* of medical and nurse clinicians was illustrated by their tendency to:

- *support* resorting to personalized and hence organizationally opaque systems for establishing the accountability of clinicians;
- *rank* clinical autonomy issues over information issues (nurse clinicians are equivocal);
- *oppose* using a hierarchical/surveillance model of clinical unit management;

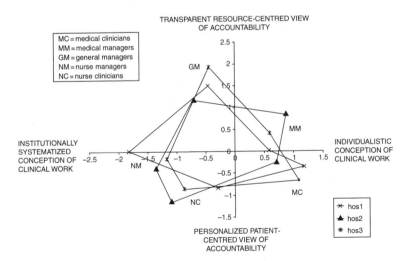

Figure 8.1 Discriminant analysis of professions in three Australian hospitals

Table 8.2 Personalized vs socially-abstracted approaches to clinical work organization and accountability

Assessment of	MC	MM	GM	NM	NC
Personalized opaque accountability	−.287	.285	1.13	.153	−.203
Importance of information issues relative to clinical autonomy issues	.271	−.061	−.977	−.357	−.039
Hierarchical and financially-driven approaches to clinical unit management	.276	−.383	−.593	−.077	.732
Organizationally transparent clinical and financial accountability systems	.103	.240	−.032	.218	.287
Stakeholder inclusive approaches to setting clinical standards	.304	−.022	−.388	.204	.330

Notes: MC = medical clinicians; MM = medical managers; GM = general managers; NM = nurse managers; NC = nurse clinicians. Shaded scores indicated values congruent with the direction of reform. Unshaded scores indicate values at variance with the direction of reform.

- *oppose* organizationally transparent clinical and financial accountability; and
- *disagree* with using stakeholder inclusive approaches to setting clinical standards.

In contrast, the responses of staff with managerial responsibilities tended in the opposite direction, and this was especially the case with lay managers.

The factors that comprised the dimension set out on the horizontal axis in Figure 8.1 are set out in Table 8.3. These factors drew attention to differences between medical clinicians' and medical managers' *individualistic* conceptions of clinical work *performance* as compared with the *collective* orientations of nurse clinicians and nurse managers.

The *individualistic* orientations of medical clinicians and medical managers were illustrated by their tendency to:

- *deny* the importance of institutional shortcomings as causes of clinical practice variation;

Table 8.3 Individualistic vs institutionalized collective concepts of clinical work performance

Assessment of	MC	MM	GM	NM	NC
Institutional shortcomings as causes of clinical practice variation	.688	.411	−.156	−.429	−.362
More systematized approaches to clinical work	.590	.421	−.291	−.465	−.033
The appropriateness of a medical ascendancy model for clinical unit management	−.388	−.144	.448	.766	.129
Team based clinical work systematization as a model for clinical unit management	.319	.141	.141	−.429	−.472
The autonomy effects of protocol based service provision	.389	.136	−.122	−.554	−.337
Self generated knowledge as a basis of setting clinical standards	−.144	−.289	.328	.731	.172

Notes: MC = medical clinicians; MM = medical managers; GM = general managers; NM = nurse managers; NC = nurse clinicians. Shaded scores indicated values congruent with the direction of reform. Unshaded scores indicate values at variance with the direction of reform.

- *reject* the introduction of more systematized and integrated approaches to service delivery to address hospital resource issues;
- *subscribe* to a medical ascendancy model of clinical unit management;
- *reject* team-based systematization as a model for clinical unit management;
- *assess* being expected to follow protocols as restricting their autonomy; and
- *support* basing clinical standards on self-generated knowledge.

In contrast, the *institutionalized/collective* orientations of nurse clinicians and nurse managers were illustrated by their opposing stance on each of these matters. For example, in contrast to their medical counterparts, nurse clinicians and nurse managers tended to:

- *accept* the importance of institutional shortcomings as explanations of clinical practice variation;
- regard involvement in team based management as *enhancing* their autonomy;

- assess expectations that they follow protocols as *enhancing* their autonomy; and
- *reject* the view that clinical standards can be based on self-generated knowledge.

The leadership challenge of reform

As noted earlier, the success of reform within participating hospitals can be judged from its impact on the value/rule basis of relationships within clinical settings. Among other matters, the reforms necessitate clinicians to:

- recognize interconnections between the clinical and financial dimensions of care;
- participate in processes which are oriented to bring clinical work within the ambit of work process control;
- accept the multidisciplinary and hence team-based nature of clinical service provision and accept the need to establish structures and practices which are capable of supporting this; and
- adopt a perspective which balances clinical autonomy with transparent accountability.

Judged against these criteria, professions varied markedly in the *following* they accorded to particular aspects of the programme of reform.

As summarized in Table 8.4, whereas general managers and nurse managers were inclined to support all aspects of reform, this was not the case with the remaining professional groupings. Medical clinicians and managers rejected all aspects of reform although medical managers did recognize 'the need to accept interconnections between the clinical and resource dimensions of care'. While nurse clinicians supported systematizing clinical work and strongly supported team-based service provision, their stances on accountability issues and resource issues were similar to those of medical clinicians.

The problem for senior managers (the now designated leaders of reform) was that, in the absence of 'clinician buy-in', there was little that they could do to bring about the required changes within their hospitals. Put simply, progress on the reform agenda within individual hospitals required resolution of subcultural differences on:

- intersections between the clinical and resources dimension of care;
- understandings about the prevalence and causes of clinical practices variances;

Table 8.4   Professional responses to reform

Reform focus	MC	MM	GM	NM	NC
Recognize interconnections between the clinical and financial dimensions of care	Deny	Recognize	Strongly Recognize	Recognize	Strongly deny
Adopt a perspective which balances autonomy with transparent accountability	Reject	Reject	Strongly accept	Accept	Reject
Participate in processes which are oriented to bring clinical work within the ambit of work process control	Reject	Reject	Accept	Accept	Accept
Accept the multidisciplinary and hence team-based nature of clinical service provision	Reject	Reject	Accept	Accept	Accept

Notes: MC = medical clinicians; MM = medical managers; GM = general managers; NM = nurse managers; NC = nurse clinicians.

- who should be involved in setting clinical standards;
- what should be taken into account in setting clinical standards;
- the appropriate model of clinical unit management;
- the appropriateness of clinical work process control;
- the multidisciplinary nature of clinical work; and
- individualism versus collectivism.

The clinical directorate structure introduced as part of the programme of hospital reform (devolving managerial and budget responsibilities for a service to a team of clinicians) meant that medical and nurse managers were best-placed to promote this change agenda. Perforce their position, medical and nurse managers were located at the intersection of clinical and managerial constructions of what was projected as required and appropriate for improving the effectiveness and efficiency of clinical service provision.

But the marked differences between clinical and managerial perspectives noted above, meant that medical and nurse managers' capacity to jointly engage in implementing reform depended on the extent to which they had developed a shared discourse. This could then be used in a number of ways. Firstly, to establish a clinical/managerial identity separate from their clinical colleagues, and, second, to provide a basis for mediating between nursing, medical and managerial conceptions of clinical work. The issues posed by these requirements within the participating hospitals are highlighted further in the data presented in Table 8.5.

The data suggest that despite the authoritative promulgation of new organizational arrangements, medical managers were ambivalent about their roles. For example, the data of Table 8.5 show that in 1999, some 15 years since the commencement of hospital reform, 35 per cent of medical managers continued to display the attitudes, values and beliefs of medical clinicians displayed in Table 8.4. Moreover, the data in Table 8.4 suggest that the 28 per cent who were secure in their identity as medical managers, differed from medical clinicians only in their willingness to recognize interconnections between the clinical and resource dimensions of care. On all other factors, these medical managers were of the same mind as their medical colleagues.

Medical managers and medical clinicians were united in their concern to preserve an *individualistic* conception of clinical work. The evidence therefore suggests that many medical managers were defining their roles in terms which were much more limited than is claimed for them. Evidence from ethnographic case studies has shown that the effects of medical managers' limited conceptions of their roles are registered at a number of levels. For example, while the information systems being introduced into hospitals have the capacity to focus more directly

Table 8.5 The extent to which members of each profession identified with their own 'prototypes'

Percentage	MC	MM	GM	NM	NC
MC	61.9	10.2	5.1	10.2	12.7
MM	34.9	27.9	20.9	14.0	2.3
GM	7.7	5.8	67.3	11.5	7.7
NM	1.9	1.9	7.7	69.2	19.2
NC	5.1	1.7	6.8	16.9	69.5

Notes: MC = medical clinicians; MM = medical managers; GM = general managers; NM = nurse managers; NC = nurse clinicians.

on output and outcome, their use in mapping and managing the work of clinicians was being kept to a minimum (Iedema *et al.*, 1999).

Similarly, despite sustained efforts on quality improvement and the promotion, development and implementation of clinical guidelines and standards, both these initiatives remain subject to continued contestation, particularly among medical clinicians. This suggests that medical managers are denying themselves, and being denied, the practical and discursive tools necessary to address the resource and clinical practice issues that are at the core of current hospital reforms. Put in terms of the concerns of this chapter, in the absence of a *following* for reform among their medical colleagues, medical managers abdicate their leadership role.

Initiating leadership

In light of these findings, the CEOs in the participating hospitals invited the Centre for Clinical Governance (UNSW) to conduct workshops within the hospitals. (Each of the workshops, an average, were attended by 10 nurse manager, 12 medical managers, eight medical clinicians and three general managers.) The workshops were cast as forums in which clinicians and managers could have their say on reform. The aim was to encourage those attending to 'take the lead' in establishing 'responsible autonomy' as an organizing principle in the delivery and management of health services.

The workshops progressed through a series of case studies set in a hypothetical hospital around issues similar to those that the workshop participants were experiencing. They operated at three levels. Firstly, they introduced technical material about reforms being pursued and explored interconnections between these instrumental dimensions. Second, by illustrating the way that technical issues and concerns are shaped by the dense social fields within which they emerge, the workshops called into question values, attitudes and beliefs integral to how medical and nursing staff construe their work and their relations with both one another and with management. Finally, the workshops encouraged clinicians to break away from the 'habitus' (Bourdieu, 1994) of their professional identities and put at risk both behaviours and related positionings which they preferred to remain taken-for-granted.

In the course of the workshops, the positions taken by medical clinicians confirmed those mapped out in Figure 8.1. As the workshops progressed, these positionings became increasingly overt and direct, and questions about the way entrenched practices, values and beliefs limited the possibility of change became more pressing following the presentation of the survey results. These results, as noted above, pointed to marked differences between professions' conceptions of clinical work and of what was permissible and possible to improve performance. Thus the survey findings brought to the fore unspoken dimensions of medical, nursing and managerial practice and the ways these dimensions have affected the conduct and structuring of relations within the hospitals.

There was frequent contestation over the ways in which the hospital was to be defined and how the 'production management' theme of reform efforts violated these identifications. When the workshop addressed proposals to *more closely link resource and clinical dimensions of care*, advocates of this agenda were met with rejoinders such as: '...the doctor–patient contract is the only contract I'm here for'.

The tenor and manner of these comments was exemplified by one medical clinician who, with vehement sarcasm (his feet stretched out on the table in front of him), noted that there were '...fundamental differences between us and Kellogg's Cornflakes'. In other words, the hospital was a vehicle for realizing care as a humanistic/moral calling, not a factory used for the production of 'widgets'.

A similar identification was mobilized to reject the *centrality of work standardization* through the use of clinical pathways with comments such as:

> '...medicine isn't some production line',
> '...we'll end up like trained monkeys doing cookbook medicine', and
> '...variance is a tricky issue...every person is unique...clinical practice is an art'.

The identification of the hospital as a locale for the enactment of trust-based referral networks was mobilized during a discussion on the centrality of clinical pathways and work-process control for improving quality and effectiveness. Some medical clinicians were quick to point out the benefits that derived from the trust-based informality of conventional clinical referral:

> I see it as a sign of health and vigour... [it produces]...a kind of cohesiveness which allows them [doctors] to solve problems by talking to each other in corridors and ringing each other up...

The commitment to uni-professionalism evident in this comment highlights medical resistance to the *multidisciplinary nature of care and to team-based clinical work organization*. Other indications of this resistance were found in comments such as:

'...you'll get enormous resistance from patients and their families
not to have their doctor', and
'...consensus means nobody agrees'.

These responses contrasted with the widespread acceptance of clinical
pathways and clinical work-process control by nursing staff:

clinical pathways aren't new to nursing. We've been talking about
them for ten or more years and a lot of this information is old and
repetitive.

Strong, at times bitter, critiques of the anti-teamwork arguments (and
the personalities making them) were frequently shared *backstage* by the
nurses although they rarely participated publicly.

Medical staff blunted, if not terminated, reform-oriented discussions
primarily by emphasizing *accountability issues* which, they claimed,
were not recognized in pathways or the reform agenda. Comments
included:

'...they're not going to like big brother looking over their shoulder',
and
'...in the final analysis the person who's ultimately responsible,
sueable, legally responsible and so on is the person who has their
name on the end of the bed'.

Another strategy was to raise 'definitional issues' before ways forward
could be found. In the words of one medical manager:

[we need to resolve] what is a clinical pathway, what's a critical pathway, what are clinical indicators, what's a protocol, what's an algo-
rithm, what's the difference between all those...

Medical managers acted to protect medical individualism and self-
appraisal by also questioning the evidentiary basis of hospital reform
especially that focused on medical participation in designing, costing
and implementing clinical pathways:

we haven't been presented with the other models for costing...and
I don't think we've been presented with the evidence why they are
the best way to go.

In effect, the workshop sessions became forums in which participants acted out 'well-rehearsed renditions' of discursive and embodied stances in realizing membership of their professional subcultures. It is in precisely these reactions and embodied behaviours that the import of the case study for the potential of leadership in health is found.

Discussion: 'leading where followers want to go?'

This discussion has taken the issue of leadership beyond traits, styles and contingencies. Rather, leadership is construed as a modality of authority. While leaders build coalitions, mobilize bias and power, and craft strategies and tactics in a deeply political sense, it is also the case that followership is a condition for leading.

Judged against this criterion, the 'leadership project' in our three hospitals was failing. There were markedly different attitudes between professional groups towards their willingness to invest in, and accept, the authority of reform-oriented managers, particularly where the reforms in question affect the interests of nominated professional groups. What is involved here becomes apparent when we consider differences in the follower–leadership nexus of nurse managers and medical managers. While significant aspects of current hospital reforms are in line with what has been termed nursing's professionalization project, they run counter to the interests of medicine (Wicks, 1999; Witz, 1990; Zadoroznjy, 1998; Degeling *et al.*, 2001). Under these circumstances the capacity of nurse managers to command a following is much greater than that of their medical counterparts.

On a broader front, the change leadership capacity of medical managers is constrained by the structural position of medicine within society and the system of power and authority in which medical clinicians are enmeshed. Despite criticism within policy circles, medicine remains a profession with legislative and ideological backing for its monopoly position in the labour market. The legitimacy (and hence strength and resilience) of this position is continually reinforced as actors in both health policy circles and within clinical encounters continue to enact an ensemble of practices, values and meanings that underwrite medical preeminence. Equally, a medical manager's authority is circumscribed by clinicians' membership of a specialty college or society. It is these bodies which determine a specialist's rights of practice and which influence his/her career progression. Under these circumstances, medical managers find that, before they can lead, they need to establish the legitimacy of their newly acquired role among colleagues who claim autonomy as a defining characteristic of their professional work.

In summary, the processes of leading and following that are central to implementing reform cannot be construed as socially disembodied processes directed to achieving instrumental purposes external to the actors involved. Rather, 'leading' and 'following' are partial and partisan, and circumscribed by participants' position-takings. Leading/following is shaped by the professional subcultures and 'regulatory ideals' with which staff of each profession are imbued. It is reflected in how each professional subculture, on the basis of past and present experience of their positions within the ongoing structuring of relations within hospital settings, identify, embody and perform their interests and concerns.

Mainstream leadership theorists assume that cultural factors within, for example, a hospital can be altered, negated or removed simply by raising the awareness of those involved and in the ability of followers-to-be to step outside of their embodied self. This assumption collapses the politics of following to a reasoned debate about preferred states of social being, and does not address how and why individuals and professions advantaged (or disadvantaged) by the existing structuring of relations act to maintain this. Thus, this approach avoids or ignores significant aspects of how relations within hospitals have been structured over time and are restrained by the actors' continuing activity.

The data and analysis presented in this chapter call into question the claims made in the name of leadership and the normative principles from which its paradigm proceeds. Within our case-study hospitals, marked differences in the responses of medical, nursing and managerial staff to significant aspects of the reform programme were the source of a *dance macabre* which manifested in conflict and organizational stasis.

Two factors are important here for the 'leadership project'. These outcomes occurred within organizations that were under significant and well-recognized pressure to change. Second, in responding to their organizations' changed circumstances, the senior management élan of each hospital had adopted strategies that, in broad terms, were consistent with what is proposed under the rubric of change leadership. The literature on leadership, even that of a 'transformational hue', provides little basis for explaining what had or had not transpired in these hospitals or for identifying where ways forward were to be found. Our findings suggest that these shortcomings can be traced, in part, to the teleological, a-social, rationalist and mechanistic conceptions of following and followership that underpin leadership theorization. Put simply, most 'conventional' organization theory proceeds from an unstated assumption that followers are actors who, when asked to follow, empty themselves of their interests and divorce themselves from their personal histories, their social identities, and the regulating impact of the professional regimes which they embody.

There are two related problems with this view. First, it is apparent that leading and following, as with any other form of social action, are functions of two related things: individuals' embodied performance of their professional identity, which, in turn, answers to their profession's 'regulatory ideal' (Foucault, 1978). Each profession's 'regulatory ideal' references the ensemble of values, meanings and rules which institutionalize the profession's definition of disease, and determine what is required, both clinically and organizationally, for the proper conduct of its work. Moreover, a professional regulatory ideal generally 'forecloses and/or disavows other identifications' (Butler, 1993, p. 5), and does so through naturalizing particular embodiments and performances while denying others.

Supporting evidence for this is provided by both the questionnaire and the workshop data, which show that the nursing, medical and managerial discourses and embodied 'regimes' derive their demarcations and definitions to a considerable extent from the tensions that obtain among them (see again Figure 8.1), rather than from rationally discrete and cognitively independent ideals and 'logical' principles. One example of what is being referred to here can be seen in how the individualistic dispositions of medical staff are inversely proportioned to the self-protective collectivism of nurses on the one hand, and to the level of concern with work-process control of the lay managers on the other (see Degeling *et al.*, 1998, 2001).

Conclusion

We challenge the current use of the term 'organizational leadership' because we contest the discourse through which leadership is construed. In our view, leadership discourses fail to appropriately consider the political and the embodied dimensions of workers' performance of professional self on the one hand, and their profession-specific ideals, regimes and normative regulations on the other. The call for 'leadership' is a *rhetorical abstraction* promoting an instrumental-mechanistic view of organization and work. Such instrumentalism can neither be posited nor assumed, since workers' interests, conflicts and claims to power on the one hand, and their embodiments of professional regimes and ideals on the other, radically exceed its logic.

References

Allport, G. W. (1937) *Personality* (New York: Holt).

Bass, B. M. (1985) *Leadership and Performance beyond Expectations* (New York: Free Press).

Bass, B. M. (1990) *Bass and Stogdill's Handbook of Leadership: Theory, Research and Managerial Applications*, 3rd edn (New York: Free Press).

Bourdieu, P. (1994) 'Rethinking the State: Genesis and the Structure of the Bureaucratic Field', *Sociological Theory*, 12: 1, pp. 1–18.

Braithwaite J. (1995) 'Organisational Change, Patient Focused Care: An Australian Perspective', *Health Services Management Research*, 8: 3, pp. 172–85.

Braithwaite, J. (1999) *Incorporating Medical Clinicians into Management: An Examination of Clinical Directorates*, doctoral thesis (Sydney: University of New South Wales).

Bryman, A. (1996) 'Leadership in Organizations', in S. Clegg, C. Hardy and W. Nord (eds), *Handbook of Organization Studies* (London: Sage), pp. 276–92.

Burns, J. M. (1978) *Leadership* (New York: Harper & Row).

Butler, J. (1993) *Bodies That Matter: On the Discursive Limits of 'Sex'* (New York: Routledge).

Cardona, P. (2000) 'Transcendental Leadership', *Leadership and Organization Development Journal*, 21: 4, pp. 201–7.

Degeling, P. (1993) 'Policy as the Accomplishment of an Implementation Structure: Hospital Restructuring in Australia', in M. Hill (ed.), *New Agendas in the Study of a Policy Process* (London: Harvester-Wheatsheaf), pp. 25–56.

Degeling, P. (1994) 'Unrecognised Structural Implications of Casemix Management', *Health Services Management Research*, 7: 1, pp. 9–21.

Degeling, P., Hill, M. and Kennedy, J. (2001) 'Mediating the Cultural Boundaries between Medicine, Nursing and Management – the Central Challenge in Hospital Reform', *Health Services Management Research*, 14: 1, pp. 36–48.

Degeling, P. J., Kennedy, J., Hill, M., Carnegie, M. and Holt, J. (1998) *Professional Subcultures and Hospital Reform* (Sydney: Centre for Hospital Management and Information Systems Research, The University of New South Wales).

Degeling, P., Macbeth, F., Kennedy, J., Maxwell, S., Coyle, B. and Telfer, B. (2002) *Professional Subcultures and Clinical Governance Implementation in NHS Wales: A Report to the National Assembly for Wales* (Durham: Centre for Clinical Management Development, University of Durham).

Degeling, P., Sage, D., Kennedy, J. and Perkins, R. (1999) 'The Impact of Reform on Hospitalization-based Professional Sub-Cultures – a Comparison of Some Australian and New Zealand Hospitals', *Australian Health Review*, 22: 4, pp. 172–88.

Di Maggio, P. J. and Powell, W. W. (1983) 'The Iron Cage Revisited: Institutional Isomorphism and Collective Rationality in Organisational Fields', *American Sociological Review*, 35, pp. 147–60.

Fiedler, F. E. (1967) *A Theory of Leadership Effectiveness* (New York: McGraw-Hill).

Fiedler, F. E. (1993) 'The Leadership Situation and the Black Box in Contingency Theories', in M. M. Chemers and R. Ayman (eds), *Leadership Theory and Research: Perspectives and Directions* (New York: Academic Press).

Fiedler, F. E. and Garcia, J. E. (1987) *Improving Leadership Effectiveness: Cognitive Resources and Organisational Performance* (New York: Wiley).

Foucault, M. (1978) *The History of Sexuality Vol. I* (Harmondsworth: Penguin).

Gibb, C. A. (1947) 'The Principles and Traits of Leadership', *Journal of Abnormal and Social Psychology*, 42, pp. 267–84.

Giddens, A. (1984) *The Constitution of Society: Outline of the Theory of Structuration* (Cambridge: Polity).

Greene, C. N. (1975) 'The Reciprocal Nature of Influence Between Leader and Subordinate', *Journal of Applied Psychology*, 60, pp. 187–93.

Griffith, J., Sahney, V. and Mohr, R. (1995) *Reengineering Health Care: Building on CQI* (Michigan: Health Administration Press).

Harrison, S. (1988) *Managing the NHS* (London: Chapman & Hall).

House, R. J., Spangler, W. D. and Woycke, J. (1991) 'Personality and Charisma in the U.S. Presidency: A Psychological Theory of Leader Effectiveness', *Administrative Science Quarterly*, 36, pp. 364–96.

Iedema, R., Degeling, P. and White, L. (1999) 'Professionalism and Organisational Communication', in R. Wodak and C. Ludwig (eds), *Challenges in a Changing World: Issues in Critical Discourse Analysis* (Vienna: Passagen Verlag), pp. 127–55.

Kerr, S., Schriesheim, C. A., Murphy, C. J. and Stogdill, R. M. (1974) 'Toward a Contingency Theory of Leadership Based Upon the Consideration and Initiating Structure Literature', *Organisational Behaviour and Human Performance*, 12, pp. 62–8.

Korman, A. X. (1966) '"Consideration", "Initiating Structure" and Organizational Criteria – a Review', *Personal Psychology*, 19, pp. 349–61.

Kotter, J. P. and Heskett, J. L. (1992) *Corporate Culture and Performance* (New York: Free Press).

Lowin, A and Craig, C. R. (1968) 'The Influence of Performance on Managerial Style: An Experimental Object Lesson in the Ambiguity of Correlational Data', *Organisational Behaviour and Human Performance*, 3, pp. 440–58.

Pollitt, C., Hunter, D. and Marnoch, G. (1988) 'The Reluctant Managers: Clinicians and Budgets in the NHS', *Financial Accountability and Management*, 4: 3, pp. 213–33.

Pollitt, C. (1990) *Managerialism and the Public Services: The Anglo-American Experience* (London: Blackwell).

Schein, E. H. (1985) *Organisational Culture and Leadership* (San Franciso: Jossey-Bass).

Stogdill, R. M. (1948) 'Personal Factors Associated with Leadership: A Survey of the Literature', *Journal of Psychology*, 25, pp. 35–71.

Stogdill, R. M. (1974) *Handbook of Leadership: A Survey of Theory and Research* (New York: Free Press).

Weber, M. (1990) 'Legitimate Authority and Bureaucracy', in D. Pugh (ed.), *Organization Theory: Selected Readings*, 3rd edn (London: Penguin).

Wenger, E. (1998) *Communities of Practice* (Cambridge: Cambridge University Press).

Westley, F. R. and Mintzberg, H. (1989) 'Visionary Leadership and Strategic Management', *Strategic Management Journal*, 10, pp. 17–32.

Wicks, D. (1999) *Nurses and Doctors at Work: Rethinking Professional Boundaries* (St Leonards, NSW: Allen & Unwin).

Willmott, H. (1993) 'Strength is Ignorance: Slavery is Freedom: Managing Culture is Modern Organisations', *Journal of Management Studies*, 26, pp. 561–85.

Wilson, C. K. and Porter-O'Grady, T. (1999) *Leading the Revolution in Health Care: Advancing Systems, Igniting Performance*, 2nd edn (Maryland: Aspen).

Witz, A. (1990) 'Patriarchy and the Professions: The Gendered Politics of Occupational Closure', *Sociology*, 24: 4, pp. 675–90.

Zadoroznjy, M. (1998) 'Transformation in Collective Identity of Australian and US Registered Nurses', in H. Keleher and F. McInerey (eds), *Nursing Matters* (Melbourne: Churchill Livingstone, Harcourt Brace & Co.).

9

The Dynamics of Decision-Making: Leading Change in Resource Distribution of Health Care

Alexandra Harrison and Craig Mitton

Introduction

Why does a good idea work in one health care programme and not in another, even when both are part of the same regional health authority? Two case studies are presented that involve introducing a method of resource allocation, Programme Budgeting and Marginal Analysis (PBMA), that was new to the regional health authority in Calgary, Alberta, Canada. The success of the method in one programme is contrasted with the challenges experienced in introducing the approach in the second programme. Lessons learned from the differences in the adoption of the innovation between the two programmes are examined in the context of a framework that explicitly incorporates aspects of organizational behaviour.

When 17 Health Regions were established in Alberta, Canada in 1994, to replace more than 200 individual boards, it was anticipated that 'the Regional Health Authorities Act would promote coordination and integration of health services' (Alberta Health, 1994). The new health regions exhibit many features of integrated health care delivery systems (Gilles, 1993). Horizontal integration has been accomplished by consolidating hospital services, and vertical integration is also apparent since each region has been required to merge the previously independent organizations responsible for public health, acute care, home care and continuing care under a single board with a single administrative structure. However, despite these macro level organizational changes, most budgets still reflect historical spending patterns rather than an integrated approach to deciding on priorities that will benefit the heath region or the population as a whole.

Programme Budgeting and Marginal Analysis (PBMA) is a technique for examining existing patterns of resource use and developing recommendations for the reallocation of resources. It begins by examining how resources are currently spent, and then looks at incremental gains and costs of changes in spending within or across programmes. As the need to set priorities and allocate resources is a universal challenge in health organizations, an economic framework like PBMA, which aids decision-makers in determining how best to spend limited resources, has a widespread appeal. In fact, PBMA has been used at least 78 times in about 60 health regions internationally, across a diverse array of programme areas (Mitton and Donaldson, 2001).

The two case studies reported in this chapter were part of an Alberta-based comprehensive project to evaluate the PBMA process. The analysis of the cases highlights the organizational behaviour aspects of a PBMA 'Calgary' framework that has emerged from this research project. The findings from this research have parallels in international comparisons of the PBMA resource allocation process as well as lessons that are relevant to understanding leadership in health care organizations.

The next section describes the setting in which this work was carried out, as well as two priority-setting case studies and the PBMA process itself. The findings from the two case studies are then presented, followed by a description of the PBMA Calgary framework. The discussion links the PBMA health economic work more directly to aspects of organizational behaviour with an emphasis on leadership in health care organizations, and finishes with concluding comments.

Method

Setting

Alberta is one of 10 Canadian provinces, which have constitutional jurisdiction over the delivery of health services. The province covers an area of 255,000 square miles and has a population of over two and a half million people. In June 1994, the Regional Health Authorities Act was proclaimed, which established provincial health regions in Alberta for the delivery of health services.

The Calgary Health Region (CHR) is one of 17 Regional Health Authorities created. The region provides primary and secondary care for citizens in the Calgary area (about 900,000 people), tertiary care for surrounding regions and certain quaternary services for the entire province. The region now has a single regional board, regional medical staff of about 1500 physicians, and a regional senior management structure with a single chief executive officer.

The CHR provides services across the full continuum of care, with an annual budget of about $1.5 billion (Canadian). The region is organized into seven major portfolios: each of four acute care hospitals is in a different portfolio, with its own site manager; mental health services has its own portfolio; and there are two community-based portfolios. There is a matrix organizational structure so that regional departments (such as surgery and medicine), and regional programmes (such as seniors' health and heart health) are also assigned to one of the seven portfolios. Each of the portfolios is co-led by an executive director and a medical director.

Two case studies

Two case studies reported here were conducted in the Calgary Health Region as part of a comprehensive assessment of the feasibility of using PBMA in a Canadian setting. One PBMA exercise was conducted in the Infant Head Cranial Remodelling Programme. This is a small programme, with a budget of approximately $300,000, in the Child and Women's Health portfolio, and is located at the Alberta Children's Hospital. There is a part-time programme administrator for this programme who reports to the Director of Ambulatory Care, who in turn reports to the Executive Director of the Child and Women's Health portfolio. There is one medical liaison for the Cranial Remodelling Programme, representing five physicians who spend at least some time with this programme.

The Musculoskeletal (MSK) Programme is much larger. It is a major medical division within the CHR, with a total budget of about $15 million (Canadian). The medical division head is the Chief of Orthopedics, and there are numerous administrators who coordinate activity across the continuum of care in this area and who each report to the Executive Director of the Rockyview Hospital, a community-based adult acute-care and teaching hospital in Calgary.

PBMA process

The PBMA process is built around five questions about resources:

1 What resources are available in total?
2 In what ways are these resources currently spent?
3 What are the main candidates for more resources and what would be their effectiveness?

4 Are there areas of care that could be provided to the same level of effectiveness with fewer resources, which would release resources to fund candidates from #3?

5 Are there areas of care which, despite being effective, should receive fewer resources because a proposal from #3 is more effective (per dollar spent)?

The first two questions relate to programme budgeting, while the latter three pertain to the marginal analysis. Programme budgeting is a means of describing the pattern of spending within a health authority and its distribution between groups in the population (Gold *et al.*, 1997). The programme budget can classify expenditure by programme (that is, disease group), by service inputs grouped by sector of care (that is, primary care, acute care), or by other means such as population demographics (Miller *et al.*, 1997). The second stage, marginal analysis, can be used to examine the historical provision of services in health care, and propose options for improving the efficiency and equity of programmes (Donaldson *et al.*, 1995). Although this technique is often used to analyse potential changes in service options within a particular programme, marginal analyses can also be utilized within health authorities across programmes of service (Mooney *et al.*, 1986; Viney *et al.*, 1995).

To apply PBMA, a specific programme area and set of objectives must be defined; a programme budget is then developed to map the relevant activity and cost data. An expert panel, representing key stakeholders including administrators and clinicians, is set up to assess the impact of potential shifts in resources on the overall health of the target population. Scenarios which involve increases and reductions in spending on services are presented to the panel. The panel then develops a list of priorities based on services which should be expanded or contracted, and the impact of these proposed changes is evaluated by examining evidence on effectiveness and cost from the literature, as well as local data on needs and outcomes. Finally, key decision-makers must decide whether the resource shifts recommended by the expert panel will actually be implemented. The final decisions should take into account locally relevant, predefined criteria.

Findings

Infant Head Cranial Remodelling Programme

The Cranial Remodelling Programme provides orthotic headbands to infants who are born with a misaligned head. The case study was conducted both as a research project and to aid a group of decision-makers who faced a real challenge of maximizing the service provided in a specific programme with constrained resources. The objective of the PBMA exercise was to provide a framework for the Infant Cranial Remodelling Programme to make recommendations for resource allocation to improve programme efficiency, patient care and access to services.

The working group (expert panel) consisted of the medical lead (a neurosurgeon), two nurses, a rehabilitation therapist and the programme administrator. After an introductory meeting, which included the Executive Director of the Child and Women's Health portfolio, the group decided to pursue the project and met three more times during the following four months. The Alberta Children's Hospital site manager and a representative from Finance also attended the meetings as observers. The research assistant reviewed relevant literature and presented to the group an initial list of potential areas for service expansion and resource release. The working group assessed the list and added additional items. After examining the potential costs and benefits of the suggested list, the group developed five recommendations:

- Further develop the prevention/education component of the cranial programme.
- Hire a full-time programme coordinator for the cranial programme.
- Discontinue all anthropometric measurements.
- Pursue a significant price reduction with current manufacturing company.
- Examine alternative manufacturers with lower headband prices.

It is anticipated that implementation of the first two points would require $37,000, while the latter two changes could release up to $140,650. The third point neither saves nor releases actual dollars, although time, as a resource, would be saved, which could be reallocated elsewhere. Some aspects of this PBMA exercise were successful: the group met and developed recommendations that identified areas for resource expansion and resource release. However, due in part to the busy schedules of the clinical and administrative staff, in the end only the third recommendation was acted upon immediately. The others have not been explicitly followed-up to date, although, anecdotally, more focus has been placed on education for families whose children are affected by this medical problem.

Lessons from the Infant Head Cranial Remodelling Programme

The expert panel working group made significant strides towards improving the efficiency of the Infant Cranial Remodelling Programme. The PBMA framework enabled the various options for expansion and resource release to be examined in an explicit and evidence-based manner, and if implemented the recommendations could result not only in improved patient benefit but also significant programme savings. The PBMA process does not actually include the final step of making a decision. Rather, PBMA provides an explicit framework through which the expert working group navigates to make recommendations for further action.

That said, a key issue arising from this case study was the uncertainty about follow-up on some of the recommendations. It was made clear to the group that the purpose of the exercise was to identify potential changes, not to carry out those changes. However, discussion on how the specific recommendations were going to move forward could have taken place during the final marginal analysis session and might have facilitated the implementation phase. One previously published PBMA study also raised the issue of follow-through as a particular challenge (Haas *et al.*, 2001), although this was not a problem with other case studies in Alberta. The lack of clarity surrounding follow-through suggests that resources should be earmarked at the outset of the project to facilitate this follow-through.

In summary, the lack of follow-up in this case study emphasizes the need to clearly define expectations about implementation at the outset of the exercise. Despite this, the priority-setting exercise was successful in that options for redesigning the Cranial Remodelling Programme were identified and recommendations for change made.

Musculoskeletal Health Programme

After preliminary discussions in the Fall of 1999 with the Chief of Orthopedics and the Executive Director of the portfolio in which the MSK programme is located, a PBMA exercise was considered in the area of arthroplasty (that is, hip and knee replacements). The stated objective of the exercise was to apply PBMA in order to identify how the mix of arthroplasty services might be changed to improve the benefit to this patient population within the available resources. However, as the project progressed, it appeared that the intention of the surgeons was really to find ways to do more surgeries with the resources available in this area.

Despite initial interest, the PBMA exercise was not actively pursued in this area because a number of other components of a project examining MSK services more broadly took centre stage. Consultants from a US-based health care consultant firm were hired to identify areas where there was less than optimal use of resources, and to recommend how the process could be improved. The extensive report from the external consultants made the use of the PBMA framework redundant. Despite this, however, one manager in MSK was keen to use PBMA, and therefore a more focused exercise was considered to make specific recommendations on redesigning the surgical services. The rationale for using PBMA was that it was not clear how the recommended changes would actually be implemented. Ultimately, however, the PBMA project in MSK was abandoned completely by mutual agreement of the researchers and the project Chair.

Lessons from Musculoskeletal Health (MSK)

Although the PBMA framework was not actually used in the MSK programme, a number of lessons can be learned from the MSK case study, particularly around barriers to implementation of the PBMA framework. First, a high-level champion must be behind the PBMA exercise. While a member of senior management does not have to be intimately involved in each step of the process, such an individual must buy into the process to the extent that they are willing to direct managers who would be involved at the operational level of an exercise to earmark time and energy for the project. This was not present for the PBMA project in the MSK programme.

A second problem was the organizational design in MSK. One component of this was that the organizational reporting relationships for the MSK programme were unclear. In addition, the MSK programme did not have its own programme budget. With vertical budget silos spanning a number of operational areas (such as the operating room, various medical and post-surgical wards and so on), MSK did not have an organizational structure to foster reallocation across the areas in the programme. As Jick (1993) observes, the process of change is influenced by both formal and informal processes. In the case of MSK, neither the formal organizational structure nor the culture of the informal relationships (between administrators and physicians) supported an environment in which a mechanism for priority-setting like PBMA could be adopted and used in routine decision-making. In the MSK programme, there had been a large number of structural and personnel changes in the months and years preceding the PBMA activity. There appeared to be a lack of trust, based in part on the accumulation of power in certain medical portfolios, which further undermined the necessary informal working relationships that might have circumvented the structural barriers.

Another issue apparent in the MSK case study was a misalignment of incentives between physicians and administrators. The surgeons' main objective was to do more arthroplasty surgeries but this group was not affected by the broader resource impact of this objective. Although meeting need is also an objective for the administrators in the MSK programme, they have to address needs in many areas across the continuum of services, with surgery being just one service area. These broader service needs must be met within a fixed budget.

Overall, the MSK case study was useful from a research perspective, even if PBMA did not directly influence the decision-making process. Key factors were identified to foster the success of a priority-setting framework like PBMA, including the need for a health region champion, an organizational structure that allows allocation across programme areas, an organizational culture of trust between physicians and administrators, a culture that is willing to change from the status quo, and better alignment of incentives between physicians and the health region.

The Calgary PBMA framework

Previous work in the PBMA literature has tended to examine the PBMA process in isolation. That is, the focus has been on defining a programme, developing a programme budget, striking a marginal analysis expert panel, developing incremental wish lists and resource release options, and then making recommendations for potential service redesign. After the case studies were conducted during this project, it became clear that there were a broader set of influences that were contributing to the success or failure of a given PBMA exercise. Using data from the two PBMA case studies described above, and several other applications of the PBMA process in Alberta, a framework that incorporates the PBMA process was developed. This Calgary framework positions the PBMA process within the context in which it is to be applied (see Figure 9.1) (Mitton and Donaldson, 2002).

The 'PBMA process' box in Figure 9.1 represents the standard PBMA steps outlined above, with a number of the key lessons learned from the case studies in Alberta listed underneath. These points can be taken as suggestions for future PBMA exercises. For example, the programme budget is not an essential component of the PBMA

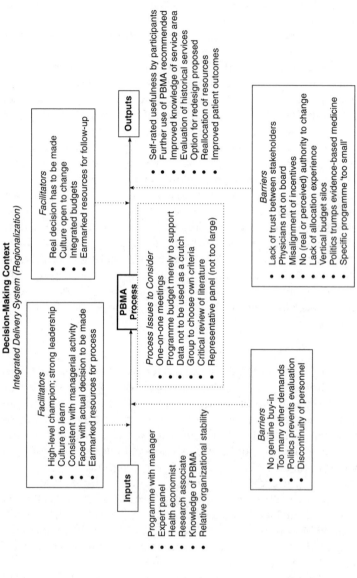

Decision-Making Context
Integrated Delivery System (Regionalization)

Inputs

- Programme with manager
- Expert panel
- Health economist
- Research associate
- Knowledge of PBMA
- Relative organizational stability

Barriers

- No genuine buy-in
- Too many other demands
- Politics prevents evaluation
- Discontinuity of personnel

Facilitators

- High-level champion; strong leadership
- Culture to learn
- Consistent with managerial activity
- Faced with actual decision to be made
- Earmarked resources for process

PBMA Process

Process Issues to Consider

- One-on-one meetings
- Programme budget merely to support
- Data not to be used as a crutch
- Group to choose own criteria
- Critical review of literature
- Representative panel (not too large)

Facilitators

- Real decision has to be made
- Culture open to change
- Integrated budgets
- Earmarked resources for follow-up

Outputs

- Self-rated usefulness by participants
- Further use of PBMA recommended
- Improved knowledge of service area
- Evaluation of historical services
- Option for redesign proposed
- Reallocation of resources
- Improved patient outcomes

Barriers

- Lack of trust between stakeholders
- Physicians not on board
- Misalignment of incentives
- No (real or perceived) authority to change
- Lack of allocation experience
- Vertical budget silos
- Politics trumps evidence-based medicine
- Specific programme 'too small'

Figure 9.1 Calgary framework for PBMA process

framework; it merely serves to outline the existing services in terms of activities and resources. Other tools, such as the business plan, can serve this purpose.

The model identifies a number of 'inputs' that should be in place for the PBMA process to be conducted. These include having a programme in which priority questions are being asked, with a manager who has overall responsibility for the programme, and someone associated with the project who is knowledgeable about the PBMA process. There are numerous potential 'outputs' from any given PBMA exercise. As Mooney *et al.* (1997) identifies, these outputs include the direct results of resource reallocation and patient outcomes, but can be expanded to include a broader list of outcomes such as the evaluation of historical services and improved knowledge of a given service area.

Barriers and facilitators to the PBMA process are also included in the model. For example, from the MSK case, it became apparent that some PBMA exercises will not even get off the ground, thus the need for barriers and facilitators after the input box but before the process commences. Similarly, following the PBMA process, there may be factors which facilitate or prevent recommendations from being reached or followed up. For example, the cranial remodelling exercise resulted in a number of recommendations for redesign, some of which were not (at least in the short term) acted upon.

As well as depicting PBMA activity in Alberta, the Calgary framework can also serve as an 'evaluation framework' for future PBMA studies.

Decision-making

The findings from the Alberta case studies that have been incorporated into the Calgary framework are very consistent with what is known about organizational change (Kotter, 1996; Lorenzi *et al.*, 2000), including the importance of leadership, the challenge of politics, and the need for a supportive organizational culture. An interesting theme that emerged from a number of the case studies was an obsession of some clinicians and managers for data. In the MSK exercise, this obsession in part immobilized the decision-making process. It is understood that relevant data is needed to support the decision-making process, but managers still have to make a decision even if data is not available, and even if that decision is to implicitly maintain the status quo of service delivery in their programme. In situations without sufficient data, it is not clear why making an (implicit) decision to provide the same set of services is acceptable, whereas making an explicit decision to change the set of services is not. It may be that managers will reject change unless there is compelling evidence to do so, even if there is no clear evidence that what is being done currently is maximizing benefit for the given resources. This finding can serve as a warning for others interested in introducing change. The issue of decision-making with incomplete data may need to be explicitly identified.

Discussion

International application of PBMA

While programme budgeting has its roots in the US defence sector in the 1950s and 1960s, it was not until the mid-1970s that the apparent logic of the framework was recognized for health care (Pole, 1974). Through the late 1970s and early 1980s, a number of programme budgeting and marginal analysis exercises surfaced in the UK (Mooney, 1977; Gray and Steele, 1979; Mooney, 1984). With the advent of the purchaser–provider split in the UK in the early 1990s, the application of PBMA appeared to 'take off'. However, commentators have argued that the formation of an internal market is not necessary for the use of a framework like PBMA (Madden *et al.*, 1995), as evidenced by the proliferation of examples in which the framework has been used in recent years in Australia, New Zealand and, most recently, Canada.

Although there is limited international comparative analysis of the application of PBMA, one survey of authors of PBMA, found a number of common threads in attempting to identify potential factors for its successful implementation (Mitton and Donaldson, 2001). These included the presence of a high-level champion, continuity of personnel over time, and the involvement of a university-based health economist. It would also seem that decision-makers appreciate a non-vested party (such as a university-based researcher) facilitating the priority-setting activity. Finally, the survey of authors highlighted that the aim of PBMA is generally not viewed to be just about resource reallocation, but also found that changes in organizational culture, particularly around how decision-makers think about economic principles, and how they approach priority-setting activity, are valuable byproducts of such work. These findings are consistent with the information that emerged in the Alberta work that has been incorporated into the 'Calgary' framework.

Organizational issues

The MSK case highlighted a number of structural barriers to implementing PBMA in health care organizations. As indicated previously, one challenge was that the MSK programme was comprised of a number of components funded from different budgets. Another related issue was the relationship between the surgeons and the Health Region. Ideally, a PBMA exercise will identify opportunities for resource release and resource utilization that will enhance services provided to the population served by a Health Region. It appeared during the discussions about PBMA in the MSK programme that there was not agreement among the stakeholders about the intent of the PBMA exercise. The administrators were interested in how the spectrum of MSK services might be optimized, whilst the surgeons were interested in how to reorganize resources so that more surgeries could be performed. For a PBMA exercise to be effective, there needs to be agreement at the outset on the purpose or objective of the exercise. In addition to the structural barriers, the MSK programme had its organizational culture undermined by ongoing organizational change. Other authors have suggested that organizational stability is needed for PBMA to be effective (Peacock, 1998), and it may be that stability is important to foster organizational relationships and allow trust to develop. Trust was evident in the cranial project and a variety of professional groups were able to come up with recommendations for the programme. However, lack of trust was a barrier in the MSK programme.

The classic models of innovation have been instrumental in shaping thinking about the stages of innovation (Rodgers, 1995). However, the early models have limitations, one of which, as Fitzgerald *et al.* (1999) note, is that the majority of diffusion models are context free. In contrast, organizational models of the diffusion of innovation underscore the importance of understanding the organizational environment, particularly the social culture (Lockyer *et al.*, 1994). In a similar vein, a major limitation of the PBMA process described in the economic literature is the lack of recognition of the organizational context. The Calgary framework that emerged from this study begins to address this limitation by explicitly identifying organizational factors that may influence the success of the PBMA process. Rodger's (1995) definition of an organization as 'a stable system of individuals who work together to achieve common goals through a hierarchy of ranks and a division of labor' does not reflect the reality of today's health care organizations and regions.

Challenges for health care organizations and leadership

Health care organizations present a number of organizational and leadership challenges. The highly complex nature of such organizations relates to several key characteristics which include public and political demands, as well as industrial, scientific and professional issues (Dawson, 1999).

Shortell and Kaluzny (2000) observe that it is the confluence of professional, technological and task attributes that make the management of health services organizations particularly challenging. Health care has a highly professionalized workforce whose primary loyalty is with their professional group rather than the organization. These professionals are often carrying out complex and highly specialized work activities that are very interdependent, but with little organizational control over physicians whose clinical decisions affect most of the work and expenditures that occur in the organization.

The challenging nature of health care organizations presents challenges for leadership in these institutions. Some of the definitions and interpretations of leadership articulated by Bass (1995) that are particularly relevant include: (a) leadership as the focus of group processes, (b) as the exercise of influence (which implies a reciprocal relationship between the leader and followers), and (c) as an instrument to achieve goals. Smircich and Morgan (1982) speculate that leadership is the management of meaning and is essentially a social process defined through interaction. It involves a process of defining reality in ways that are sensible to the lead. The leaders guide the attention of those involved in a situation in ways that are designed to shape the meaning of the situation. The need to 'manage meaning' in health care is evident when one looks at differences between managers and physicians. Physicians see themselves as responsible and accountable to their patients; they work with short time frames due to the immediate feedback from patients; and are influenced by strong collegial relationships with other physicians. Managers, however, have an allegiance to the organization with a shared sense of responsibility, and often delayed feedback that occurs in a hierarchical authority structure (Pointer and Sanchez, 1994).

Possibly because of the structural and cultural challenges among groups in health care, methods to coopt professionals into processes that will accomplish organizational aims are in evidence. Two examples are quality improvement and PBMA.

Team organizational processes

A variety of activities to align professional activities with organizational priorities are emerging in health care. Quality-improvement activities have shifted the focus away from searching for the individual 'bad apples' to improving systemwide processes to improve care. The evolution in vocabulary is continuing from 'quality assurance', to 'quality improvement', to 'preventing medical error' and, more recently, 'patient (or health system) safety'. There is increasing recognition by policy-makers and health care providers that many adverse events are related to well-intentioned individuals working in less than optimal systems.

PBMA is also a team process. It requires input from stakeholders to make decisions about where resources will be reallocated. Leadership is required for this to be successful, and leadership is needed to manage the team process. This could be why respondents to the international survey of PBMA use (Mitton and Donaldson, 2001) have found the involvement of a University researcher to be helpful. It was also evident both in the Alberta experience and in the international survey of authors that high-level leadership support is required.

PBMA is evidence-based, but not evidence-driven. Since there are increasing expectations that physicians will incorporate the best available evidence into their clinical practices, evidence-based management decisions will be more compatible with the ethos of evidence-based clinical practice. It is known that evidence alone is not enough to change physician practice (Rappolt, 1997). When clinical practice guidelines are developed by a distant group of experts, they will not automatically be adopted locally. The adoption process is dependent on collegial communication (Lockyer, 1999), since the construction, interpretation and application of evidence is a social process (Fitzgerald *et al.*, 1999). What is needed is careful review by local opinion leaders and then application by individual physicians based on their 'clinical judgement'. In a similar manner, PBMA requires 'management judgement' by local experts (clinicians and managers) to apply the evidence appropriately to the decision at hand, since data alone cannot provide all the answers. The review of available data (such as historical utilization or findings from the literature) requires interpretation by the expert panel, analogous to using clinical judgement with practice guidelines. Both tasks may require action without complete information. PBMA may thus be an example of the evidence-based management (Stewart, 2002) of the future.

Conclusion

The relentless pace of change in health care shows no signs of easing. Health care organizations continue to face an increasingly complex environment and will need to adapt both structures and processes to deal the ongoing challenges. Recent reports also highlight this need. The most recent report *Health Care Reform in Alberta* (2001) recommends 'implementing alternative approaches for paying physicians and providing a better alignment between physicians and regional health authorities'. The Institute of Medicine in the United States (2001) suggests that leaders of health care organizations need to allow new and more flexible roles and responsibilities for health care providers. PBMA provides a glimpse of this 'brave new world'.

References

Alberta Health (1994) *Regional Health Authorities User's Guide* (Edmonton, AB: Alberta Health).

Bass, B. (1995) 'Concepts of Leadership', in J. L. Pierce and J. W. Newstrom (eds), *Leaders and the Leadership Process* (Burr Ridge, Illinois: Irwin McGraw-Hill).

Donaldson C. (1995) 'Economics, Public Health and Health Care Purchasing: Reinventing the Wheel?', *Health Policy*, 33, pp. 79–90.

Dawson, S. (1999) 'Managing, Organising and Performing in Health Care: What Do We Know and How Can We Learn?', in A. Mark and S. Dopson (eds), *Organizational Behaviour in Health Care – the Research Agenda* (London: Macmillan – now Palgrave Macmillan), pp. 7–24.

Gray, A. and Steele, R. (1979) 'Programme Budgeting in the Health Sector', *International Journal of Management Science*, 7: 5, pp. 451–8.

Fitzgerald, L., Ferlie, F., Wood, M. and Hawkins, C. (1999) 'Evidence Into Practice? An Exploratory Analysis of the Interpretation of Evidence', in A. Mark and S. Dopson (eds), *Organizational Behaviour in Health Care – the Research Agenda* (London: Macmillan – now Palgrave Macmillan), pp. 189–206.

Gilles, R., Shortell, S., Anderson, D., Mitchell, J. and Morgan, K. (1993) 'Conceptualizing and Measuring Integration: Findings from the Health Systems Integration Study', *Hospital and Health Services Administration*, 38: 4, (Winter), pp. 467–89.

Gold, L., Raftery, J. and Soderlund, N. (1997) *Costing Diseases at DHA Level: A Standardised Approach?*, Presented at the Health Economists' Study Group, University of York.

Haas, M., Viney, R., Kristensen, E., Pain, C. and Foulds, K. (2001) 'Using Program Budgeting and Marginal Analysis to Assist Population Based Strategic Planning for Coronary Heart Disease', *Health Policy*, 55, pp. 173–86.

Institute of Medicine (2001) *Crossing the Quality Chasm: A New Health System for the 21st Century* (Washington, DC: National Academy Press).

Jick, T. D. (1993) *Managing Change: Cases and Concepts* (Boston: Richard D. Irwin).

Kotter, J. P. (1996) *Leading Change* (Boston: Harvard Business School Press).

Lockyer, J., Mazmanian, P., Moore, D., Harrison, A. and Knox, A. (1994) 'The Adoption of Innovation', in D. Davis and R. Fox (eds), *The Physician as Learner, Linking Research to Practice* (Chicago, Ill: American Medical Association), pp. 33–45.

Lorenzi, N. M. and Riley, R. T. (2000) 'Managing Change: An Overview', *Journal of the American Medical Informatics Association*, 7, pp. 116–24.

Madden, L., Hussey, R., Mooney, G. and Church, E. (1995) 'Public Health and Economics in Tandem: Programme Budgeting, Marginal Analysis and Priority Setting in Practice', *Health Policy*, 33, pp. 161–8.

Miller, P., Parkin, D., Craig, N., Lewis, D. and Gerard, K. (1997) 'Less Fog on the Tyne? Programme Budgeting in Newcastle and North Tyneside', *Health Policy*, 40, pp. 217–29.

Mitton, C. and Donaldson, C. (2001) 'Twenty-five Years of Program Budgeting and Marginal Analysis in the Health Sector, 1974–99', *Journal of Health Services Research and Policy*, 6: 4, pp. 239–48.

Mitton, C. and Donaldson, C. (2002) 'Setting Priorities and Allocating Resources in Health Regions: Lessons from a Project Evaluating Program Budgeting and Marginal Analysis (PBMA)', *Health Policy*.

Mooney, G. (1977) 'Programme Budgeting in an Area Health Board', *The Hospital and Health Services Review*, November, pp. 379–84.

Mooney, G. (1984) 'Program Budgeting: An Aid to Planning and Priority Setting in Health Care', *Effective Health Care*, 2: 2, pp. 65–8.

Mooney, G., Haas, M., Viney, R. and Cooper, L. (1997) *Linking Health Outcomes to Priority Setting, Planning and Resource Allocation* (New South Wales, Australia: Center for Health Economics Research and Evaluation).

Mooney, G., Russell, E. and Weir, R. (1986) *Choices for Health Care: A Practical Introduction to the Economics of Health Provision* (London: Macmillan – now Palgrave Macmillan).

Peacock, S. (1998) *An Evaluation of Program Budgeting and Marginal Analysis Applied in South Australian Hospitals* (Melbourne: Center for Health Program Evaluation, Monash University).

Pointer, D. P. and Sanchez, J. P. (1994) 'Leadership: A Framework for Thinking and Acting', in S. Shortell and A. Kaluzny (eds), *Health Care Management: Organization Design and Behaviour* (Albany, NY: Delmar Publishers), pp. 86–112.

Pole, J. (1974) 'Programs, Priorities and Budgets', *British Journal of Preventive and Social Medicine*, 28: 3, pp. 191–5.

Premier's Advisory Council on Health (2001) *A Framework for Reform*, Province of Alberta, Edmonton, Canada, December.

Rappolt, S. G. (1997) 'Clinical Guidelines and the Fate of Medical Autonomy in Ontario', *Social Science and Medicine*, 44: 7, pp. 987–97.

Rogers, E. M. (1995) *Diffusion of Innovations*, 4th edn (New York: The Free Press).

Shortell, S. M., Gillies, R. R., Anderson, D. A., Erickson, K. M. and Mitchell, J. B. (2000) *Remaking Health Care In America*, 2nd edn (San Francisco: Jossey-Bass)

Shortell, S. and Kaluzny, A. (2000) 'Organization Theory and Health Services Management', in S. M. Shortell and A. D. Kaluzny (eds), *Health Care Management, Organizational Design, and Behavior* (New York, NY: Delmar Publishers), pp. 3–29.

Smircich, L. and Morgan, G. (1982) 'Leadership: The Management of Meaning', *Journal of Applied Behavioural Sciences*, 18: 3, pp. 257–73.

Stewart, R. (2002) *Evidence Based Management: A Practical Guide for Health Professionals* (Oxford: Radcliffe Medical Press).

Viney, R., Haas, M. and Mooney, G. (1995) 'Program Budgeting and Marginal Analysis: A Guide to Resource Allocation', *NSW Public Health Bulletin*, 6: 4, pp. 29–32.

Part III

Taking Health Care Forward in the Twenty-First Century

10

Role Innovation in the NHS: A Preliminary Evaluation of the New Role of Nurse, Midwife and Health Visitor Consultant*

Sally Redfern, David Guest, Jenifer Wilson-Barnett, Riccardo Peccei, Patrice Rosenthal, Philip Dewe and Amanda Evans

Introduction

This chapter describes an early evaluation of the establishment of the role of nurse, midwife and health visitor consultant in the National Health Service in England and Wales. It was in 1998, after three decades of various developments of senior clinical roles in the nursing and midwifery professions, that Prime Minister Tony Blair announced his intention to establish consultant posts in nursing, midwifery and health visiting (public health nursing). These consultants were expected to have the same status in their professions that medical consultants have in theirs though the number would be nothing like that available to medicine. Consultant nurse and other specialist nursing roles have been introduced in the USA since the 1970s, but it was not until the 1980s and 1990s that specialist nurses and advanced nurse practitioner roles became commonplace in the UK (Wilson-Barnett *et al.*, 2000), and 2000 when the first consultant roles were introduced on a national scale with a government-defined brief, though a few self-styled pioneering consultant posts had been established before this (Wright, 1991; Manley, 2000, 2001). The announcement from the Department of Health was

---

* The study was funded by the Department of Health, England. The views expressed are the authors' and not necessarily those of the Department of Health. We are grateful to the consultants for responding to our requests for information so willingly.

clear in its expectation that the new consultants would improve service provision and outcomes for patients, strengthen leadership and increase retention of expert practitioners by establishing a new career opportunity in clinical practice (DoH, Health Service Circular, 1999/217). Each post was to have an ambitious brief:

- an expert practice function;
- a professional leadership and consultancy function;
- an education, training and development function; and
- a practice and service development, research and evaluation function. (DoH 1999/217)

Specific criteria for appointment were set out including the expectation that 50 per cent of the role would be practice-based, and that partnerships between the NHS and local universities would be set up to enhance the education and research functions. The role was to be introduced into a wide range of health service contexts that, though containing standard features, in practice are quite different kinds of setting.

The Department of Health commissioned our team to evaluate the establishment of the new role in its earliest stages of development. The first posts were filled during 2000 and our evaluation includes all consultants in post in February 2001. This preliminary study ended in June 2001 (see Guest *et al.*, 2001). The aim here is, first, to explore role innovation by comparing levels of activity and function in the new role with previous roles, and then to describe consultants' initial perceptions and experiences in the role.

Background to development of new roles in nursing

The new role of consultant nurse, midwife and health visitor emerged on a national scale in the UK in the year 2000, though its establishment can be traced through statutory professional and government policy documents published during the 1990s. Table 10.1 lists guidelines and policy documents that emerged over the decade and indicates ways in which perceptions of roles in these professions and the training required for them have evolved.

Factors contributing to the case for the consultant role have been noted by Read *et al.* (1999). These include provision of guidelines by professional bodies to help nurses widen the scope of their practice; management flexibility in changing skill-mix to overcome difficulties in staffing services; and policy drivers such as the need to expand primary care

Table 10.1 Statutory and government policy documents leading to establish-ment of consultant nurse, midwife and health visitor posts in England and Wales

1991	Department of Health, NHS Executive	*Junior Doctors: The New Deal*
		• Moves to reduce junior doctors' hours and extend the nursing role
1991	Department of Health	*The Patient's Charter*
		• Leading to new standards and expectations of nurses and the need for expanded roles and different ways of working
1992	United Kingdom Central Council for Nursing, Midwifery & Health Visiting (UKCC)	*The Scope of Professional Practice*
		• Nurses given authority to expand their practice after appropriate preparation
1994	Department of Health	*The Greenhalgh Report*
		• Six activities could be undertaken by nurses (taking patient histories, venous blood sampling, cannulation, intravenous drug administration, patient referral for investigations writing discharge letters)
1994	UKCC	*The Future of Professional Practice*
		• Elements of advanced practice defined
1997	Department of Health	*Junior Doctors' Hours: The New Deal*
		• Shorter (72) hours a week for junior doctors • More medical tasks taken over by nurses
1997	Department of Health	*The New NHS: Modern and Dependable*
		• Reconfiguration of the workforce with more permeable boundaries between roles • New measures to ensure high standards, accountability and evidence-based practice

Table 10.1   continued

1997	UKCC	*Post-Registration Education and Practise Project*
		• Continuing education and professional development required • Three levels of practice introduced: primary, specialist, advanced
1998	Department of Health, NHS Executive	*Nurse Consultants* (HSC 1998/161)
		• Plans announced
1999	Department of Health, NHS Executive	*Making a Difference*
		• Strengthening the nursing, midwifery and health visiting contribution to health and health care • Competencies were seen as essential to workforce planning rather than professional qualifications
1999	UKCC	*A Higher Level of Practice*
		• Recommendations for new roles of of nurse practitioner and clinical nurse specialist

and community-based services as well as shorten junior doctors' hours. Expansion of nursing functions that incorporate elements of clinical leadership, expertise in implementing evidence-based practice, extended technical and medical skills, and abilities in practice development are seen by policy-makers to help in resolving problems for health service delivery and taking health care forward in the twenty-first century.

Drivers for change have also come from nurses as they demonstrate their increasing clinical competence and potential for role expansion and leadership, though establishing criteria that distinguish between different levels of expert practice continues to evade the profession. Clinical nurse specialists and nurse practitioners in the UK have led the way over the last two decades as individual pioneers (Wilson-Barnett and Beech, 1994; Read and Roberts-Davis, 1998). Positive evaluations have been made of development units in various specialties of nursing, midwifery and health visiting (Turner Shaw and Bosanquet, 1993; Pearson, 1995, 1997; Christian and Norman, 1998; Redfern and Murrells, 1998) and of nurse-led units set up for intermediate care of older people (Pearson *et al.*, 1988; Griffiths and Evans, 1995; Griffiths and Wilson-Barnett, 2000). The *Exploring New Roles in Practice* (ENRiP) report (Read *et al.*, 1999) showed that 838 posts representing new roles in nursing, midwifery and allied health professionals in the acute sector of the NHS had successfully breached traditional role boundaries. The main influence of these new roles is seen to lie in the clinical credibility of the practitioners. They are change agents with ambitions to improve quality and continuity of care and, where appropriate, they provide plans for reorganizing health service delivery.

Retaining their credibility as experts in practice is a priority in the consultant role initiative, as indicated by the requirement that post-holders should keep a 50 per cent expert practice function. Whether it is realistic for the new consultants to be active in all the functions specified by the Department of Health, that is in leadership, education, research, development and evaluation as well as expert practice, is one of the questions that the research will explore. The new role of nursing officer grade 7, introduced following the 'Salmon' management reforms of the late 1960s (Ministry of Health and Scottish Home and Health Department, 1996), failed because of overambitious and wide-reaching goals for the role and lack of adequate preparation and planning for its establishment (Wilson-Barnett, 1973). Our study, conducted 30 years later, raises similar concerns.

The ENRiP project and a more recent evaluation of advanced nurse practitioners (Wilson-Barnett *et al.*, 2000) highlight a lack of managerial and professional support. Major concerns are to do with authority, accountability and responsibility in the new roles. Most of the post-holders assessed their roles positively but identified considerable pressures associated with high expectations, work overload, role confusion and lack of management, administrative and peer support. The Wilson-Barnett report revealed that, at times, medical and nursing practitioners were in open conflict over the way the posts are configured, and these aspects are important to investigate with respect to the new consultants. We have looked at their initial experiences with respect to job control, job demands, workload, role clarity, role conflict and rewards. Expectations of the role held by health service policy decision-makers and managers, as well as the nursing and medical professions, are high. Could unrealistic demands lead to a consultant role that cannot be sustained?

How effective the new consultant roles are for patients is an important but methodologically tricky question for evaluators. Reviews of the UK research on clinical nurse specialists and advanced nursing practitioners show generally positive results in terms of outcomes for patients, professional staff and economic parameters (Wilson-Barnett and Beech, 1994; Shewan and Read, 1999; Reynolds *et al.*, 2000). Research on nurse-led units demonstrates that nurses can run services safely but do not necessarily save on costs of the service (Griffiths and Wilson-Barnett, 2000). Rapid response and accessibility seem to be key for patients when judging nursing services. Nurses are deemed to be the more appropriate practitioners for providing care to patients with enduring problems from stroke, rheumatoid arthritis and Parkinson's disease, for example, whereas doctors are considered best for making diagnoses and prescribing medications (Jahanshah *et al.*, 1994; Forster and Young, 1996; Reynolds *et al.*, 2000). There is evidence from these reviews of blurring of professional boundaries occurring some time before the new consultant role was introduced.

Not surprisingly, given the newness of the NHS-defined consultant role, we have found very little research yet published evaluating it in the UK, although consultants themselves have described their experiences in the first months in the role (Pennington, 2000; Gosling, 2001; Scullion, 2001; Pottle, 2002). However, a three-year action research study on a self-styled consultant nurse post in England which predated introduction of the NHS-defined role, has been completed (Manley, 2000, 2001). Manley investigated the development and organizational impact of one nurse consultant working in an intensive care unit, and reported the consultant's leadership role as crucial to achieving successful change in nursing practice and the wider hospital culture. Another English study is a survey of members of a forensic mental health team about the post of forensic mental health consultant (Chalder and Nolan, 2001) which pointed to the risk of burnout if the role is not clearly defined. There have been more role evaluations of consultants published in other countries, most notably the USA (Hewitt and Tellier, 1996; Popejoy *et al.*, 2000; Stichler, 2002), Australia (Blackford and Street, 2001; Jannings and Armitage, 2001) and the Netherlands (Simonetti and Tjia, 1995). Most of these studies focus on consultants within certain specialties, such as public health nursing, community nursing, cancer and palliative care, and they highlight the value of the consultant in promoting such activities as facilitating inter-agency working and continuity of care, improving quality of care through practice-based research and on-the-job teaching, and health promotion activities such as publicizing implications of smoking and drinking alcohol during pregnancy.

In summary, there is substantial support for the initiative to introduce consultant posts in nursing, midwifery and health visiting into the UK, though very few evaluations have yet been published on their role and impact. Previous research evaluations on specialist and advanced nursing practitioners in this country confirm that they can usefully expand their roles without harming patients, though there is less clarity about the essential elements within practice that make these roles unique or expert. Published work shows that certain professional, organizational and resource constraints hamper the potential of some specialist/advanced posts to make a difference, though other research demonstrates benefits to patients. It is against this background and experience of previous innovations in the roles of nurses, midwives and health visitors that the present evaluation of the new consultant role was set up.

Research methods and sample

The research has three components:

- *Accounts of incidents and experiences.* A sub-sample of 32 consultants were interviewed by telephone at intervals (3–5 per individual over June–November 2000, number of interviews = 138). Consultants were selected across region and role category to assess early evolution of the role. They included four midwives, three health visitors, and 25 nurses – adult-generalist (7), adult-specialist (5), mental health (5), elderly (4), child (2), learning disability (2). Questions focused on specific experiences in establishing the role and on perceived challenges and learning across the four prescribed elements of the job (clinical practice, education/staff development, leadership/consultancy, research/evaluation).
- *A role network analysis.* Ten case studies of consultants in their role context included interviews with the consultants and key members in their role network, informal observation and document analysis. The participating consultants were two midwives, two health visitors/child specialists and six nurses – adult-specialist (1), adult-generalist (1), mental health (2), elderly (1), learning disability (1). The aim was to understand perceptions of the new role among network members and any implications for members' own roles and for the effectiveness of the unit. Visits of one or two days per case were made between August and November 2000.
- *A questionnaire survey.* Questionnaires were sent in February/March 2001 to all consultants in post including those selected for the interviews and case studies (158 in total). Questions asked for views about the consultants' roles, levels of involvement in various activities

compared with their previous job and their initial experiences. Specific questions and attitude scales included items on evaluation of the role in terms of job control and complexity, clarity, conflict, workload and rewards. After one reminder, the final response in time for the analysis was 153 questionnaires. A few of these were from consultants who were very new to their post and who did not answer all the questions. The extremely impressive response rate of 95 per cent demonstrates the support and commitment of the consultants in contributing to this evaluation.

Results

Involvement in activities specified by the Department of Health

The Department of Health specified 22 activities considered to be appropriate for the consultant role in its guidelines (DoH, 1999/217) and these are structured around the four core functions of expert practice, leadership, training and research and development as indicated in Table 10.2. Table 10.3 shows that involvement in every function is reported as significantly greater in the current compared with the previous job. Similarly, average scores calculated for each of the 22 activities separately are significantly greater for the current job except for one (supervising staff, in the training function).

Table 10.4 shows the patterns of involvement across the different functions for the four main consultant types, classified as hospital-based, community-based, mental health and midwives. Consultants' level of involvement in the 22 activities tends, on the whole, to be very high with nearly two-thirds reporting a great deal of involvement in the activities overall. There is considerable variation for the total sample across the four functions with nearly all (90%) of the consultants reporting deep involvement in leadership activities. Over two-thirds (68%) reported high involvement in research and development activities compared with training and expert practice activities, which drop to about half the group (50% and 48% respectively). This pattern of involvement tends to occur for each consultant type with reported activity being highest for the leadership and R&D functions and lowest for training and expert practice. A statistically significant difference across the groups, however, for the expert practice function, indicates that over twice as many consultant midwives are deeply involved in expert practice activities compared with community-based and mental health consultants. In fact, the midwives reported greater involvement for all the functions compared with the other groups.

Table 10.2 Functions and activities of the consultant role

Expert Practice (expert practice function)

- Making referrals to other professionals
- Prescribing medicines/aids/equipment as directed in the group prescribing protocol
- Managing complete programmes of care
- Developing clinical protocols, documentation systems and guidelines
- Monitoring effectiveness of current therapeutic programmes
- Integrating different aspects of practice to improve quality and health outcomes

Leadership and Consultancy (leadership function)

- Advising and supporting colleagues where standard protocols do not apply
- Developing best practice
- Promoting best practice
- Generating and implementing new solutions that will best meet the needs of patients and clients
- Offering expert advice to own and other professions on care practices, delivery and service development

Education, Training and Staff Development (training function)

- Identifying and responding to individual and team training needs
- Mentoring staff
- Supervising staff
- Engaging in professional development of staff
- Teaching staff and students in partnership with colleges/universities

Practice and Service Development, Research and Evaluation (research and development function)

- Promoting evidence-based practice
- Setting, monitoring and auditing standards
- Evaluating local services against best practice
- Carrying out research
- Disseminating and networking on improving practice
- Developing and sustaining new partnerships/networks to improve delivery systems and health outcomes

The last item in Table 10.4 shows that consultants reported spending, on average, 44 per cent of their time working with patients/clients, and this proportion is similar across consultant type. Thus, even though fewer community-based and mental health consultants reported high involvement in expert practice activities, they seem to be spending, on average, much the same amount of time

Table 10.3 Levels of involvement in role functions in present and previous job (all consultants)

Function	Average involvement score* (mean)		
	Present job	*Previous job*	*Difference score*
Expert practice	3.79	3.06	.73**
Leadership	4.56	3.69	.85**
Training	3.86	3.45	.42**
Research & development	4.17	3.22	.94**
Total (22 activities)	4.08	3.34	.74**

Note: * Responses were rated on a 5-point scale: 1 = not involved at all; 2 = minor involvement/contribution; 3 = moderate involvement/contribution; 4 = major involvement/contribution; 5 = I take the lead in the activity. ** $p < .001$.

Table 10.4 Pattern of involvement across functions: overall and by consultant type

	Consultant type				
Involvement function	*Total sample (n = 147)*	*Hospital -based (n = 78)*	*Community -based (n = 34)*	*Mental health (n = 25)*	*Midwives (n = 10)*
Total involvement (% highly† involved*)	65	72	56	48	90
Expert practice function (% highly involved**)	48	56	38	24	80
Leadership function (% highly involved)	90	88	94	88	90
Training function (% highly involved)	50	50	44	52	70
R&D function (% highly involved)	68	69	68	56	90
Average % of time spent working with patients/clients	44	47	41	43	41

Notes: † score of 4 or above on 5-point scale; * statistically significant difference across the four consultant types at $p < .05$ level; ** statistically significant difference across the four consultant types at $p < .01$ level.

with patients as the other groups. It should be noted that the averages reported in the table mask considerable variation in time spent working with patients/clients. Nearly a quarter (24%) of the total sample reported spending 30 per cent or less of their time working with patients, and a similar proportion (23%) reported spending between 60 per cent and 80 per cent of their time with patients. The average of 44 per cent is quite close to the target of 50 per cent working in practice set by the Department of Health.

Role innovation

Two dimensions of role innovation are relevant to the establishment of consultant nurse, midwife and health visitor posts. The first measures changes in individual consultants' overall level of involvement in the different activities and functions between their present and previous job. The second concerns changes in the individuals' overall pattern of involvement, or role profile, between their present and previous job. For the first dimension, the consultants reported, on average, a 19 per cent increase in their overall involvement across the 22 activities, with the greatest increase (23%) occurring in the research and development function and the smallest increase (10%) in the training function. No significant difference emerged across consultant type.

For the second dimension of role innovation we adapted and extended the function-specific measures so that we could classify the consultants into different role profiles according to their level of involvement. For each function, we distinguished three main levels of involvement: low (average involvement scores of 3 or below on the 5-point scale), medium (average scores between 3 and 4), and high (average scores of 4 and above). On this basis we then identified five distinct role profiles or models of consultant activity. These are described below together with average total involvement scores associated with each profile:

- *Low-involvement model*: includes respondents who reported low involvement in at least three of the four functions with, at most, only medium involvement in the remaining function (total involvement score = 3.27).
- *Medium-involvement model*: includes respondents who reported medium levels of involvement in two or more functions with, at most, low involvement in the remaining function (total involvement score = 3.96).
- *Single-focus model*: includes respondents who reported high involvement in one of the four functions with medium or low involvement in the remaining three functions (total involvement score = 4.12).

- *Dual-focus model*:   includes respondents who reported high involvement in two of the four functions with either medium or low involvement in the other two (total involvement score 4.47).
- *High-involvement model*: includes respondents who reported high involvement in three or more functions (total involvement score 4.71).

Comparing the previous job with the present job the proportion of consultants adopting the low-involvement model is 68 per cent vs 22 per cent, medium involvement model 12 per cent vs 14 percent, single-focus model 16 per cent vs 29 per cent, dual-focus model 1 per cent vs 19 per cent and high-involvement model 5 per cent vs 18 per cent. Neither pattern of profiles varies significantly across consultant type. These results indicate that, overall, the establishment of the new consultant role was accompanied by a substantial amount of role innovation and role expansion.

Perceptions and experiences of the consultant role

How do consultants feel about the new role? Questions asked of those interviewed included details of challenges they were facing during their first few months and what new things they were learning (see Table 10.5).

Some of the early challenges focus on consultants wanting to make an impact and improve practice, as one said when speaking of preserving time for clinical practice:

Table 10.5   Challenges and learning identified by interviewed sample (*n* = 32)

Challenges	Learning
• Improving practice and service delivery	• Balancing desire for rapid change against need to win over reluctant staff
• Improving, developing and confirming clinical credibility	• Need for patience, and persistence, change takes time
• Prioritizing demands, managing breadth of job	• Leadership skills of listening, challenging, involving, sharing
• Expanding knowledge and skills	• Declining external requests and management responsibilities
• Deciding where to begin in introducing change	• Finding support networks
• Selling the consultant role to other professionals	• Not getting upset by criticism and opposition

I feel that that [clinical time] has to be a priority really, otherwise I'm not gonna make a difference. I feel that my particular priorities here are trying to protect the normal [childbirth] and prevent unnecessary intervention. (cohort 1, consultant 4, interview 2)

Another focused on providing value for money:

Well, you know the job isn't done, by any stretch of the imagination, and there is a need to produce some tangible changes. I mean, after all I'm being paid a, quite a lot of money to do that, so I've to demonstrate that's happening. (cohort 1, consultant 2, interview 5)

Making an impact is difficult to achieve if they lack confidence in their clinical competence or are unsure where to start in introducing change, yet have to handle an exponential increase in demands made on them by others. The stimulation of facing new challenges was fulfilling for many, however:

I mean, there are times when you think, I can't see the wood for the trees. But, you know, you have an hour and everything seems to sort of get done. And if something else happens that is a new challenge, a new stimulation. So I have to say I'm really enjoying the stimulation. And y'know, I really am very fulfilled by the role. (cohort 4, consultant 2, interview 2)

They described themselves as being on a very steep learning curve in having to gain leadership skills such as patience, diplomacy and persistence in persuading staff to accept change. As one said:

I had found it very difficult because I had a vision of how I thought the service should be developed. But they [the nurses] needed to own it. The challenge was meeting them again this week and realizing that they haven't really moved forward with the ideas, and trying to keep my mouth shut and...getting them to own it. I'm pleased to say by the end of the meeting, 3.5 hours the meeting went on, they're completely – it's as if it's their idea. But the challenge was to sell mine as if it was their idea. (cohort 2, consultant 8, interview 3)

And coping with the burgeoning demands meant having to learn which requests they could turn down without jeopardizing the viability of new support networks and making progress:

I think I've learned to say no this week. …It's taken a long time! In actual fact, [name of manager] who I was able to talk to quite effectively in the general manager's absence, said to me a few weeks ago, 'you know, you're taking so much on, I do worry that you're going to be able to keep this up.'…I'm having to take a chunk of everything at the moment to define my role, to see what it is I need to do and who I need to know and what can come first,…so I can effectively prioritize where we can take action. And so I've taken on everything. …And now I feel that I've reached the point where I can look at it and be selective. And I think that's a good place to be because I'm getting tired. …Oh, I still feel good about it. There's a big difference between being tired and being burnt out. (cohort 3, consultant 1, interview 3)

Moving to the questionnaire survey, we can see how much the perceptions of the interview cohort are reflected in job-related perceptions asked of the whole group. Table 10.6 summarizes the proportion of 'high' scorers on the following job factors, each represented as a rating

Table 10.6 Task characteristics, role stressors and perceived job rewards: overall and by consultant type

% high scorers*	Consultant type				
	Total sample (n = 147)	Hospital -based (n = 78)	Community -based (n = 34)	Mental health (n = 25)	Midwives (n = 10)
Task characteristics					
Job control	79	82	76	80	60
Job demands	39	41	41	32	30
Role stressors					
Work overload	47	47	44	56	30
Role clarity**	50	60	44	28	40
Role conflict	11	9	18	16	0
Job rewards					
Career opportunities	52	54	56	44	40
Growth opportunities	84	86	85	80	80

Notes: * Score of 4 or above on 5-point scale; ** statistically significant difference across the four consultant types at $p < .05$ level.

scale of items completed by the consultants as follows (for details of the scale items, see the full technical report, Guest *et al.*, 2001):

- Job control: measured using a 5-item scale (alpha .87).
- Job demands: 7-item scale (alpha .78).
- Work overload: 3-item scale (alpha .78).
- Role clarity: 3-item scale (alpha .87).
- Role conflict: 3-item scale (alpha .74).
- Career opportunities: 3-item scale (alpha .79).
- Growth opportunities: 3-item scale (alpha .83).

These items were selected because of their relevance to the lessons learned from previous evaluations of new roles in health care practice, notably the ENRiP study (Read *et al.*, 1999) referred to earlier.

Levels of reported job control and autonomy are high and levels of difficulty and complexity, as represented by the job-demands factor, relatively low. This may not be surprising given the overall high level of competence, experience and expertise of these consultants (64 per cent hold a masters or doctorate degree and 30 per cent hold professional diplomas/certificates in addition to the basic qualification in nursing or midwifery). In contrast, the relatively high reported work overload (47%) and low role clarity (50%) suggest that half the consultants have too much to do and are unclear about their duties and responsibilities. There is a significant difference between consultant groups on perceived role clarity, with fewer high-scoring mental health consultants. Otherwise the differences between the groups are not statistically significant. Job rewards, in terms of perceived opportunities for career progression, were rated highly by half the group (52%), and opportunities for personal growth by the majority (84%).

To probe the findings on work overload and role clarity further, we ran regression analyses on each with individual and structural job variables as predictors (individual variables: age, gender, marital status, dependent children, tenure, educational qualifications, professional qualifications, perceived job competence; structural variables: role involvement in previous job, new to job, new to organization, pre-entry job clarity, detailed job description, perceived resource adequacy, perceived support from line manager, professional manager, senior medical staff, colleagues, senior management). The independent variables account for 38 per cent of the variance in role clarity, compared with only 9 per cent of the variance in work overload. Significant predictors of role clarity are perceived job competence (beta .25), pre-entry role clarity (beta .26) and perceived support from the consultant's line manager (beta .21). Only job tenure (beta .33) emerges as a significant predictor of work overload, but the positive association suggests, somewhat alarmingly, that quantitative overload gets greater as time in the job increases.

Discussion

The evaluation of the introduction of a new and complex role can be usefully considered in terms of behavioural, affective and performance outcomes. Behavioural outcomes include whether the activities undertaken correspond to the role specification. Affective outcomes address how consultants feel in this role and how much their initial reactions are shaped by their experience of the role and by the support they receive. Performance outcomes concerned with performance standards and effect of the role on patients must wait until the consultants have been practising for longer than the period of this preliminary study. Although we collected some information from consultants on patients' views of the role, this evaluation is concerned with the early stages of role settlement and adjustment as people find their feet in the role and begin to work out how to perform in it.

The results suggest that consultants are able to cope with the complexity of the work and the professional rewards are high, but work overload and role ambiguity are challenges that need careful handling to avoid the job becoming unmanageable. Work overload seems to be a fairly predictable problem for incumbents of new roles in the nursing professions as demonstrated by the early evaluation of the role of the nursing officer (Wilson-Barnett, 1973) and the more recent ENRiP research (Read *et al.*, 1999). Our finding that workload increases with length of time in the job needs confirmation. It may be that consultants find it difficult to control their workload in the first few months while they are settling in and adjusting to new demands. After a year or so they may have clarified their priorities and be able to confidently refuse certain demands without jeopardizing their impact. In the meantime, managers and consultants themselves need to be alert to the negative consequences, such as burnout, of too heavy a workload. The ENRiP report and the survey of the forensic nurse consultant post (Chalder and Nolan, 2001) also identified a strong risk of burnout.

Our results support ENRiP's findings on role ambiguity. The ENRiP team reported unclear boundaries and ambiguity about the purpose of the new roles, and only half the consultants in our study reported high role clarity and this proportion dropped to about a quarter of the mental health consultants. The implication is that many are unclear about their new responsibilities, they do not know what is expected of them and do not have a clear idea of what has to be done in the job. Further investigation through regression analysis suggests that role clarity would be enhanced if clarity before starting the job were higher and support from line managers greater in the early months. The importance of good management support was underlined strongly in the ENRiP report. Perceived competence also emerged as a predictor of role clarity which suggests that clarity may improve over time as consultants gain confidence in their competence.

Innovation emerges as a strong feature of the new role of consultant in nursing and midwifery. That is to say, generally speaking, the new role is not an existing role with a new name. There is a significant increase in activities within the four centrally specified functions of leadership, research and development, training and expert practice. The classification of consultants into one of the five 'involvement' models shows that, compared with their previous job, far fewer fit the low-involvement model. Instead, they moved to embrace a model that is either dual-focused, single-focused or high-involvement, with midwives, in particular, the consultants for whom role innovation is most pronounced (though note the small sample of midwives surveyed). These results indicate that consultants are working more than before in the activities specified by the Department of Health though the nature of their involvement varies, with some increasing their involvement in all four functions and others prioritizing one or two functions over the others. This variability is not necessarily surprising nor cause for concern given the wide range of specialties, client groups and health service settings represented. More research is needed to investigate the patterns of involvement across consultants working in different specialties in order to understand how they craft their roles and responsibilities according to the priorities within their different jobs. We have now embarked on a follow-up study to investigate these patterns further and undertake a more systematic evaluation of the impact of the consultant role on quality of practice and patient outcomes.

Establishment of the new consultant role in the last decade of the twentieth century has set the scene for nursing, midwifery and health visiting to introduce significant change to health care in the UK. This preliminary study has confirmed the potential of consultants in these professions to make a difference to practice. The follow-up study will show how the new roles are unfolding and becoming embedded into routine practices, and what impact consultants are having on conventional role configurations in health care and on career aspirations and fulfilment among the nursing, midwifery and health visiting professions.

References

Blackford J. and Street A. (2001) 'The Role of the Palliative Care Nurse in Promoting Continuity of End-of-Life Care', *International Journal of Palliative Nursing*, 7: 6, pp. 273–8.

Chalder, G. and Nolan, P. (2001) 'The Role of the Forensic Nurse Consultant Observed', *British Journal of Forensic Practice*, 3: 3, pp. 23–30.

Christian, S. and Norman, I. (1998) 'Clinical Leadership in Nursing Development Units', *Journal of Advanced Nursing*, 27, pp. 108–16.

Department of Health (DoH) (1991) *Junior Doctors: The New Deal* (London: NHS Management Executive).

Department of Health (DoH) (1991) *The Patient's Charter: Raising the Standard* (London: HMSO).

Department of Health (DoH) (1994) *The Interface between Junior Doctors and Nurses: A Research Study for the Department of Health* (Macclesfield: Greenhalgh & Co. Ltd).

Department of Health (DoH) (1997) *Junior Doctors' Hours: The New Deal* (London: NHS Executive).

Department of Health (DoH) (1997) *The New NHS: Modern, Dependable* (London: The Stationery Office, CM3852).

Department of Health (DoH) (1998) *Nurse Consultants* (London: NHS Executive, Health Service Circular), http://www.open.gov.uk/doh/coinh.htm

Department of Health (DoH) (1999) *Nurse, Midwife and Health Visitor Consultants: Establishing Posts and Making Appointments* (London: NHS Executive Health Service Circular 1999/217).

Department of Health (DoH) (1999) *Making a Difference: Strengthening the Nursing, Midwifery and Health Visiting Contribution to Health and Healthcare* (London: Department of Health).

Forster, A. and Young, J. (1996) 'Specialist Nurse Support for Patients with Stroke in the Community: A Randomised Controlled Trial', *British Medical Journal*, 312, pp. 1642–6.

Gosling, J. (2001) 'A Week in the Life of...a Urology Nurse Consultant', *Professional Nurse*, 16: 9, pp. 1378–9.

Griffiths, P. and Evans, A. (1995) *Evaluation of a Nursing-led Inpatient Service: An Interim Report* (London: King's Fund Centre).

Griffiths, P. and Wilson-Barnett, J. (2000) 'Influences of Length of Stay in Intermediate Care: Lessons From the Nursing-led Inpatient Unit Studies', *International Journal of Nursing Studies*, 77: 3, pp. 245–55.

Guest, D., Redfern, S., Wilson-Barnett, J., Dewe, P., Peccei, R., Rosenthal, P., Evans, A., Young, C., Montgomery, J. and Oakley, P. (2001) *A Preliminary Evaluation of the Establishment of Nurse, Midwife and Health Visitor Consultants.* Research Paper 007 (The Management Centre, King's College, London 2001) http:// /www.kcl.ac.uk/depsta/pse/mancen/Research Papers/Ncp.htm

Hewitt, J. B. and Tellier, L. (1996) 'A Description of an Occupational Reproductive Health Nurse Consultant Practice and Women's Occupational Exposures During Pregnancy', *Public Health Nursing* 13: 5, pp. 365–73.

Jahanshah, M., Brown, R. G., Whitehouse, C., Quinn, N. and Maselen, C. D. (1994) 'Contact with a Nurse Practitioner: A Short Term Evaluation Study in Parkinson's Disease and Dystronia', *Behavioural Neurology*, 7: 1–7.

Jannings, W. and Armitage, S. (2001) 'Informal Education: A Hidden Element of Clinical Nurse Consultant Practice', *Journal of Continuing Education in Nursing*, 32: 2, pp. 54–9.

Manley, K. (2000) 'Consultant Nurse Outcomes: Part 2 Nurse Outcomes', *Nursing Standard*, 14: 37, pp. 34–9.

Manley, K. (2001) 'Consultant Nurse: Concept, Processes, Outcomes', unpublished PhD thesis (University of Manchester and RCN Institute, London 2001).

Ministry of Health & Scottish Home & Health Department (1996) *Report of the Committee on Senior Nursing Staff Structure (the Salmon Report)* (London: HMSO).

Pearson, A. (1995) 'A History of Nursing Development Units', in J. Salvage and S. Wright (eds), *Nursing Development Units: A Force for Change* (London: Scutari Press).

Pearson, A. (1997) 'An Evaluation of the King's Fund Centre Nursing Development Unit Network 1989–1991', *Journal of Clinical Nursing*, 6, pp. 25–33.

Pearson, A., Durant, I. and Punton, S. (1988) 'The Feasibility and Effectiveness of Nursing Beds', *Nursing Times*, 84: 9, pp. 48–50.

Pennington, J. (2000) 'Nurse Consultant: Could It or Should It Be You?', *Journal of Diabetes Nursing*, 4: 5, pp. 136–9.

Popejoy, L. L., Rantz, M. J., Conn, V., Wipke-Tevis, D., Grando, V. T. and Porter, R. (2000) 'Improving Quality of Care in Nursing Facilities: Gerontological Clinical Nurse Specialist as Research Nurse Consultant', *Journal of Gerontological Nursing*, 26: 4, pp. 6–13.

Pottle, A. (2002) 'Becoming a Nurse Consultant', *Nursing Times*, 98: 1, p. 39.

Read, S., Lloyd Jones, M., Collins, K., McDonnell, A. and Jones, R. (1999) *Exploring New Roles in Practice: Implications of Developments Within the Clinical Team* (ENRiP). (Report for the Department of Health by a team from Sheffield University, England).

Redfern, S. and Murrells, T. (1998) 'Research, Audit and Networking Activity in Nursing Development Units', *NT Research*, 3: 4, pp. 275–88.

Reynolds, H., Wilson-Barnett, J. and Richardson, G. (2000) 'Evaluation of the Role of the Parkinson's Disease Nurse Specialist', *International Journal of Nursing Studies*, 37, pp. 337–46.

Scullion, J. (2001) 'Respiratory Nurse Consultant: The Role', *Nursing Times*, 97: 34, p. 44.

Shewan, J. A. and Read, S. M. (1999) 'Changing Roles in Nursing: A Literature Review of Influences and Innovations', *Clinical Effectiveness in Nursing*, 3, pp. 75–82.

Simonetti, G. P. C. and Tjia, P. F. (1995) 'From Consultation to Innovation: The Development of Nursing Consultancy in the Utrecht Comprehensive Cancer Centre Area, The Netherlands', *European Journal of Cancer*, 31: 975, p. S306.

Stichler, J. F. (2002) 'The Nurse as Consultant', *Nursing Administration Quarterly*, 26: 2, pp. 52–68.

Turner Shaw, J. and Bosanquet, N. (1993) *A Way to Develop Nurses and Nursing* (London: King's Fund).

United Kingdom Central Council for Nursing, Midwifery and Health Visiting (1992) *The Scope of Professional Practice* (London: UKCC).

United Kingdom Central Council for Nursing, Midwifery and Health Visiting (1994) *The Future of Professional Practice* (London: UKCC).

United Kingdom Central Council for Nursing, Midwifery and Health Visiting (1997) *PREP – The Nature of Advanced Practice* (London: UKCC).

United Kingdom Central Council for Nursing, Midwifery and Health Visiting (1999) *A Higher Level of Practice* (London: UKCC).

Wilson-Barnett, J. (1973) 'A Description of the Working Environment and Work of the Unit Nursing Officer', *International Journal of Nursing Studies*, 10, pp. 185–93.

Wilson-Barnett, J., Barriball, L., Reynolds, H., Jowett, S. and Ryrie, I. (2000) 'Recognising Advancing Nursing Practice: Evidence from Two Observational Studies', *International Journal of Nursing Studies*, 37, pp. 389–400.

Wilson-Barnett, J. and Beech, S. (1994) 'Evaluating the Clinical Nursing Specialist: A Review', *International Journal of Nursing Studies*, 31: 6, pp. 561–71.

Wright, S. (1991) 'The Nurse as Consultant', *Nursing Standard*, 5: 20, pp. 31–4.

11

Leading Clinical Practice Change: Evidence-Based Medicine (EBM) in the United States and United Kingdom*

David A. Chambers and Sue Dopson

In recent years, researchers, policy-makers, and clinicians have been struggling with the often complex relationship between science and clinical practice. Leaders among all three constituent groups have seized on a number of initiatives to develop improvements in everyday practice, organizing their efforts behind concepts of 'quality improvement', 'system reorganization', 'total quality management' and, more recently, 'evidence-based medicine'.

Along the way, a number of projects have been funded to use evidence on the best possible treatment for a specific medical condition as ammunition for leading clinical practice change in local health care settings. Many of these projects have been conceived as 'demonstrations' of local change that can ideally be replicated throughout a country and even beyond. The demonstration project leaders have found evidence-based change to be an incredible challenge from the beginning, facing barriers from health care organizations, professions, political institutions and financial constraints, among others. Few of the projects ever pass the first implementation test and go 'national'.

While the projects have proliferated throughout the world, little work has been done to compare the experiences of these projects, to draw together a larger knowledge base about the complexity of evidence-based change. This chapter analyses a series of evidence-based change projects in the United States and United Kingdom to understand the influences on leading the implementation of change in health care settings. The study intends to link the findings from demonstration projects in both countries to develop a general framework for evidence-based change that applies usefully to all contexts. We will discuss traditional assumptions

---

* The views expressed in the chapter are those of the authors and do not necessarily reflect the official position of the National Institute of Mental Health or the US DHSS.

of commentators about evidence-based change and explore a model of change that goes beyond these assumptions to better address the complexity of the field. Finally, we will address the implication of the research findings on work in both countries, and implications for taking healthcare forward in the twenty-first century.

Introduction

In the United Kingdom, where the NHS has provided universal care to all of its citizens since 1948, the rationing system (while not described as such) is based on determining what can be provided within the constraints of a given amount of money budgeted by the government to every level of service. The NHS has reorganized every eight years, starting in 1974, and the latest reorganization has tried to place the responsibility for meeting standards of care with general practitioners in a series of Primary Care Groups (NHS, 1998) Waiting lists for procedures continue to plague the system, as funding can only account for a certain number of each procedure per year, leaving some people with only the option of turning towards private health care or simply waiting months for treatment.

In the United States, no comprehensive national system exists, and rationing remains largely based on individual income. The primary funding for health care comes through employment-based insurance schemes which cover 60 per cent of the population (Bodenheimer and Grumbach, 1995). Care is often delivered through a managed care organization, which may have one of several general structures. Some organizations have physicians as their employees, some contract with independent practices to provide care for their patients; others operate on a fee-for-service basis. For people whose jobs do not include health benefits, or for the unemployed segment of the population, almost no health care is provided other than volunteer and community clinics. The government supports the extreme poor and the elderly, through Medicaid and Medicare programmes, respectively. For many who have coverage, the standard at which they receive health services is the best in the world; for others, it is non-existent.

Within both countries, the difficulty of preserving a standard of care across regions remains at the forefront of policy discussions. The reality is that geographical location determines access to a battery of tests, diagnostic machines and clinical expertise, and newspapers frequently spotlight cases in which lack of access to a specific treatment leads to the death of an otherwise non-terminal patient.

Policy-makers in both countries have proposed programmes to improve the quality of the nation's health and reduce the gap between services in different regions. Projects to draft treatment guidelines for specific conditions have been commissioned in both countries, condition-centred clinics have been established to more effectively treat patients with similar profiles, and attempts to educate physicians about medical evidence have been established as part of medical education programmes and continuing medical education for established health care professionals. The recent attention to evidence-based medicine encompasses many of these efforts, providing a rally cry for policy-makers to influence clinical practice change.

The definition of evidence-based medicine (EBM), and the associated evidence-based change, suggests that the movement is about finding the best possible treatment for every disease to raise care to the highest possible level. Irrespective of costs, evidence-based medicine tries to eliminate sub-standard care and implement more effective procedures, pharmaceuticals and devices. EBM gives an opportunity for health care leaders to have the science to support their policy decisions. However, as Glaziou (1998) notes, 'Some policy makers are turning to evidence-based medicine, not so much as a means of improving patient care, but as a means of containing costs' (p. 7). Sometimes this can result in better care for patients, but often the projects are concerned only with maintaining current standards, not raising them.

Evidence-based medicine has evoked various and vigorous commentaries from leaders in research, practice and policy. Within these commentaries, several assumptions are made. These assumptions are powerful in the sense that they subtly but significantly shape the planning and implementation process of demonstration projects, whether or not conscious in the minds of the participants in the projects; they include:

1 That evidence presented to the clinician will lead directly to change;
2 Evidence is irrefutable;
3 Evidence is permanent, unchangeable;
4 Change is a rational process; and
5 Context is irrelevant to change.

The next section highlights the relevant literature that challenges these assumptions.

Previous studies of evidence-based change

Over the past few years, researchers have evaluated a number of evidence-based initiatives, bringing together a number of findings that have informed the case study analysis in this study. The initiatives have primarily focused on different sites within the UK, as the USA is only just beginning to incorporate evidence-based medicine into the policy debate. They represent a number of different approaches to evidence-based change, with consistent findings regarding the importance of evidence (content of change), the local context, and the process through which change is attempted. We have presented a summary of the details of key studies in Table 11.1.

Challenging the evidence

Synthesizing the information from these empirical studies, there are common issues related to how the 'evidence' is used which challenge the first three of the assumptions discussed. Wood *et al.* (1998) chose four case studies in which 'the degree of evidential controversy' (p. 28) varied across the cases; 'Three of the cases were controversial, one was not. Higher controversy meant finding a means of proceeding given the uncertain evidence' (p. 28). As they discussed:

> The solidity of evidence may be more implied than real. Our research suggests that evidence is not a full and transparent cause, but is a socially and historically constructed effect. Our empirical data show that scientific evidence is not clear, accepted, or bounded. There is no such entity as 'the body of evidence.' There are simple (more or less competing) bodies of evidence able to support almost any position. Much of what is called evidence is, in fact, a contested domain, constructed of the debates and controversies of opposing viewpoints in search of ever more compelling arguments. (p. 40)

In summary, the study found that 'evidence from trials and published material in prestigious journals may be influential in setting indirect climates of opinion, yet they rarely change practice on their own' (*ibid.*). Huby and Fairhurst's (1998) study suggested:

> the dichotomy often drawn between on the one hand, 'evidence based practice' as scientific and objective and, on the other, 'experience based practice' as idiosyncratic and subjective is unhelpful in promoting medical practice based on systematic evaluation of

Table 11.1 Summary of key previous evaluations: research design, project details

	Design	No case studies	Face-to-face interviews	Telephone interviews	Written questionnaires	Document analysis	Dates
Dopson and Gabbay (1995)	Single stage case studies on four clinical topics	4	58 (purchasing managers, clinicians, and public health)			Yes	2 years, 1993–94
Wood et al. (1998)	Two stages: 1. Overview survey across whole region	4	71 (mainly front-line clinicians)			Yes	2 years, 1995–97
	2. Case studies, one per clinical topic, selected on evidence of clinical change elicited from first stage		48 (mainly clinicians and clinical managers)			Yes	

Table 11.1 continued

	Design	No case studies	Face-to-face interviews	Telephone interviews	Written questionnaires	Document analysis	Dates
Dawson et al. (1998)	Embedded case studies, 2 clinical topics in each of four hospitals	8	256 (clinical staff of various professions and grades) plus 20 informal interviews with managers		256 (same as interviews)	Yes	2 years, 1995–97
Huby and Fairhurst (1998)	One case study on a single clinical topic	1	24 (consultants and GPs)				1 year
Mant et al. (1997)	'Before and after' study in an intervention and a control hospital	1	28 (Senior and middle grade obstetric and midwifery staff)			Yes	3 years, 1991–94
Oxman et al. (1995)	Systematic review of 102 trials of interventions to improve health services					Yes	4 years, 1990–93
Bero et al. (1998)	Systematic review of published research on implementation in health sector					Yes	

existing evidence. Experience based practice is underpinned by socially constructed knowledge produced through interaction between trial data and the context in which it is used. Thus it is more objective than is often recognized. The production of scientific trial data is influenced by social processes and more subjective than it might appear. (pp. 11–12)

Fitzgerald *et al.* (1999) agreed that the evidence used in projects is quite subjective. Namely, what might be sufficient evidence to convince one clinician that a change in practice is needed may not necessarily be enough for another. In order to make substantial changes, Fitzgerald *et al.* (1999) argued that projects need to incorporate multiple views of evidence, which allows for more subjectivity ('picking and choosing what each clinician finds compelling') among the targets for change. The studies' findings clearly relate to research on the foundation of medical knowledge and questions one of the major assumptions of evidence-based medicine, that medical evidence is regarded as scientific truth.

Similarly, researchers discussed the importance of basing the use of evidence on realistic models of how evidence is assessed (Fairhurst and Huby, 1998). Too often, project teams used evidence that convinced them (the individual team members) without considering whether their analysis of the evidence was similar to the process through which other clinicians assess evidence. To remedy this, Huby and Fairhurst advocate developing assessment strategies that 'should be built on existing structures of coordination and debate and extend local consensus about the significance of trial data, matching local resources to local need' (p. 2). This speaks to the importance of understanding and even improving clinicians' assessment skills, leading to recent attempts to incorporate research assessment skills training into medical school residency programmes (see for example, Lovett, 1999; Green, 2000; Neale *et al.*, 1999).

Ferlie *et al.* (1999) also argue that the presenter of the evidence can have a significant impact on its success in dissemination. In their study,

There were perceived hierarchies of evidence, where relative position relates to the credibility of the source as well as the 'hardness' of the data. Practitioners were more likely to accept advice coming from eminent colleagues within their own particular field. For example, knowledge generated within general surgery was not seen as persuasive to orthopedic surgeons. Even within a single profession, there were alternative definitions of 'evidence.' Some surgeons saw surgery as more of a craft, pointing out that techniques – even if backed by research – did not readily transfer. (p. 14)

This supports the use of opinion leaders to transmit the evidence, even though systematic reviews have questioned whether they add any effectiveness (Oxman, 1994). In any case, the exploration of who presents the evidence seems a central issue in evidence-based change.

Furthermore, one cannot guarantee that evidence is relevant to the topic and authoritative enough to convince clinicians to change their practice, as the Clinical Standards Advisory Group (1998) has pointed out. Dopson *et al.*'s (1998) case study on glue ear echoed this point, underscoring the clinicians' perception that evidence is always evolving:

> Many in our sample whatever their clinical role, commented on the confusing and evolving state of the evidence...[The bulletin on evidence used to influence practice] has not proved to be particularly helpful for our group of interviewees in clarifying appropriate practice...Clinical practice is very subtly shaped by a variety of influences...Experience (69% of our respondents rated this of high importance) of the condition built up over time is the most significant influence on practice. (Dawson *et al.*, 1998, p. 18)

The collective findings about evidence from these previous studies refute the original assumptions of evidence-based medicine that where strong evidence is available advocating change in clinical practice, a change should occur. There are too many issues that conflate this presumably simple question of whether the evidence is strong. The subjectivity of evidence, its relation to experience and other factors influencing practice, its continual change over time, its frequent inaccessibility, and the multiple ways in which it is assessed all contribute to the need to discuss evidence not just as a static body of truth that will change practice immediately. As these studies have shown, the central question of whether evidence affects clinical practice is very difficult to answer.

Is evidence-based change rational?

Previous studies of evidence-based change initiatives have challenged this assumption. Dawson *et al.*'s (1998) study, for example, concludes, 'Clinical practice is shaped by many different influences' (p. 18). Therefore, the ideal project should develop processes that include multiple interventions, as Bero *et al.* (1998) note: 'Specific strategies to implement research based recommendations are necessary to ensure practice change, and existing studies suggest that more intensive efforts to alter practice are generally more successful (p. 9).

Howitt and Armstrong's (1999) study discussed the need to understand implementation on both practitioner and patient for any clinical topic and resulting intervention:

> The first level of implementation, assessing evidence on effectiveness, is essentially population-based as it advises on the proportion likely to benefit out of a defined group of patients with the condition... further assessments of this evidence need to be made. Firstly, a practitioner based assessment to identify individuals who may benefit from the treatment and secondly, the individual patient has to make the decision as to whether, given the advantages and disadvantages, the treatment is worth taking. (p. 1325)

According to this study, these two assessments are generally neglected, which inhibits implementation, regardless of the intervention.

Not all interventions have been found to be equally effective, leading to a challenge of the assumption that context is irrelevant to change. If interventions are effective in one setting, but not another, the question arises as to how the two settings (or contexts) differ. Bero *et al.* (1998) found that more interactive methods of presenting the evidence (that engage local clinicians) – including local consensus processes, interactive educational meetings, and systems to remind patients and physicians about proper treatments – were more effective than traditional lectures and memos. Davis *et al.* (1995) found that conferences had generally little impact on clinical change, while more systematic attempts to engage local practices were effective, but rarely used. As one can recall from the systematic reviews of translating research into practice, no one intervention is guaranteed to effect change (Oxman, 1994; NHS Centre for Reviews and Dissemination, 1999).

The previous studies have questioned whether the use of a number of relatively traditional methods of improving the process of change actually has any impact on change in specific projects. Use of opinion leaders (called 'project champions' by Ferlie *et al.*, 1999), management and clinician commitment to change, attention to local contexts, and involvement of professional groups were all found to enhance the likelihood of evidence-based change (Ferlie *et al.*, 1999; Eve *et al.*, 1997). Negative influences on project success were seen to include antagonistic stakeholders, methods that necessitated changes in professional roles, and change driven by external forces (Ferlie *et al.*, 1999). The previous studies also spotlighted several major factors (opinion leaders, senior commitment to change) and specific interventions to change clinical practice (guidelines, audit), all of which are utilized in the cases we examine in this study.

Selecting a model to analyse evidence-based change projects

Given the empirical evidence, what conceptual models might exist that help us explore the complexity of leading change to clinical practice? Strategic change has been discussed in terms of a number of different perspectives, each having extensive literature that underpins the perspective. Briefly, change has been viewed as a rational action, involving a series of sequential steps towards a specific outcome. It has also been seen as a response to the external environment, described with respect to a series of influences that cause the organization to adapt. Change has been viewed as a process of diffusing an innovation throughout an environment, and as a cultural shift of an organization. While each of these perspectives adds important insight to the influences behind change, none of them sufficiently addresses the complexity of the change process, location and substance.

In a search for a more integrative view of change, we found the work of Pettigrew, Ferlie and McKee (1992) to be effective in handling the complexity through an analysis of the context, content and processes of change. This enables more considered exploration of the material by acknowledging the individual nature of change through its unique setting, evidence, and methods chosen by the project teams.

An application of the model to evidence-based change to clinical practice

The simplest conceptualization of the model, as applied to evidence-based change to clinical practice, is that which appears in Figure 11.1 below. Pettigrew refers to context as occurring on both inner and outer levels. 'Outer context' refers to the 'national economic, political, and social dimensions' of the location of the change initiative, as well as 'the perception, action and interpretation of policies and events' at national and global levels within health care (Pettigrew *et al.*, 1992). Outer contextual issues include the influence of historical background on health care settings, the effect of government on clinical practice change, and institutionalized traditions and national trends which impact how health care is provided. As Backer (1995) points out:

Changing clinical practice requires setting the process of change itself into a larger context. Tools for change (education and training, task forces, legislation, strategic planning, and so on) cannot be viewed merely in the context of change in physician practice or even change in health care, but must be examined against the total context of change that is occurring in society. (p. 352)

Pettigrew *et al.* (1992) explain that

content refers to the particular area or areas of transformation under study...The content of change can also be classified according to a set of more abstract features which may affect adaptability: some changes will be radical, others incremental; some technological (where there is some evidence of premature diffusion) and others centered on changes to roles (where there may be important barriers to rapid diffusion). (p. 7)

Pettigrew describes process as involving

streams of activity over time. The processes through which strategic changes are made seldom move directly through neat, successive stages of analysis, choice, and implementation. Powerful, internal characteristics transform the process. One of the defining features of process is ambiguity (e.g. Mintzberg, 1979; Quinn, 1988). Process derives its force from economic, political, and personal imperatives. Their interaction means a constant adjustment, assessment, and decision process. (Pettigrew and Whipp, 1993).

Process has usually been discussed in its constituent parts – individual strategies developed to change practice (that is guidelines, continuing medical education, audit), involvement of specific groups (such as senior clinicians, patients, managers and so on), or allocated resources. This model views process as a continuous path, continually subject to the forces that govern evidence and context.

As Pettigrew (1985) points out, few studies exist which attempt to go beyond the superficial analysis of a change event and investigate the 'how' and 'why'. Change, to Pettigrew, is a natural process, combining the external pressure of the environment and internal management. He suggests that change originates with a small number of people in an organization who see a gap between the demands of the environment

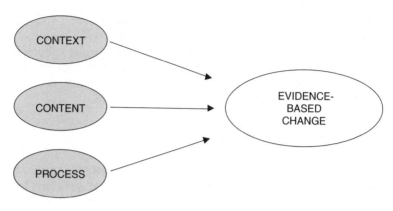

Figure 11.1   Pettigrew *et al.*'s (1992) three dimensions of evidence-based change

and the performance of the organization.. For change to be successful, the gap must narrow (Pettigrew, 1985).

One of the major strengths of the use of Pettigrew's framework for change is in its ability to examine a case of strategic change over time, using issues from context, content and process of the change to evaluate how well a project has been able to accomplish its objectives. Several of the other change frameworks assume that organizational change occurs at a single point in time, in effect recasting the organization into 'before' and 'after' stages. For many industries, the amount of evidence available continues to change, the organizations themselves continue to adjust to political, cultural, scientific and economic pressures, and the people involved in the change do not necessarily remain with the organization. This framework is flexible enough to deal with the impact of all of these changes, the 'unintended consequences of change', in addition to the intended change specified by the project.

Introducing the projects

The study that we were involved in considered seven cases of project leaders attempting to use medical evidence as a lever to change clinical practice in the United States and the United Kingdom, seeking to understand how to enact evidence-based change. The clinical topics included cardiac rehabilitation, leg ulcers (England); stroke rehabilitation, schizophrenia (Wales); anticoagulation services for patients with irregular heartbeats, community-acquired pneumonia, and venous thrombosis (USA). The four United Kingdom cases were funded by the government, and were part of two larger initiatives – the PACE (Promoting Action toward Clinical Effectiveness) programme in England, and the Welsh National Demonstration Projects. The full details of the evaluations of these initiatives are available elsewhere (Dopson *et al.*, 1998; Locock *et al.*, 1999). Two of the cases in the USA were part of a larger university medical centre guideline project, while the third was a collaboration of university, government and private enterprise (MAST trial). Six of the seven projects were created in a local setting, with an eventual goal of wider dissemination; the seventh was supervised nationally, but administered locally.

The purpose of the study was to understand the common lessons from evidence-based change across different local and national contexts and clinical topics, and to examine levers and barriers to change that could apply to all projects, to varying degrees, as well as test and extend a model that could apply to general strategic change. The common thread between the projects was the attempt to use evidence to strategically influence changes in clinical practice. Each of the projects had central project teams, and additional senior managers and clinicians supervising, and targeted an audience of front-line clinicians in primary care.

The studies report findings derived from a data-set gathered through interviews, surveys and documentary evidence. For each project, we gathered data from all members of the project team through a series of semi-structured interviews of 45 minutes to 90 minutes in length. We also interviewed senior managers and clinicians who were peripherally involved with each of the projects for between 30 and 90 minutes, and front-line clinicians at each site to get the perception of the target audience to each change. In addition, we surveyed clinicians about their knowledge of each project, collected data on the influences on clinical practice as reported by clinicians, and examined all documents pertaining to each project. Using the Pettigrew model, findings are presented in terms of the three dimensions of change.

Findings

Context: how the local setting affects an effort to lead to clinical practice change

Leading change to clinical practice in a specific setting requires an understanding of the issues that exist in that local context. In both US and UK cases, the patterns related to the context of change were quite similar. All cases found the distance between project team and implementation site to be a key factor influencing the dissemination of evidence. In cases where the project teams frequently visited the implementation sites, the project leaders reported an ability to make connections with local clinicians and influence their practice. When they stayed away from the sites, the project teams found it hard to interact with the local clinicians and collect information about the success of their dissemination efforts.

In addition, both US and UK cases found a number of organizational barriers to change practice in local contexts. Both found that instability in the local setting made implementation impossible, whether the instability occurred because of political factors (NHS reorganization, university politics), or market variables (the threat of insolvency for managed care organizations). Cases in both countries also found resources to be a major barrier, limiting changes in practice for treatments not covered by national or local health plans, and in generating money to pay for dissemination strategies. Also apparent across national boundaries were the conflicts among stakeholders that prevented the implementation strategies, specifically in cases involving referral of patients from one local context to another. In the UK, for example, the Bro Taf stroke project team failed to convince consultants in multiple wards to refer admitted patients to the stroke unit; they also could not keep track of all relevant patients because of the many wards where patients were admitted. In the USA, the MAST trial team found the separation of managed care organization from GP practice difficult to overcome to get patients from private practices to an anticoagulation clinic at a managed care organization.

All cases acknowledged the importance of involving professional groups in change, though little insight was provided as to how best to get them involved. Thoughts returned to traditional methods of involving groups (opinion leaders, continuing medical education and so forth), but these methods were questioned even by the project teams that employed them.

Overall, the cases highlight very similar contextual influences on evidence-based change in both countries, leading us to conclude that all of these issues are relevant to implementation of change, regardless of national or local setting. These cases confirm many of the findings from previous studies, regarding the need to overcome tensions between clinicians and managers, economic restrictions on health care, and the requirement of the medical profession to remain autonomous. However, this study concludes that organizational and financial barriers are critical aspects of context that need to be more carefully considered. Project teams and researchers will more effect-ively create and evaluate these projects if they can understand and incorporate this complexity and influence of context into their efforts.

Content: how evidence is used to lead to clinical practice change

The patterns in the data about the use of evidence in UK and US evidence-based change projects were quite similar for both countries. All projects had to deal with the question of what types of evidence could best be used to lead to changes in clinical practice. Responses in both countries dealt with the variability of the evidence available for each clinical topic, and the difficult choice between use of scien-tific evidence (from randomized control trials) and other sources of evidence. All of the cases showed that no definitive 'evidence' could convince all clinicians to change; the subjectivity of evidence must be understood to better influence clinicians, regardless of national and local context.

Cases in both countries also dealt with the importance of how the evidence should be presented. The cases showed that multiple methods of disseminating the research were more effective at engaging clinicians than any one strategy, which supports the reviews of interventions (Oxman *et al.*, 1995; Bero *et al.*, 1999). However, no case has found a dissemination strategy that will always work to engage clinicians, or even which strategies are preferred by clinicians. This suggests that further research on dissemination is needed in all contexts.

In the UK, respondents spoke of the importance of using evidence from local patients, indicating success in engaging clinicians by show-ing that the evidence related to their own patients directly. In the USA, respondents also mentioned the importance of who presents the evidence, and interestingly, whether there were negative effects of following the evidence. This final point reinforces the view that evidence is not incontrovertible, and while one can acknowledge that evidence is subjective, patient outcomes must be studied and used to guide practice.

Each of these findings does not seem limited, or determined, by the national context in which the project is set. Each can be used to guide future dissemination projects, and evaluations of them, in both countries. Change participants should not assume, as many of these cases have illustrated, that if the project team agrees with the evidence, everyone will; project teams should spend time organizing their body of evidence and carefully decide how it should be disseminated.

Process: what is the mechanism by which leaders attempt to change practice?

Respondents from both US and UK cases discussed how they perceived clinical change, with quite similar findings. Commitment to change on all levels of the organization was seen as instrumental, as was making information available to the clinician, and allowing clinicians to be involved in the change process. All cases also noted that clinicians' willingness to change varies with age, with younger clinicians being more receptive to newer ideas. Finally, respondents reflected on the importance of individual contact as necessary to change, rather than attempting wider dissemination efforts. This again seems to support the systematic reviews of dissemination (Bero *et al.*, 1999; Oxman *et al.*, 1995), which explain that one method does not work for everyone.

Respondents from all cases also reflected on their perceptions of the purposes of the projects. Generally, clinicians from the two countries had differing opinions about the purpose. The UK project teams believed that the purpose of the projects were to improve standards of care, either through actual implemented changes in practice, or through increased awareness of the evidence. In the USA, clinicians balanced the attempt to improve care with the need to contain costs, often finding the economic needs to prevail over better care. This speaks to the for-profit market in the US system, and also to the fear that costs of care will continue to increase in the future (Weisbrod, 1995). Both countries' project teams also spoke specifically about the importance of strong project leadership, insisting that the difference between success and failure often fell on the shoulders of the leader. The Royal Berkshire PACE project also found leadership to be pivotal, but leadership overall in the UK sites had less emphasis than in the USA.

A key feature of the cases in the USA, not as prevalent in the UK cases, was the monitoring of change. In both guideline projects and the MAST trial, attempts were made to use organized data collection and analysis, which helped the projects to understand the extent to which implementation was succeeding. While the measures were not considered to be ideal, their presence did help keep the project teams aware of progress. The corresponding cases in the UK did not have as organized efforts, which led to the respondents' limited knowledge about dissemination achievements.

While past research has focused on the specific methods of dissemination, these cases have shown how common views of purpose and clinician change can have a large impact on the development of the

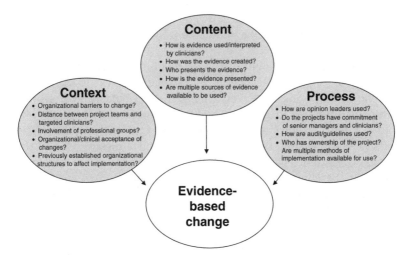

Figure 11.2 The three dimensions of evidence-based change, as shaped by the findings of this research

projects, located in a variety of practices. The data again suggest that the issues related to process span national contexts and all can be used to better prepare future project teams with implementation efforts.

As has been discussed, all three domains that were examined within the cases (content, context and process) showed remarkable similarities of influences when compared across national boundaries. Figure 11.2 documents some of the common issues. This finding directly refutes a popular comment on both sides of the Atlantic that research and practice in either country cannot inform that from the other. We have found that the differences in influences on evidence-based change are far more likely to be those of intensity, rather than of type.

A new model for looking at change

As previously discussed, Pettigrew's model appears to be the most flexible and comprehensive of the models of strategic change found within the literature. It is helpful because it alerts us to the fact that:

- Change is complex.
- There are many influences on change projects.
- Evidence is subjective.
- Contextual factors are important to change.
- A conceptual model must incorporate complexity of change.

- The general goal of evidence-based change is universal.
- Past experience/knowledge should be explored.

We found the three dimensions to be helpful as a starting point for analysis, by signalling elements of change that carry with them specific assumptions. However, after gathering data from front-line clinicians involved in each of the change projects, it became clear that a useful extension to the model was to include the target audience's dimension; that is, insights into the clinicians' view of the process of evidence-based change. We argue this is a much-neglected aspect of the change process in this arena, and a potential limit to effective leadership of change. The front-line clinicians' views can be characterized as:

- Lack of knowledge of the projects.
- A belief that projects were imposed.
- Change is more likely to be made if there are obvious benefits to clinicians.
- Often projects did not incorporate acknowledged influences on clinical practice, for example resources, colleagues, patients, organizational structure and research.
- Change will not be welcomed if projects constitute a threat to clinicians' autonomy.

Figure 11.3 incorporates the insights gathered from front-line clinicians to the Pettigrew model. This model may be useful to health services researchers in organizing and prioritizing their evaluations, and by project teams to understand the substantial task of using evidence to change clinical practice in a specific health care setting. The additional stakeholder dimensions imply an important avenue for further research – the understanding of each of the groups' views of evidence-based change.

Implications of the research

As Mark and Dopson (1999) argue, 'Absent from many of the [research] contributions...is the importance of building on existing theoretical and empirical knowledge' (p. 255). This chapter, through the development of Pettigrew's model, seeks to provide the base for future projects and evaluations, so that subsequent initiatives and evaluations can advance understanding of evidence-based change.

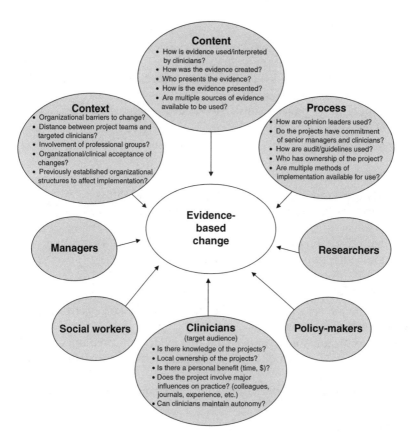

Figure 11.3   The expanded framework for evidence-based change, including context, content, and process dimensions, and mediated by target audience of change and other stakeholder views (including those not researched in the study)

However, this 'snapshot' of evidence-based change does not aim to provide a 'laundry list' of questions for each dimension, but to suggest methods through which participants in evidence-based change can acknowledge the complexity of the field. Further questions can and should be added to each dimension; the questions in Figure 11.3 simply relate the data from this empirical study.

There are also a number of general policy implications of this research as indicated below:

United Kingdom

- Clinical governance systems must exist as part of the solution to change practice, not the solution itself.
- Future government-led projects must appreciate top-down difficulty, and employ bottom-up strategy.
- Clinician-led projects must have added emphasis on management skills.
- Clinical change is constrained by organizational instability.

United States

- Managed care turbulence make clinical change difficult.
- Distance between providers and purchasers is a major barrier to change.
- University hospitals have difficulty with residents rotating, and guidelines implemented in specific sites.

All Contexts

- Future project teams should seek to decrease distance between clinicians and projects.
- Project teams should understand that evidence is multidimensional.
- Policy-makers must question assumptions of evidence-based change to clinical practice.
- The importance of the sustainability of change must be recognised.

Conclusions

One objective of this study is to offer hindsight gained from past project teams to those of the future. If future leaders of evidence-based change can understand the complexity and the multiple factors that influence clinical practice, perhaps the next wave of projects will have more positive results.

For academics, this chapter has sought to alter a model of evaluating clinical practice change. Using Pettigrew's model of strategic change, the presentation of the projects' histories and the incorporation of front-line clinician data into project analysis may assist in developing a much deeper understanding of evidence-based change.

Finally, this chapter has attempted to bring new knowledge to the continuing challenge of leading the improvement of health care services, based on an ever-growing body of evidence on the effectiveness of new treatments. This is no easy task; new evidence continues to be produced far faster than we can collect and process it. We can only hope that those leading the change will understand the importance of its complexity. Only with that understanding can these demonstration projects ever achieve their ultimate goal – to improve national and, indeed, global health.

References

Backer, T. E. (1995) 'Integrating Behavioral and Systems Strategies to Change Clinical Practice', *Journal of Quality Improvement*, 21: 7, pp. 351–3.

Bero, L., Grilli, R., Grimshaw, J., Harvey, E., Oxman, A. and Thomson, M. A. (1998) 'Closing the Gap between Research and Practice – an Overview of Systematic Reviews of Interventions to Promote Implementation of Research Findings by Health Professionals', in A. Haines and A. Donald (eds), *Getting Research Findings into Practice* (London: BMJ Books), pp. 27–35.

Bodenheimer, T. and Grumbach, K. (1995) *Understanding Health Policy: A Clinical Approach* (Norwalk, CT: Appleton & Lange).

Clinical Standards Advisory Group (1998) *Clinical Effectiveness* (London: Clinical Standards Advisory Group).

Davis, D. A. *et al.* (1995) 'Changing Physician Performance: A Systematic Review of the Effect of Continuing Medical Education Strategies', *JAMA*, 274: 9, pp. 700–5.

Delbecq, A. J. and Van de Ven, A. H. (1971) 'A Group Process Model for Problem Identification and Program Planning', *Journal of Applied Behavioral Science*, 7: 4, pp. 466–92.

Dopson, S. and Gabbay, J. (1995) *Getting Research Into Practice and Purchasing (GRiPP)* (London: NHS Executive).

Dopson, S., Gabbay, J. and Locock, L. with Chambers, D. (1999) *Evaluation of the PACE Programme: Final Report*. Templeton College, University of Oxford and Wessex Institute for Health Research and Development, University of Southampton.

Dopson, S., Miller, R., Dawson, S. and Sutherland, K. (1998) 'Case study of Glue Ear', *Quality in Health Care*.

Eve, R. *et al.* (1997) *Learning from FACTS: Lessons from the Framework for Appropriate Care Throughout Sheffield (FACTS) Project* (Sheffield: School of Health and Related Research, University of Sheffield).

Ferlie, E., FitzGerald, L. and Wood, M. (2000) 'Getting Evidence into Clinical Practice? An Organisational Behaviour Perspective', *Journal of Health Services Research and Policy*, Royal Society of Medicine Press.

Ferlie, E., Wood, M. and Fitzgerald, L. (1999) 'Some Limits to Evidence-Based Medicine: A Case Study from Elective Orthopedics', *Quality in Health Care*, 8: 2, pp. 99–107.

Fitzgerald, L., Ferlie, E., Wood, M. and Hawkins, C. (1999) 'Evidence into Practice? An Exploratory Analysis of the Interpretation of Evidence', in A. Mark and S. Dopson (eds), *Organisational Behaviour in Health Care* (London: Macmillan – now Palgrave Macmillan).

Friedman, J. and Hudson, B. (1974) 'Knowledge and Action: A Guide to Planning Theory', *Journal of American Institute of Planners*, January.

Glaziou, P. (1998) 'Using Cost-Effectiveness for Subsidy Decisions', *Heart*, 79: 1, pp. 7–8.

Green, M. L. (2000) 'Evidence-Based Medicine Training in Internal Medicine Residency Programs: A National Survey', *Journal of General Internal Medicine*, 15: 2, pp. 129–33.

Howitt, A. and Armstrong, D. (1999) 'Implementing Evidence Based Medicine in General Practice: Audit and Qualitative Study of Antithrombotic Treatment for Atrial Fibrillation', *British Medical Journal*, 318: 7194, pp. 1324–7.

Huby, G. and Fairhurst, K. (1998) 'How Do General Practitioners Use Evidence? A Study in the Context of Lothian Health Policy and Practitioners' Use of Statin Drugs', final report to CSO (Edinburgh: Primary Care Research Group, Department of General Practice, University of Edinburgh, August 1998).

Locock, L., Chambers, D., Surender, R., Dopson, S. and Gabbay, J. (1999) *Evaluation of the Welsh Clinical Effectiveness Initiative National Demonstration Projects: Final Report*. Templeton College, University of Oxford and Wessex Institute for Health Research and Development, University of Southampton.

Lovett, P. (1999) Personal Interview, University of California-San Francisco, Evidence-Based Medicine Residency Program coordinator.

Mant, J., Hicks, N., Dopson, S. and Hurley, P. (1997) *Uptake of Research Findings into Clinical Practice: A Controlled Study of the Impact of a Brief External Intervention on the Use of Corticosteroids in Pre-term Labour* (Oxford: Division of Public Health and Primary Care).

Mark, A. and Dopson, S. (eds) (1999) *Organisational Behaviour in Health Care* (London: Macmillan – now Palgrave Macmillan).

Mintzberg, H. (1979) *The Structuring of Organizations: A Synthesis of the Research* (Englewood Cliffs, NJ: Prentice Hall).

Neale, V., Roth, L. M. and Schwartz, K. L. (1999) 'Faculty Development Using Evidence-Based Medicine as an Organizing Curricular Theme', *Academic Medicine*, 74: 5, p. 611.

NHS (1997) *The New NHS: Modern, Dependable*. Government White Paper. Presented to Parliament by the Secretary of State for Health by Command of Her Majesty, December 1997. London: HMSO.

NHS (1998) *A First Class Service: Quality in the New NHS*. London: HMSO.

NHS Centre for Research Dissemination (1999) *Effective Health Care – Getting Evidence into Practice*, 5: 1 (University of York: NHSCRD).

Oxman, A. D., Thomson, M. A., Davis, D. A *et al.* (1993) 'No Magic Bullets – a Systematic Review of 102 Trials of Interventions to Improve Professional Practice', *Canadian Medical Association Journal*, 153, pp. 1423–31.

Pettigrew, A. and Whipp, R. (1993) *Managing Change for Competitive Success* (Oxford: Blackwell Business).

Pettigrew, A., Ferlie, E. and McKee, L. (1992) *Shaping Strategic Change* (London: Sage).

Pettigrew, A. M., McKee, L. and Ferlie, E. (1989) 'Managing Strategic Service Changing in the NHS', *Health Services Management Research*, 2: 1, pp. 20–31.

Pettigrew, A. M. (1985) *The Awakening Giant: Contingency and Change in ICI* (London: Blackwell).

Quinn, J. B. (1980) *Strategies for Change: Logical Incrementalism* (Homewood, IL: Irwin).

Sackett, D. L. (1996) 'A Doctor's Dilemma (Economic and Ethical)', Office of Health Economics Annual Lecture, 1996.

Sackett, D. L., Rosenberg, W. M. C., Gray, J. A. M., Haynes, R. B. and Richardson, W. S. (1996) 'Evidence-Based Medicine: What it is and What it isn't', *British Medical Journal*, 312, pp. 71–2.

Weisbrod, B. A. (1995) 'Rising Health Care Costs: What is Causing it? What Can Be Done About it?', Inaugural lecture for the John Evans Professor of Economics. Northwestern University, Evanston, Illinois, 28 November 1995.

Wood, M., Ferlie, E. and FitzGerald, L. (1998a) *Achieving Change in Clinical Practice: Scientific, Organisational and Behavioural Processes* (University of Warwick: Centre for Creativity, Strategy and Change).

Wood, M., Ferlie, E. and FitzGerald, L. (1998b) 'Achieving Clinical Behaviour Change: A Case of Becoming Indeterminate', *Social Science and Medicine*, 47: 11, pp. 1729–38.

12

Alternative Future Paths for Ontario Hospitals: An Exercise in Scenario Planning

Gale Murray

Background to the Ontario hospital scenario planning exercise

Hospitals throughout the developed world have been undergoing some form of restructuring and Canadian hospitals have been no exception. In Canada most provinces have restructured to devolve authority to regional health authorities that in turn have merged and closed hospitals and integrated them into the broader continuum of care. The most populated province in Canada, Ontario, has chosen another path. Since the late 1980s Ontario hospitals had been engaged in voluntary mergers and programme rationalization. In 1996, however, hospital restructuring moved from locally driven initiatives to a legislated, centrally driven and province-wide initiative under the auspices of an independent body, the Ontario Health Services Restructuring Commission (HSRC).

In 1999, the Ontario Hospital Association (OHA) commissioned The Change Foundation to review the interim results of HSRC-directed hospital restructuring and to assess whether the HSRC restructuring would position Ontario hospitals for future success. Two reports were presented. The first, *Hospital Restructuring at the Mid-point* (Murray, McGrath and Croskery, 1999) concluded that hospital restructuring to date has been responding to a short-term government fiscal imperative to cut hospital costs and increase their efficiency, rather than to any transformational view of hospitals or health care for the future. The second report, *Alternative Paths for Ontario Hospitals* (Murray, McGrath and Croskery, 2000) suggested Ontario hospitals and their association needed to identify strategic directions to adapt successfully to the broader rapidly changing environment. This report utilized scenario planning to develop future-oriented enterprises for hospitals.

Scenario planning

The scenario method enables organizations to see more clearly the future environment in which their actions or the impact of these actions or decisions will occur, and to gauge how well those actions and decisions fit the prevailing forces, trends, attitudes and influences (Ackoff, 1970; Van der Heijden, 2000; Godet, 2000).

Scenario planning is not new to the health field. The World Health Organization (WHO) commissioned Canadian health futurist, Dr Trevor Hancock, to develop a set of scenarios for health promotion on the global level (Hancock, 1997). In the United Kingdom, the National Health Service (NHS) created the Hemingford scenarios (Hadridge *et al.*, 1995); scenario planning, it was claimed, was the method to shift NHS strategic thinking towards recognition that change is inevitable, necessary and an opportunity (*ibid.*). Furthermore it was an acknowledgment of the value to be gained from intuition and creativity, as well as analysis (Masini and Vasquez, 2000).

Underlying scenario planning is the premise that the larger forces of society will determine a society's organizations and systems. Thus it is necessary to understand the emerging social forces and drivers of change, in order to create a successful health care organization or to build a successful health care system. Scenarios are not an end in themselves. They are a management tool used to improve the quality of executive decision-making. Moving from the scenarios to strategy development to action is the most critical phase of the scenario process. Like scenarios themselves, the implementation has to be tailored to the needs of the organization, and adapted to local contexts (Wilson, 2000).

As part of the HSRC-directed restructuring, the hospitals of Ontario were contemplating capital improvements. The hospital sector, like any business contemplating the investment of billions of dollars in capitalization and the significant realignment of its services and programmes entailed in restructuring, needed to be certain that the investment would pay a return. The primary return required is the reasonable certainty that restructuring will contribute to hospital success in the world they will face in the next 10 to 25 years – the period of time that it will take to amortize the funds expended for restructuring. To increase the certainty of future success, it is useful to scope out likely future scenarios and to consider strategies to address these scenarios. While it is expected that the world will change more in the next quarter-century than it has in the last one, it is impossible to forecast the detail. We know we are at the edge of a series of breakthroughs on many fronts in health care, but it is difficult to know where and when innovation will occur. In response to this dilemma, a number of countries, health jurisdictions and organizations have utilized the development of scenarios. These scenarios can assist better understanding of the future, and thereby improve planning and decision-making around such key strategic decisions as:

- Investing or pulling back.
- Engaging or disengaging in particular businesses or services.
- Establishing or closing down projects.
- Creating new relationships.
- Knowing how to best think about the impact of today's decisions on the future.

Analytical approach in alternative paths

The analytical approach utilized in *Alternative Paths for Ontario Hospitals* is for the most part the scenario-building methodology of Peter Schwartz (1996) as presented in *The Art of the Long View: Planning for the Future in An Uncertain World*. In this study, the scenario planning began with the identification of the *focal issue* (hospital restructuring), the *key forces* in the local (micro) environment and the macro-environmental *driving forces* that shape the local forces. The key factors and drivers were ranked according to their certainty and importance. The next step was to select *scenario logic* – key drivers that differentiate the scenarios such as a health versus health care focus or a public versus market orientation, and so on. The scenarios were then elaborated, adding detail based on the key trends.

Where the methodology in this analysis differs somewhat from Schwartz's is in the development of implications. The 'implications' are proposed, and options for response are then identified in the form of a number of enterprise models for hospitals to consider given the future scenarios. The Foundation then translated this research into a series of workshops for hospitals to both test the validity of the drivers and scenarios, to further develop the range of enterprise options and to promote the uptake of the research into hospital strategic-planning

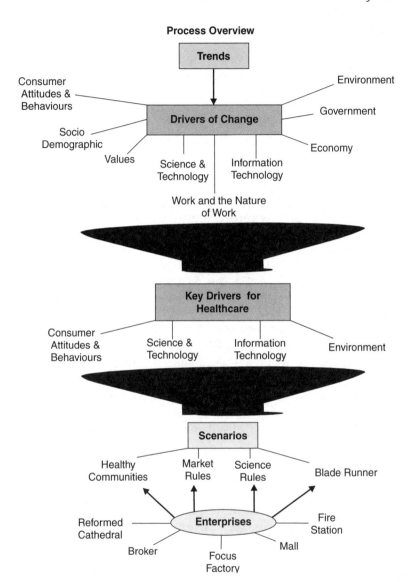

Figure 12.1 Process overview

practice (Figure 12.1 presents an overview of the process). The analysis was accomplished through review by and input from a series of expert panel discussions.

The drivers of change

In this scenario-planning process, the research team proposed to an expert panel of health care providers, policy analysts and academics a series of drivers of change (at the macro level) and their likely impacts on the health care industry and hospitals (the micro level). Table 12.1 lists the nine drivers of change agreed by the expert panel as the most important to health, health care, and hospitals for the next 10 to 25 years.

While all the drivers of change are important in shaping broad social change, they are not all equally important to health, health care and hospitals, nor are all drivers as certain in their likely development and impacts as others. Both uncertainty and importance are of critical importance to scenario planning because it is through their elaboration that the risks and opportunities for organizations can be identified. In this analysis the drivers of change were initially established by a panel of OHA senior managers and trustees and their ratings were then presented to the broader expert panel for further validation.

The key drivers of change for hospitals

Given this analysis of importance and uncertainty, consumer attitudes and behaviours, science and technology and information technology emerged as the key drivers for hospitals to consider as they planned for the future. The environment was the wild card, and as such is believed to be the most dynamic and volatile variable for all enterprises.

Table 12.1 Key drivers of change and their importance and certainty

Key drivers	Importance and certainty	
Consumer attitudes and behaviours*	Very important	Degree of uncertainty
Socio-demographic	Important	More certain
Values	Important	More certain
Science and technology*	Very important	Degree of uncertainty
Work and the nature of organizations	Important	Uncertain
Information technology*	Very important	Degree of uncertainty
Economic	Less important	More certain
Government organization and policy directions	Less important	More certain
Environment* – the wild card	Very important	Very uncertain

Changing consumer attitudes and behaviours underlies the range and types of services and products made available not only in the general marketplace but also in the health care system. The emerging trend in consumer attitudes particularly relevant to the hospital industry is the very high interest and concern of consumers in their health (health promotion and disease prevention), and not only health care.

Science and technology are drivers not only of consumer expectations but also direct drivers of change within health care. Hospitals have become citadels of high tech in response to both quality and efficiency concerns and consumer expectations. Since hospitals are naturally early adopters of clinical research and technology, their operations are being transformed with new knowledge and technology such as genetic screening and therapy, robotics and micro-robotics. Even the site of delivery is evolving with remote diagnostics, therapies and monitoring.

Information technology is accelerating consumers' interest in health and health care as well as increasing their sense of control in these domains. The Internet in particular with its rapidly increasing numbers of health-related sites gives consumers access to vast amounts of information on health matters. Consumers may at times hold more information on their health issues than the professional health provider. Concurrently, information technology is also an enabler of many new forms of diagnostics, intervention and delivery sites in health care.

Convergence reinforces and amplifies the impact of these change drivers. Taking the example of mapping the human genome, science could not have managed it without the computing power generated by the IT revolution; and without consumer acceptance of genetic screening and therapy, science cannot apply the genetic knowledge it has gained.

Selection of scenario logic

Once the key drivers of change were rated for their importance and uncertainty they were analysed for the critical variables, or axes of change, within them that will ultimately affect the future of hospitals. These appeared to be:

- health – health care
- free market – protected public sector
- scientific orientation – subjective orientation
- stable environment – environmental breakdown

Four scenarios for the distant future, that is 25 years out, were built around the dichotomies of these axes. For example if the world should become more health oriented over the next twenty-five years then it would likely correlate with an environment that is more stable since the environment is a key determinant of health. Similarly a greater sense of community, also a determinant of health, would be expected. Since health and control have been related in a number of studies it is likely that the locus of control would be closer to the individual and family. Scientific and subjective reality could equally be present in this scenario.

With four axes (and eight dichotomous variables) it is possible of course to develop multiple scenarios. However, the researchers and expert panel chose to build on four scenarios that had previously been developed by the Foundation and which in the view of the expert panel seemed to capture the most likely futures for hospitals. These included futures oriented to health and community, science and technology, markets and societal decline. The story lines of the four scenarios were then fleshed out such that the details in the story can bring insight and understanding into the longer-term possibilities for hospitals. For this discussion the scenarios have been condensed.

Future scenarios

Healthy Communities in 2025 (Hancock, 1997)

In this scenario the variables of health, strong public sector, incremental innovation and a stable environment are used to create a possible future. In this future, individuals and their communities have a strong effect on the population's health; human development has become central to the whole of society, and public policy has recognized this and moved in the direction of supporting the determinants of health. The economic ethos has shifted to sustainability and is strongly related to social and ecological sustainability. There has been a conscious redistribution of wealth through tax credits to ensure that all families are able to provide for their children's well-being and to care for family members.

There is a dramatic compression of morbidity of people over age 65 and they use less traditional health care resources. Fewer hospitals and institutional beds reflect improved lifestyle, closer community ties, and the support of caregivers. Fewer hip replacements, heroic interventions and cardiac surgical interventions are done. On the other hand, there are more local hospital beds for diagnosis and respite care. Birth and death take place at home.

The Market Rules in 2025 (Yamada, 1997)

In this scenario the variables of health care, free market orientation, high rate of scientific invention and an unstable environment are developed. Consumer choice and control expand with increasingly global markets for health and health care products and services. Dramatic increases in availability of services and products for disease and disability as well as for prevention, wellness and quality of life are spurred by the ongoing biotechnology and micro-processing revolutions. The distribution of wealth, however, is becoming increasingly concentrated correlating with significant variations of health status across income and ethnic lines.

Hospitals become much more like private-sector businesses. The most successful hospitals increase their local market share for profitable activities and sell Canadian health care services across the border to American individuals and insurers.

Science Rules in 2025 (Naylor, 1997)

In this scenario the variables of health and health care, public orientation, scientific values, continuous improvements through scientific breakthrough and an improved and stable environment are explored. In this future, science has become an increasingly respected part of everyone's life. This is reflected in the economy at large as well as in health care. Patients demand more from their clinicians in terms of effective care and personal interaction. There are changes in professional boundaries and a focus on the evidence base of medicine. In this scenario, care is 'needs-tested' and utilization is controlled on the basis of need and efficacy of treatment. Regulations improve air and water quality, and reduce occupational health hazards. Healthy lifestyle promotion and prevention efforts and prophylactic coronary drugs reduce morbidity for those over 65.

All governments in North America recognize their obligations to support a strong public infrastructure for economic development and the health of the population. This infrastructure includes health research across basic science, biomedicine and biotechnology, population health and health services. The governments recognize that advanced scientific research requires large-scale investment and critical mass that are best directed and supported by central government funding agencies and large research networks.

Blade Runner – Economic Decline and/or Environmental Catastrophe (Glouberman, 1997)

The dominant variables in this scenario are health care, central control, science and environmental decline. In this scenario the main urge is survival and to try to wait for a better day. Things have gone wrong; *pax Americana* has failed, as have many businesses and even crops. Small regional warfare has begun and is kept contained to the areas where it occurs. The pollution in the physical environment has continued with publicly supplied water suspect for contamination and most people testing and treating their water. The social fabric of Canada has become less stable as reflected in more crime and family breakdown.

In this scenario the health-care focus is on emergency care. Basic and essential health care to save lives has become the priority. Services and products are provided at the minimum level in the public system. The widespread use of new diagnostic procedures results from computer technology that is more user friendly.

From scenarios to strategy: hospital enterprises of the future

From a consideration of the implications for hospitals of the scenarios, five ideas emerge for future hospital enterprises that could be sustainable in any or all of the scenarios. These are: 'Reformed Cathedral', 'Focus Factory', 'Health Mall', 'Broker' and 'Fire Station' (Murray, McGrath and Croskery' 2000). These five enterprises were provocatively named by the expert panel and research team to draw attention to key characteristics and to stimulate new perceptions of what hospitals could be in the future. Each of these enterprises has a strong focus on the earlier identified drivers of change for hospitals: consumer attitudes and beliefs, science and technology and information technology as well as markets, suppliers and partners. This is in contrast to traditional hospital restructuring which has focused on governance changes; that is, mergers, amalgamations and closures, infrastructure reduction or renewal, and programme rationalization.

The enterprise concepts are framed into the general form of a business plan for the purpose of both having a common understanding of what the enterprises would look like and to test for viability and rigour. In this discussion, highlights of these business plans are presented. Although five enterprises are presented, by combining the different attributes of any enterprise, additional enterprise models can be created.

'Reformed Cathedral'

Hospitals at the turn of the millennium can be likened to great secular cathedrals. Their impressive edifices reflect their substantial economic, intellectual and political power in whatever community they are located. But like religious cathedrals they risk 'empty pews' as science, consumers and information technology create new opportunities for products and services, delivery sites and methods of delivery for health promotion, disease prevention and health care.

This enterprise shifts hospitals from their current isolation in silos where they focus on acute episodes of care to full service networks. As 'reformed cathedrals' (Figure 12.2) hospitals very much engage with the broadly defined health care community developing, implementing and sustaining an integrated network of services for a community of people (geographic or otherwise) across the continuum of care. The 'reformed cathedral' would offer a broad range of services across many different sites and by a variety of delivery methods.

The hospital as 'reformed cathedral' speaks to the key trends of a stronger orientation to health promotion and disease prevention, optimal development of information technology to link services and clinicians irrespective of location, and continued development of a health care system that is rationalized as to access through objective

Reformed Cathedral

Structure:
- Hospital at the centre
- Satellite clinics
- Access through levels of care

Business:
- Health and health care

Management:
- Representative management team

Services
- Full spectrum
- Womb to tomb

Marketplace
- Community image: hospital is core to the system which manages healthcare
- Large service population (500,000 to 1,000,000)
- Community relations is key

Supplier
- Multidisciplinary providers and provider teams
- Intra-system referrals

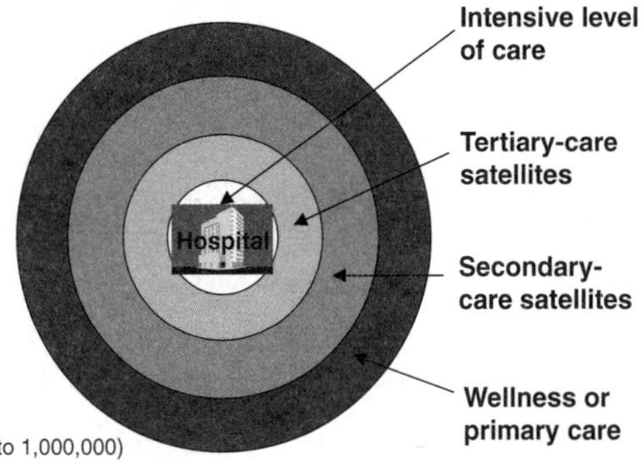

Intensive level of care

Tertiary-care satellites

Secondary-care satellites

Wellness or primary care

Figure 12.2 Reformed Cathedral

criteria for eligibility, and delivers care based on evidence. As such this enterprise can respond to the Healthy Community scenario with the emphasis on health and community; to the Science Rules scenario emphasizing evidence-based care and rationality in health care organization; and to Blade Runner (environmental and economic decline) in terms of providing a minimum range of services based on a triage of care requirements It could be viable in the Market Future scenario if there are competing 'reformed cathedrals' offering consumers alternative integrated care-delivery systems such as the Health Maintenance Organizations (HMOs) in the USA.

'Focus Factory'

This enterprise option transforms the generalist hospital to a specialty enterprise. The organization's main advantage is its leading-edge research and development for continuous improvement of its products and services. Processes are in place to reduce cycle time and procedures are developed to reduce costs and improve quality.

The hospital as 'focus factory' (Figure 12.3) is responsive to the growing specialization in knowledge and rapidly evolving new technologies and therapies supported by breakthroughs in science. Consumers are able to access the latest product and service they have previewed on the

Focus Factory

Structure:
• Special service delivery

Business:
• Production

Management: Traditional Model
• Horizontal
• Door to floor

Services:
• Disease focus
• Treatment focus
• Wellness focus   Focus Factory

Marketplace:
• Community image: the'expert'
• Dense population – volume

Supplier:
• Health management team

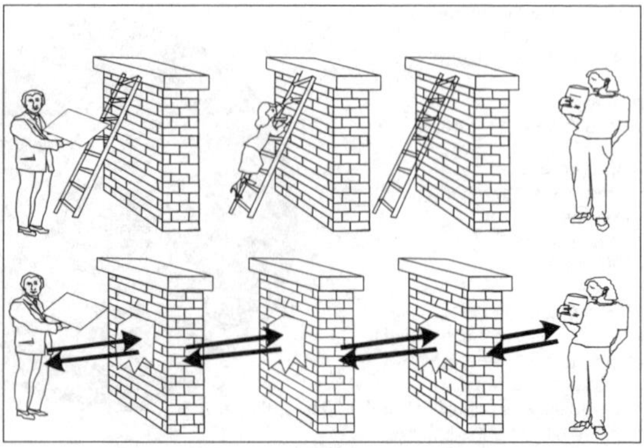

Smooth flow of information and processes
........Break down the silos

Figure 12.3   Focus Factory

Internet for their specific health or health care issue. Although the majority of 'focus factories' would service health care issues, this enterprise could also specialize in health and wellness. In the current publicly-funded health care system, this type of specialization is seen in cancer-care diagnosis and treatment. In the private sector it can be seen in the proliferation of private wellness centres.

The 'focus factory' could respond through different adaptations to three of the future scenarios – Healthy Communities, Market Rules and Science Rules. It is not likely to be successful in the Economic Decline scenario, which would likely mitigate against multiple delivery organizations.

'Health Mall'

The 'health mall' (Figure 12.4) provides 'one-stop shopping' for health and health care services. These services include both publicly insured ones as well as those funded through private insurance and/or direct consumer payment. Hospitals act as the anchor (similar to a department store in retail malls), attracting customers and offering a variety of

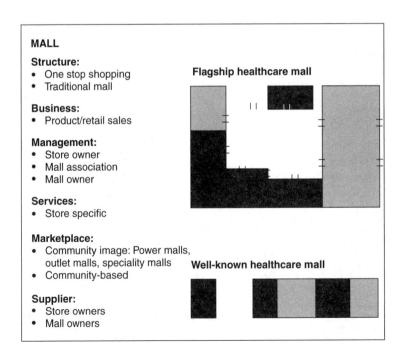

Figure 12.4 Health Mall

services or products. The development of 'health malls' by hospitals responds to the consumer requirement for choice and the trend for personalized services. It is viable in the future scenarios of Healthy Community and Market Rules Scenario.

'Broker'

The 'broker' is a referral network of service providers and consumers, with knowledge and connectivity as its main products. The goal of this enterprise is to connect the consumer with the best health or health care service and with a provider of this service. The hospital as 'Broker' (Figure 12.5) is a response to the increasingly differentiated services available due to breakthroughs in science and technology, particularly e-health breakthroughs. It is also a response to an increase in consumer demand for choice supported by their increased access to information via the Internet. The 'Broker' assists the consumer to navigate these many options for health and health care, and can also add a case management dimension to complex care requirements.

This enterprise responds to the plurality of health and health care services and products envisioned in the Market Rules scenario. It could

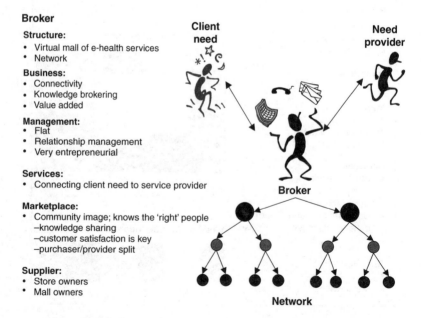

Figure 12.5   Broker

also be used to ration services in the Science Rules scenario such that access is based on need and efficacy. The technology breakthroughs in Science Rules scenario could provide capacity to monitor clients by biosensors at home, at work or in the community. In a scenario where the emphasis is on health and wellness, the 'broker' could again be an information and access broker to quality products and services. In the Blade Runner scenario (environmental or economic decline) the broker restricts access to services by tight screening for eligibility and need.

'Fire Station'

The 'fire station' enterprise's main focus is on response to urgent or emergency need for care. Response teams within the organization are always prepared and waiting for the emergency or urgent cases. Consumers in this model (Figure 12.6) are not proactive or focused on prevention, and they have less control over the health care provided.

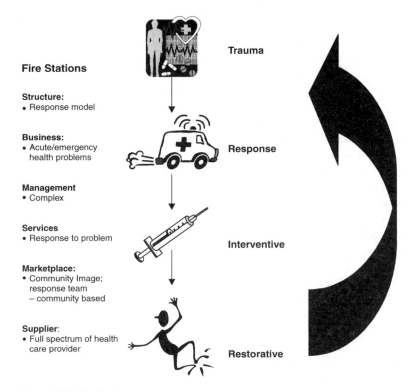

Figure 12.6   Fire Station

The hospital as 'fire station' is a highly specialized but restricted health care delivery organization. The focus is acute and emergency care. This enterprise works within the Blade Runner future scenario when health care resources are restricted to essential services, and it is also compatible with the Science Rules future scenario where service is restricted to evidence-based services supplied on the basis of medical need.

Testing the scenarios and enterprises

Alternative paths, strategic conversations

Alternative Paths for Ontario Hospitals (Murray *et al.*, 2000) proposed consideration of new enterprises responsive to significant drivers of change and emerging future scenarios. The enterprises identified were not meant to define all possible strategic directions, but were intended to be illustrative of transformational strategies oriented to the future. Following development of the scenarios and enterprises, the researchers proposed as the next step a series of 'strategic conversations' within and between the hospitals, the hospital association and the government to further evolve the alternative paths and test these enterprises for viability and rigour.

The *Alternative Paths* report material was translated into a workshop format to test in a sample of Ontario hospitals. Twenty hospitals (13 per cent of Ontario hospitals) to date including teaching, community and small hospitals as well as a hospital network have participated in the workshops. These strategic conversations are being carried out as part of the hospital's strategic planning process. Participants at each session have included board members, senior managers and clinical staff, and depending on the hospitals' preferences middle managers and partner organizations. Groups have ranged from 25 to 100 participants. The pilot workshops were facilitated by the Foundation's research team with subsequent workshops being delivered by two consultants, one of whom had been a member of the expert panel and had participated with the research team in the pilot workshops.

Each of the hospitals as part of the workshop process reviewed the drivers of change from their perspective and considered how they would respond to each of the scenarios. They identified what they would continue to do, what they would stop, and then considered the opportunities and the implications for services, infrastructure and human resources, including physicians. The responses were then reviewed for continuity and discontinuity across the scenarios. The second half of the workshop reviewed the possible enterprises against a series of questions in terms of fit and feasibility; opportunities and risks each would pose for the hospital. The outcome of the strategic conversation was to identify a number of strategies for transformation to better ensure future success. The most desired strategy was the one that could succeed in as many scenarios as possible.

The participant evaluations of the sessions are positive, but more importantly for the scenario-planning methodology, participants have rated it as an extremely effective tool for setting hospital directions for the future. The types of strategic decisions arising from the sessions have varied to date but are mostly focused on the 'reformed cathedral' and the 'health mall'; hospitals see in these the possibility of developing alternative revenue sources to supplement their insured services. The 'focus factory' has had appeal to some who do not see themselves as a viable 'reformed cathedral'. Strategies have emerged that were unthinkable before the strategic conversation – for example, partnering with a perceived threatening rival, closing emergency services, and building a health mall in conjunction with a focus factory.

Application of scenario planning in other jurisdictions

In terms of organizational design and behaviour, hospitals across the globe are more alike than not. Hospital restructuring has been a common strategic direction in most health systems, although its success, as in Ontario, has been limited even as a cost-cutting exercise. Thus hospitals are looking beyond restructuring for more transformational strategies to position them for future success. Since the scenario-planning methodology has had some initial take-up in Ontario hospitals, it is reasonable to suggest that it may well interest hospitals in other jurisdictions.

For scenario planning to be appropriate for other jurisdictions, the process for developing the scenarios must be flexible enough to allow variation. In the case of the Ontario hospitals they were able to apply and adapt the change drivers at the micro level, and thus their scenarios for their local circumstances. This suggests that the method allows for enough flexibility to be transferable beyond individual hospitals and geographic locations.

Scenario planning is not a one-time exercise, but rather a continuous strategy development. The test for its success is whether organizations do continually reflect on what is changing and what needs to change. It is too soon to establish if Ontario hospitals' strategic processes will continue to monitor change and adapt their strategy when milestones or indicators suggest that new scenarios are developing. The method used, however, in the 'strategic conversation' does parallel strategy development (Wilson *et al.*, 2000) including:

- Identifying the key elements of a successful strategy (for example, basis of competition).
- Analysing each scenario to determine the optimal setting for each strategy element (what would be the best strategy for scenario A? for scenario B?).
- Reviewing these scenario-specific settings to determine the most resilient option for each strategy element.

The workshops did not take the process as far as integrating these strategy options into an overall, coordinated business strategy due to the time constraints of a workshop method. It is expected that the hospitals will continue the process to integrate the strategic options identified in the workshops into an overall coordinated business strategy. In the follow-up evaluation the researchers will assess whether this occurred. Like scenarios themselves, organizational effort will be needed in implementation of strategies derived from scenario planning including senior management commitment, communication, education and guidance, practice and review.

Summary and conclusions

Planning for the longer-term future is something that hospitals have set aside given the financial problems of recent years and the restructuring focus on mergers, amalgamations and closures. The results to date on restructuring in Ontario have suggested that it was more about downsizing and cost-containment than about transformation of hospitals for future success. For transformation hospitals need to plan for the longer-term future of 20 to 25 years. The steps towards transformation include the consideration of the likely future scenarios for health care and hospital enterprises, and the proof of the scenario-planning process will be if the hospitals that participate in the Alternative Paths 'strategic conversations' do transform themselves into enterprises that are successful in the longer-term future. To date the workshop evaluation reports are promising. The Foundation will continue to monitor these and to further evaluate the impact of scenario planning for Ontario hospitals over the next three to five years.

References

Ackoff, R. (1970) *A Concept of Corporate Planning* (New York: John Wiley).

Gilbert, J., Murray, G. and Corbin R. (2001) *Are Consumers Becoming Patients?* (Toronto, ON: The Change Foundation).

Glouberman, S. (1997) *Framework of Variables for Consideration in Scenarios Planning* (Toronto, ON: The Change Foundation).

Glouberman, S. (1997) *Bladerunner Scenario* (Toronto, ON: The Change Foundation).

Godet, M. (2000) 'The Art of Scenarios and Strategic Planning Tools and Pitfalls', *Technological Forecasting and Social Changes*, 65, pp. 3–22.

Hadridge, P., Hodgson, T. and Thornton, S. (1995) 'Tomorrow's World', *Health Services Journal*, January, pp. 18–20.

Hancock, T. (1997) 'Future Scenarios', Panel at the Change Foundation educational conference (Toronto, ON: The Change Foundation).

Hancock, T. (1997) *Healthy Communities Scenario* (Toronto, ON: The Change Foundation).

Masini, E. B. and Vasquez, D. (2000) 'Scenarios as Seen from a Human and Social Perspective', *Technological Forecasting and Social Changes*, 65, pp. 49–66.

Murray, G., McGrath, M. and Croskery, E. (1999) *The Current Path: Hospital Restructuring at the Mid-point* (Toronto, ON: The Change Foundation).

Murray, G., McGrath, M. and Croskery, E. (2000) *Alternative Paths for Ontario Hospitals* (Toronto, ON: The Change Foundation).

Naylor, D. (1997) *Science Rules Scenario* (Toronto, ON: The Change Foundation).

Schwartz, P. (1996) *Art of the Long View* (New York, Doubleday).

Van Der Heijden, K. (2000) 'Scenarios and Forecasting: Two Perspectives', *Technological Forecasting and Social Changes*, 65, pp. 31–6.

Wilson, I. (2000) 'From Scenario Thinking to Strategic Action', *Technological Forecasting and Social Changes*, 65, pp. 23–9.

Yamada, R. (1997) *Market Rules Scenario* (Toronto, ON: The Change Foundation).

13

All Pain and No Gain? A Study of Mergers of NHS Trusts in London: Two-Year Post-Merger Findings on the Drivers of Mergers and the Processes of Merging

Gerasimos Protopsaltis, Naomi Fulop, Annette King, Pauline Allen, Andrew Hutchings, Charles Normand and Rhiannon Walters*

Mergers have been a prominent feature in the health care agenda of both the USA and the UK in the last 30 years. In the British NHS, the number of trust mergers and reconfigurations has dramatically increased over the last 10 years (99 trust mergers between 1997–2001), and these have generally been horizontal mergers of acute, mental health and community Trusts.

The literature on health care mergers identifies a number of drivers for Trust mergers, such as economic gains; improvements in clinical quality; the ability to recruit and retain staff more effectively; facilitating hospital or service closures; and securing the financial viability of smaller institutions (McClenahan *et al.*, 1999). Although numerous benefits are expected to arise from these organizational changes, studies of mergers in the corporate and health care sector show that these benefits rarely materialize, and even in the few cases where they do, it is argued that organizations can take up to two years to recover from the unintended consequences and drawbacks of the merging process (*ibid.*).

* The authors would like to thank all those staff in NHS and allied organizations who took part in this study. The study on which this chapter is based was funded by the NHS Executive London Region Organization and Management R&D Programme.

Ashenkas *et al.* (1998, p. 166) argue that despite the potential benefits of mergers, few organizations go through this process often enough to develop a pattern, simply because the process itself is often a 'painful and anxiety-producing experience...[involving] job losses, restructured responsibilities, derailed careers, diminished power and much else that is stressful'. Regardless of this, mergers in the NHS have become a repeated process (Gould, 2000).

The findings discussed in this chapter, two years post-merger, suggest that although certain gains can be achieved from full organizational merger, this is not achieved without a number of drawbacks and unintentioned negative consequences that are often overlooked or underestimated by both policy-makers and managers in the early strategic planning stages of a merger.

Background

There are two main types of mergers. *Vertical mergers* involve the combination of firms at different stages of the production process, with a single firm producing the goods or services that either suppliers or customers could provide. *Horizontal mergers* involve the combination of two or more firms producing similar goods or services (Ferguson and Goddard, 1997).

In the corporate sector and in private-sector health care, such as in the USA, merger activity is mostly driven by price competition, the desire to consolidate operations in order to remain viable, to acquire market power, and to take advantage of a monopoly situation (Alexander *et al.*, 1996). Sinay (1998) adds that in the USA, hospital merger activity initially increased with the expansion of managed care plans and the implementation of Medicare's Prospective Payment System, which changed reimbursement procedures from cost-based to case-based. In publicly-funded health care systems, however, such as in the UK where NHS Trusts do not have a strong profit-making incentive, mergers are products of a number of drivers. Meara and Millard (1998) identify eight such factors (see Table 13.1).

The majority of the literature on hospital mergers, most of which concerns the US experience, focuses on efficiency gains and savings through economies of scale as the primary drivers for merger. Some of the earlier reports from the NHS suggest that mergers were introduced to deal with the spare capacity available in the acute sector, thus creating short-run cash savings and reducing average costs by better utilizing resources and avoiding duplication (Ferguson and Goddard, 1997).

Table 13.1   Factors which might render a trust vulnerable to merger

Vulnerability factors	Comments
Size of Trust turnover limited to management cost reduction targets	For example under £20m
Lack of coterminosity with partner services	Especially relevant to community Trusts
Failure to meet financial targets	If persistent
High management cost–turnover ratio	Could be triggered by purchasers transferring elements of service elsewhere
Lack of critical mass to sustain specialist services	Especially with reference to clinical staff recruitment
Perception of poor management	Could relate to failure to develop effective services
Recognized need for service rationalization	Merger seen as a precursor
Local political factors	For example desire for coterminosity

Source: Meara and Millard (1998).

It has been argued that hospital mergers can produce some savings through improved patient volumes, operational changes, and consolidation of support and administrative services (Bojke and Gravelle, 2001; Greene, 1990; Lynk, 1995). In terms of efficiency and effectiveness indicators, a US study of 32 mergers of non-profit hospitals by Treat (1976) found that merged hospitals produced a wider range of services than non-merged hospitals. However, a review of the literature on economies of scale and scope by Aletras *et al.* (1997) found that although merging could reduce costs through management cost savings, if the size of hospitals increases past a certain size (over 300 beds) it can lead to diseconomies of scale, from increased average costs and additional sources of costs. Aletras *et al.* (1997) conclude that the evidence on whether hospital mergers generate cost savings through the exploitation of economies of scale is inconclusive and that no evidence exists to suggest that mergers reduce costs overall.

Moreover, evidence from the USA and the UK suggests that many of the expected benefits of mergers, particularly cost savings, rarely materialize post-merger and that positive effects take a long time to present themselves (McClenahan, 1999/2000; Treat, 1976; Ferguson and Goddard, 1997). For example, in the UK, cost savings from reducing management costs are estimated at £200,000–£300,000 per year, which

McClenahan (1999) suggests is less than 1 per cent of the total budgets of the merged organizations. In terms of evidence from sectors other than health care, reviews of literature from the USA and the UK suggest that in many cases efficiency declines post-merger due to unforeseen problems in integrating the merging firms (Haspeslagh and Jemison, 1992; Buono and Bowditch, 1989).

Government policy on appropriate models of service delivery has played a key role in the introduction of mergers in the UK. The 'Calman–Hine Report' (1995) highlighted the need for the creation of cancer units and centres, requiring trusts to form alliances and pull together resources. In addition, changes in medical staff training have in turn caused pressure for the concentration of services. The Calman reforms to specialist medical training, for example, may threaten the accreditation of small hospitals and departments unless they integrate into larger units (Ferguson and Goddard, 1997).

Mergers have also been introduced in order to improve clinical quality of services provided through higher concentration of specialist services. A review of the research on the volume–outcome relationship of clinical services conducted by Sowden *et al.* (1997) found that although for some procedures and specialties, quality gains can be achieved as volume increases, most research studies overestimate the level of impact of volume on quality of care.

A number of US studies (Bogue *et al.*, 1995; Weil, 2000) have found that mergers are often proposed to facilitate hospital or service closures. For a 'failing' hospital with an uncertain future, where there is excess capacity due to falling demand of specific services, a merger is often regarded the more attractive alternative to closure, since it is hoped that the hospital will continue to provide some, if not all, services post-merger.

Studies have shown that the merging process has been found to have adverse effects on hospital staff. Greene (1990) studied the merger of 36 US hospitals, concluding that despite some operational improvements, most of the merging hospital staff experienced increased stress from fear of job loss and a loss of morale and productivity for several years. McClenahan *et al.* (1999) argue that *all* mergers have negative short-term effects on staff, and may easily become a physical and/or mental health-threatening event as concerns for personal job security, changing work practices (and often environment) and apprehension about loss of autonomy, nurture fears of organizational change. It seems that mergers do not only affect remaining staff who might be disillusioned. Shaw (2001) and Allen and Sharar (2000) suggest that clinical staff and senior managers experience a 'post-merger stress syndrome', characterized by fiscal pressures, workload, feelings of lack of appreciation or reward, anger/stress, and loss/grieving.

Organizational culture is a significant yet often neglected factor in the merger process, which is an important aspect in explaining differences in work practices and approaches in the merged organizations. Handy (1993, p. 181) defines culture as an organization's 'deep-set beliefs about the way work should be organized, the way authority should be exercised, people rewarded, and people controlled'. Garside and Rice (1994) point to studies in the USA that show that a significant percentage of hospital mergers fail when issues surrounding organizational culture are ignored. The likelihood of failure is said to increase as the gap between the merging hospitals' cultures widens, which can often lead to low staff morale and productivity, job dissatisfaction, absenteeism and high staff turnover.

Mergers have also been reported to consume large amounts of time and effort from senior management; management is often unrealistic and overconfident about the time requirements and the difficulties involved in a merger (McClenahan *et al.*, 1999; Garside and Rice, 1994). Indeed, Hackett (1996) argues that ineffective management of the merger process leads to discord and disharmony, and is one of the main reasons why mergers fail.

The study reported in this chapter aims to address these issues by analysing the *process* and *impact* of mergers.

Research methodology

Aims

This study aims to increase the understanding of organizational restructuring and change in health services by focusing on the impact of the merger process on the management, organization and delivery of services, and on management costs. The study includes a management cost analysis of the financial data of merged and non-merged Trusts in London Region for 1999/2000 and 2001/2002, using regression analysis. The findings of the management cost analysis are reported elsewhere (see Fulop *et al.*, 2002; Hutchings *et al.*, 2003) We present findings of two phases of the project:

1   a cross-sectional study of all nine merged Trusts in the London area which came into existence between 1998 and 1999; and
2   the first phase of work in four case study sites, two years post-merger.

Data collection

The aim of data collection is to follow up the multifaceted processes of mergers over time and to contextualise the case studies within other mergers and reconfigurations in the London Region (see Table 13.5 in the Appendix).

The cross-sectional study

Consultation documents of all proposed reorganizations to Trusts in London Region since 1998 were collected. Nine management mergers were included in the study (Table 13.2), and 14 representatives in seven Health Authorities (HAs) involved in the mergers were interviewed.

Case studies

Our four case studies consisted of mergers in one acute, one mental health and two community NHS Trusts, all of which came into effect in 1999. Case study Trusts were selected 'purposively' (Bowling, 1997) to ensure the range of Trust types and geographical spread in London (two north, two south). The purpose of the case studies was to explore in greater depth the process of merger, assess how far the objectives of each merger had been met, and their intended and unintended consequences. In all, 22–6 interviews were conducted in each case study with a range of stakeholders, both internal and external to the trust (see Table 13.3).

Analysis of cross-sectional and case-study data

Data from the cross-sectional study and the case studies were analysed using 'contextualism', which combines the study of different perspectives and temporal and historical contexts in the analysis of organizational change and process, extracting theory from the ground up (Pettigrew, 1985).

Table 13.2   Mergers included in the cross-sectional study

Trust type	Number of mergers/ reconfigurations	Number of resulting merged trusts
Acute	5	5
Community	2	2
Mental health	1	3
Mixture of above	1	1

Table 13.3   Number of interviews in each case study site

Case study Trusts	Interviews with senior trust managers (chief executive, medical director, HR director, etc.)	Interviews with service managers (management and professional)	Interviews with external stakeholders (CHC, PCG/T, LA)	Total
Acute Trust	8	10	7	25
Mental Health Trust	9	9	5	23
Community Trust I	9	6	11	26
Community Trust II	6	6	10	22
Total	32	31	33	96

In the cross-sectional study, the analysis of the consultation documents and the interviews with HA representatives focused on the background, drivers and objectives of the mergers. The analysis drew out common reasons for the proposed mergers and highlighted noteworthy differences. The data are presented in an anonymized form so that Trusts and respondents cannot be identified.

Findings

Drivers for merger

The stated drivers for merger extracted from the merger consultation documents gave the official view of the background to and the reasons for the mergers and the favoured organizational structures. The 'unstated' drivers reported by key stakeholders internal and external to the Trusts, during the case-study interviews, concerned specific local issues with one or more of the constituent Trusts.

Stated drivers

These were obtained from an analysis of public consultation documents and confirmed by interviews with HA representatives. The need to make savings featured as a significant driver in all the consultation documents, but key stakeholders did not agree about their importance. Interviewees, however, agreed that financial pressures were a significant driver for the mergers. These included budget reductions in the

HA, either because of previous overspends or because of anticipated reductions in HA budgets in the future. Trusts' budgetary deficits were one of the central drivers for acute and community mergers, and both types of mergers sought to redress financial shortfalls in the predecessor Trusts.

Mergers were also seen as an opportunity for safeguarding specialist units and guaranteeing service developments. The specialist forensic unit attached to mental health Trust 23, for example, was expected to guarantee its survival within a larger mental health organization. (see Table 13.4 (p. 229) for the nomenclature used in referring to the different Trusts.)

Common to all Trust mergers was the need to ensure that the quality and level of service provision could be maintained in light of a number of external policy drivers, which put additional pressures on services; for example, the Turnberg Report (Department of Health, 1997). In the community and mental health Trusts, the reconfigurations were informed by pressures for local improvements to service delivery and for closer cooperation with local authority (LA) and partnership agencies. In particular, the national shift in policy towards community mental health services was seen as requiring closer collaboration with partner agencies in the local area.

In the original merger consultation documents, one of the drivers for community Trusts was the need to support primary-care development. The mergers were seen as securing organizational survival of community Trusts, but also as a way of maintaining a strategic role in future primary and community health developments. As larger organizations, all newly merged Trusts aimed to improve conditions and career prospects for staff. For the acute and mental health Trusts, staffing issues were cited as particularly important in informing the merger decisions. The need to bring together clinical and professional staff to form a larger staff and expertise base was also regarded by HA representatives as a central driver for all the mergers in our study. HA respondents argued that this 'critical mass' would help achieve the maintenance and development of services through the accumulation of a larger consultant base and clinical teams.

By merging, the newly established Trusts expected to be able to address staffing problems experienced in recent years. As larger and specialized organizations, the merged Trusts intended to improve the career and training opportunities for their staff, attracting suitably qualified staff and addressing some of the problems in the quality of the service suffered through sustained high vacancy levels.

Un-stated drivers

These were obtained through interviews with HA representatives and were drivers which were not publicly stated. Un-stated drivers often had a particular bearing on the type of reconfiguration adopted in specific cases or in addressing a specific local problem. Certain mergers were a way of imposing a new management regime on a Trust, which was seen by HAs or the Regional Office (RO) as undermanaged or 'lacking control'. By merging the Trusts, better management approaches could be introduced. For example, Trust 17 was seen as having underperforming community services, an issue that raised concern about the prospect for quality of services in the area.

There is evidence among a small number of the Trust mergers that there was an expectation that some of the financial deficits accumulated by constituent Trusts could be written off. None of the official documents explicitly stated this, but some HA representatives made reference to the fact that deficits had been part of the merger negotiations. In the merger of community Trust II, one of the constituent Trust had a considerable deficit. When the extent of this deficit became apparent after the merger, the new Trust negotiated for the deficit to be written off.

For a small number of Trusts, lobbying and pressure from central government, influential institutions and individuals, and from public pressure groups on behalf of one or more of the constituent Trusts played a role in driving the merger process. The merger of acute Trusts A and B was politically sensitive due to a long and high-profiled public campaign to avoid the closure of constituent Trust 4.

The following sections are based on the analysis of the case-study data in the second year post-merger.

Impact on service delivery

There was a general agreement in all the case studies that the mergers had affected service delivery. While the assessment of the merger by the senior management teams tended to focus on the more positive outcomes, both service managers and external interviewees were more critical. Negative effects were seen as the result of the temporary absence of 'management' and 'service focus' during the transition period. Several respondents reported a setback to service development of more than 18 months. However, respondents also stated that service improvements were beginning to show.

The more outlying community Trust services were particularly affected by the mergers and remained undermanaged for a period of months, unable to participate in local service development discussions. In community Trust II, for example, these delays held up the development of intermediate care services. The acute Trust merger experienced similar delays. Proposed changes to services in pathology, A&E and maternity are still not implemented, the services still operate quite independently from each other and delays are ongoing. A number of respondents, both within and outside the trusts, felt that this loss of focus had had some detrimental effects on patient care. Some Community Health Council (CHC) representatives believed that certain services had operated outside their statutory framework and neglected standards of clinical governance. They also pointed to periods of 'mounting complaints' and, in the case of the acute hospital merger, an increase in waiting times, which they felt was at least partly related to the merger.

In relation to the borough-based services, service delivery in the mental health Trust merger seemed to be least affected compared to the other case studies, largely because the devolution of service management to borough-based management was completed before the Trust merger. The mental health service seems to have had less success in integrating in-patient services – respondents reported an ingrained reluctance to share beds across the patch.

On the positive side, the merger allowed the mental health Trust and the two community Trusts to benefit from the sharing of clinical practice. In addition, the mergers united previously fragmented specialist services, raising their profile and enabling them to develop a stronger voice, and gain greater influence and more bargaining power. This was clearly evident in the forensic, substance misuse and Child and Adolescent Mental Health (CAMHS) services of the mental health Trust. Service managers in community Trust II regarded the changes introduced as the result of the Trust merger as freeing them from a stifling, old-fashioned and stagnating culture. The merged organizations allowed individuals to articulate and participate in a new vision of service delivery. The internal consultation on service models and the exchange of ideas was extensive, and service managers regarded the process as highly beneficial.

The impact of the merger process on staff

A number of common issues regarding the effects of the mergers on clinical and professional staff were identified in our case studies. Most importantly, our findings to date have not revealed a substantial improvement in either recruitment or retention of staff. The recruitment and retention situation did not change significantly during the early stages of the mergers, and problems varied across the four case studies. Whereas some Trusts had general recruitment and retention problems (acute Trust), others had vacancies and/or difficulties recruiting in particular services only (elderly services, learning disability, and speech and language therapy in community Trust II).

Individual staff responded in different ways to the merger. Many interviewees reported the stress they experienced related to the perceived imposed uncertainties and changes, and an increase in workload. Alongside these mainly negative responses, certain interviewees reported beneficial reactions, for example in the increased autonomy in their roles, and in being given a voice in the plans for innovation and change. The pre-merger consultation processes and the months leading up to the mergers were laced with anxieties and fears for individual staff. Many staff felt anxious about having to work alongside staff groups from another organization, which they previously considered 'rivals' (acute Trust, mental health Trust, community Trust I), and a number of people decided to look for alternative employment.

The appointment process of managers was difficult for all staff. The parts of the organization that gained new management mourned the loss of their previous managers and found it difficult to relate to the new managers, especially if they originated from the rival organization.

Organizational culture

Respondents used the term 'culture' to identify perceived deep-rooted differences between constituent Trusts, and to explain conflicts of values and priorities in the Trusts. Cultural differences were particularly relevant in explaining continuing problems and delays in forming a coherent organizational identity, and culture-related issues came into relief mainly as the result of comparing differences between constituent Trusts of the merger and between the 'before and after' phases of the merger.

Cultural differences became more apparent as the merger process developed, and were most prominent in the acute Trust merger. Some respondents regarded the differences in size of the two Trusts, different philosophies and distinct problems at their respective sites as part of an unmanageable barrier between the two previous organizations:

> There might be four miles difference between us but there is two decades in terms of culture and practice. (Executive board member, acute Trust)

Cultural differences were also used to explain delay and resistance to changes in service delivery as the result of the mergers. An example of this is the failed attempt of implementing protocol-driven clinical practice in the acute Trust merger. The clinical culture in Trust 11 was based on good links between management and clinicians, good multidisciplinary links, flexible ways of working, and commitment to modernization, and so on. As a result of this wider culture, Trust 11 had been able to implement protocols widely across the hospital. At Trust 10, the clinical culture was traditional, hierarchical, medically-led and slow to change. Introducing the protocol-driven clinical practice has been much more difficult and resistance to it remains high, as the example of the failure to implement a triage system shows.

Expectations of management cost savings and their reinvestment into patient services

The merged Trusts' finance managers believed that the clearest savings achieved were the £500,000–£750,000 associated with the reduction of management boards. Our analysis, however, showed that two years post-merger, these savings had not been made. Average management cost savings were estimated at £179,000 in the first year, and £347,000 by the second year following merger (Fulop *et al.*, 2002; Hutchings *et al.*, 2003). Moreover, there was less evidence that other savings, as the result of other rationalizations for example, had been achieved within the first financial year. There was also no evidence that any savings had been reinvested into services. Instead, the mergers highlighted additional financial problems in the Trusts and identified significant differences in the funding, staffing and resourcing of services. There were concerns about the equity of budgets for services across the merged organizations.

Opinions on the potential for other cost savings and greater financial control as the result of the mergers were also divided. A number of respondents claimed that overall savings had been nominal in their Trust. In the acute Trust merger, both the HA representatives and the Trust's staff believed that management cost savings had minimal effect on the overall financial situation of the Trust. A deficit remained (£2 million overspent in the first quarter of 2000), and the view was that the merger could only achieve its financial targets in the long term.

There was doubt that any tangible benefits had come from savings. In most cases, the Trusts were not necessarily the beneficiaries of the savings made from the mergers. According to one HA representative, whatever management cost savings were made in the mental health merger were shared out between the HAs according to fixed costs and pro-rata contributions of HAs to the Trusts, instead of reinvesting in services and facilities. In all Trusts, there was also a recognition that the merger process itself constituted a considerable financial burden and that this had been underestimated in the planning of the merger. Although management cost savings were made, external consultants were often brought to support the merging process.

Discussion

Despite the various expected gains that can be made from a merger, a number of common factors and patterns of the merger process were identified in this study, which negatively affected the management and organization of work, service provision and staff. These are the unintended consequences or drawbacks of mergers. However, it is too early to be able to assess accurately whether the merged Trusts have achieved the objectives which they set for themselves. The findings reported in this chapter are from the first stage of our study, two years post-merger. Data gathered in stage two of our case studies will reveal how the issues discussed above have played out in the third year following merger.

It is clear that the Trusts' service delivery has been affected by the mergers. The Trusts incurred delays in service development mainly as a result of the knock-on effects of delays in middle management appointments which led to setbacks in the development of the new organization and in service development of at least 18 months. Our findings confirm the results of a number of studies (Weil, 2000; Bogue *et al.*, 1995) indicating that mergers often secure the survival of smaller, inefficient hospitals.

As predicted by most studies of mergers (McClenahan, 1999/2000; Aletras *et al.*, 1997; Treat, 1976; Ferguson and Goddard, 1997), the case-study Trusts did not meet the clearly stated objective of reducing management costs by £500,000–£750,000, despite the fact that senior managers believed that these savings were made by the reduction of management boards. The lower savings achieved, particularly in the first year following merger, suggests that the implementation of mergers required more management support than had been anticipated. There was also less evidence that other savings, as the result of other rationalizations, had been achieved by the first financial year. Lastly, there was no clear evidence to indicate that savings have been reinvested into services, as it was pledged in the consultation stages of the mergers.

A prominent negative impact on staff at all levels was detected in this study – an issue that has been noted by most studies on mergers (Greene, 1990; Shaw, 2001; McClenahan *et al.*, 1999; Hancock, 1997). The merging process elicited feelings of frustration, anxiety, insecurity and fear of the unknown from staff and management at all levels, indicating that the merger process deeply affected people's work and personal lives. Consequently, many decided to look for alternate employment rather because they had no confidence in the proposed organization. Others felt anxious about having to work alongside staff groups from another organization, which they previously considered 'rivals'. Furthermore, Trust managers shared the belief that merging would improve the recruitment and retention of staff through the creation of larger, more prominent Trusts that would ultimately be seen as better employers. As such, the Trusts would be in a better position to provide staff with better opportunities, staff training and career progression. Our findings to date have revealed that there has been no substantial improvement in the recruitment or retention of staff, although in two case studies (community Trust I and mental health Trust) the merger led to improvements in training, appraisal and career development schemes.

Overall, it is evident from both our study and previous research on this topic (Hackett, 1996; Kent, 1997; McClenahan *et al.*, 1999) that the management teams involved in mergers significantly underestimated the amount of time and effort necessary for such major organizational change. The mergers examined involved bringing together two or more different organizations across geographical distances, with different policies (clinical and non-clinical) and processes. In fact, our research suggests that there was a sense of naivety on the part of the Trusts' management boards, that the merging process would have minimal impact or disruption to services. As a result, in all Trust mergers, external representatives, Trust staff and management reported that senior management had lost control over the strategic direction of the Trust and day-to-day operations at some point in the early phases of the merger. This was often the result of unforeseen circumstances emerging from the merger process itself, and took the form of timetable delays in plans for restructuring and reorganization of services. These in turn were caused by delays in mostly middle-management appointments, by financial short-falls (mental health Trust, acute Trust and community Trust II), and IT delays, which ultimately set back the organization at least 18 months.

In this study we found that little attention was paid to the perceived cultural differences of the merging Trusts. These differences became more apparent as the merger process developed, and although present in all four case studies, were most prominent in the acute Trust merger. Some respondents regarded the differences in size of the two Trusts, different philosophies and distinct problems at their respective sites as part of an unmanageable barrier between the two previous organizations. The basic incompatibility of the two Trusts has contributed to the whole range of current problems in the merged organization, including the continued tension around directors' and consultants' appointments, organizational structures. In order to begin to address such issues, management teams should recognize that without clear lines of communication, positive working relations within the Trust and across staff groups, these 'clashes of culture' will not diminish. Attempts to address the issue of organizational culture in a merger need to be part of a wider range of improving activities and cannot be in isolation from such issues as: organizational structure, financial arrangements, lines of control and accountability, strategy formulation, or human resource management activities (McClenahan *et al.*, 1999; Garside and Rice, 1994).

In light of the above, critics of mergers have argued that a full merger is not always the only or, in fact, the best option available. In cases where only parts of the organizations need to integrate, alternative strategies such as licensing, alliances, partnerships or even joint ventures can often obtain the same expected benefits but in a less-disruptive manner (Hackett, 1996; Beenstock, 1995; McClenahan *et al.*, 1999; Donnelly, 1999).

A number of lessons can be drawn from the results of our study. It is important to recognize that a merger is a long-term process, from which an organization can take up to two years to recover. Staff should be involved in the preconsultation process from the early stages of the merger, and more transparency and more realism is necessary regarding the measurable benefits and outcomes of the preferred option. Decisions about management structures and strategic goals should be made as soon as possible and with a transparent process. Otherwise, uncertainty and speculation about the future can have detrimental effects on staff and the organization as a whole. A successful integration needs to take into consideration the different cultures of the organizations.

It is of vital importance that the above lessons are incorporated into any future policy considerations or management/leadership agendas about further reorganization within the NHS. Despite political pressures and intentions to make cost savings, managers and leaders within the

NHS need to acknowledge the drawbacks and/or unintended negative consequences that mergers have on the management and organization of work, service provision and staff morale. By ignoring or underestimating the potential backlash from bringing together two or more often dissimilar organizations, managers are creating rather than solving problems. Moreover, in order to achieve a smooth transition, it must be recognized that the merger process is more difficult and time-consuming than is estimated.

Table 13.4   Merged Trusts, Constituent Trusts and Health Authorities

Trust type	Merged Trust	Constituent Trusts	Health Authorities
Acute	Trust A	Trust 1	HA 1
		Trust 2	HA 8
	Trust B	Trust 3	HA 4
		Trust 4	
		Trust 5	
		Trust 6	
		Trust 7	
	Trust C	Trust 8	HA 7
		Trust 9	HA 9
	Trust D	Trust 10	HA 1
	(Case study acute trust)	Trust 11	
	Trust E	Trust 12	HA 5
		Trust 13	HA 10
Community	Trust F	Trust 14	HA 6
	(Case study community trust I)	Trust 15	
		Trust 16	
	Trust G	Trust 17	
	Trust H	Trust 18	HA 7
	(Case study community trust II)	Trust 19	
		Trust 20	
Mental Health	Trust I	Trust 21	HA 2
	(Case study mental health trust)	Trust 22	HA 3
		Trust 23	HA 5
	Trust J	Trust 24	
Combined	Trust K	Trust 24	IIA 2
		Trust 25	HA 5
			HA 11

References

Aletras, V., Jones, A. and Sheldon, T. (1997) 'Economies of Scale and Scope', in B. Ferguson, T. Sheldon and J. Posnett (eds), *Concentration and Choice in Healthcare* (London: Royal Society of Medicine).

Alexander, J., Halpern, M. and Lee, S. (1996) 'The Short-term Effects of Merger on Hospital Operations', *Health Services Research*, 30: 6, pp. 827–47.

Allen, B. and Sharar, D. (2000) 'Post-merger Stress Syndrome', *Behavioural Healthcare Tomorrow*, 9: 1, pp. 40–4.

Ashkenas, R., Demonaco, L. and Francis, S. (1998) 'Making the Deal Real: How GE Capital Integrates Acquisitions', *Harvard Business Review* (Jan.–Feb.), pp. 165–78.

Beenstock, J. (1995) 'An Approach to Mergers Between NHS Trusts', *British Journal of Health Care Management*, 1: 6, pp. 289–391.

Bojke, C. and Gravelle, H. (2001) 'Is Bigger Better for Primary Care Groups and Trusts?', *British Medical Journal*, 322 (10 March), pp. 599–602.

Bogue, R. J., Shortell, S. M. and Sohn, M. W. (1995) 'Hospital Reorganisation After Merger', *Medical Care*, 33: 7, pp. 676–86.

Bowling, A. (1997) *Research Methods in Health: Investigating Health and Health services* (Buckingham: Open University Press).

Buono, A. and Bowditch, J. (1989) *The Human Side of Mergers and Acquisitions: Managing Collisions Between People, Cultures, and Organizations* (London: Jossey-Bass).

Calmark-Hine Report (1995) *A Policy Framework for Commissions Services* (London: Department of Health: 1).

Donnelly, L. (1999) 'Sizing the Argument', *Health Service Journal* (9 September), pp. 10–11.

Department of Health (1997) *Strategic Review of London's Health Services, Report of the Independent Advisory Panel* (Chairman: L. Turnberg) (London: Deparment of Health).

Ferguson, B. and Goddard, M. (1997) 'The Case for and against Mergers', *London Financial Times Healthcare*, iv, pp. 67–82.

Fulop, N., Protopsaltis, G., Hutchings, A., King, A., Allen, P., Normand, C. and Walters, R. (2002) 'Process and Impact of Mergers of NHS Trusts: Multi-centre Case Study and Management Cost Analysis', *British Medical Journal*, 325, 7358, pp. 24–249.

Garside, P. and Rice, J. (1994) 'Merger Mania', *Health Service Journal*, 104, 5412 (21 July), pp. 22–4.

Gould, M. (2000) 'Closed to Argument', *Health Service Journal* (13 January), pp. 11–13.

Greene, J. (1990) 'Do Mergers Work?', *Modern Healthcare*, 20: 11, pp. 24–5.

Handy, C. (1993) *Understanding Organisations* (Harmondsworth: Penguin Books).

Hackett, M. (1996) 'Are There Alternatives to Merger?', *Health Manpower Management*, 22: 5, pp. 5–12.

Hancock, C. (1997) 'Taking the Mania Out of Mergers', *Health Service Journal* (5 March), pp. 22–9.

Haspeslagh, P. and Jemison, D. (1992) 'Making Acquisitions Work', Institut Europeen d'Administration des Affaires (INSEAD), 77 – Fontainebleau (FR). (21473Q).

Hutchings, A., Allen, P., Fulop, N., King, A., Protopsaltis, G., Normand, C. and Walters, R. (2003) 'The Process and Impact of Trust Mergers in the National Health Service: A Financial Perspective', *Public Money and Management*, 23(2), pp. 103–12.

Kent, G. (1997) 'Going with the Flow', *Health Service Journal* (18 September), p. 29.

Lynk, W. (1995) 'The Creation of Economic Efficiencies in Hospital Mergers', *Journal of Health Economics*, 14: 5 (December) pp. 507–30.

Meara, R. and Millard, G. (1998) 'Managing Mergers', *The Healthcare Risk Resource*, 2: 1, pp. 7–11.

McClenahan, J. (1999/2000) 'Emerging Problems with Merger Policy', in *Health Care UK 1999/2000 : The King's Fund Review of Health Policy*, pp. 94–7.

McClenahan, J. (1999) 'Apart at the Seams', *Health Services Journal* (18 November), pp. 22–3.

McClenahan, J., Howard, L. and Macknight, A. (1999) 'Health Ever After – Supporting Staff through Merger and Beyond', *Health Education Authority*, pp. 1–25.

Pettigrew, A., Ferlie, E. and McKee, L. (1992) *Shaping Strategic Change* (London: Sage).

Shaw, J. (2001) 'Tracking the Merger: The Human Experience?', personal communication, Nuffield Institute for Health, University of Leeds.

Sinay, U. (1998) 'Pre and Post-merger Investigation of Hospital Mergers', *Eastern Economic Journal*, 24: 1, pp. 83–97.

Sowden, A., Watt, I. and Sheldon, T. (1997) 'Volume of Activity and Healthcare Quality: Is There a Link?', in B. Ferguson, T. Sheldon and J. Posnett (eds), *Concentration and Choice in Healthcare* (London: Royal Society of Medicine).

Treat, T. (1976) 'The Performance of Merging Hospitals', *Medical Care*, 14: 3, pp. 199–209.

Weil, T. (2000) 'Horizontal Mergers in the United States Health Field: Some Practical Realities', *Health Services Management Research*, 13, pp. 137–51.

14

Institutional Pressures vs Chain Effects on Radical Learning

Alison Evans Cuellar, Ann F. Chou and Joan Bloom

In the United States, state governments are experimenting with new ways of contracting and funding services in order to effect dramatic changes in publicly funded mental health services. New incentives and contracting schemes are being designed to change organizational practices, underlying which are deep, or radical, learning processes. Much of the literature on organizational adaptation and learning has asked how organizations adapt and learn and which types of learning lead to prosperity or problems for organizations (Miner and Mezias, 1996). However, from the perspective of state governments seeking change, the question is what external pressures or organizational forms can be exploited in order to effect changes in organizational practices that embody deep, radical learning. State governments have several available tools: external coercive or normative pressures and the ability to encourage organizational forms through contracting. In some organizational forms learning may be transmitted at multiple levels, which may more effectively lead to changes in practice. In choosing among organizational forms, the challenge for states is selecting the most appropriate organizational form for a given policy purpose. This in turn may depend on the level at which crucial learning occurs.

The literature on organizational learning provides little guidance to states wanting to promote learning. Although the literature acknowledges that learning may occur at individual or organizational levels (Argyris and Schon, 1996; Shaw and Perkins, 1992; Hedberg, 1981; Popper and Lipschitz, 1998), it provides little guidance on what characteristics of organizations can be leveraged to promote learning.

Theory

The study of organizations and learning has a long theoretical history with relatively less attention to empirical research (Miner and Mezias, 1996). The theoretical literature distinguishes the type, locus and content of learning. The type of learning distinguishes between incremental (also called 'single-loop') versus radical ('double-loop') learning (Hedberg, 1981; Argyris and Schon, 1978). Incremental learning is generally the result of repetition or routine, is of short duration, and impacts only part of what an organization does. In contrast, radical learning changes norms, values and world views, leading to new cognitive frameworks within which to make decisions.

The theoretical literature also distinguishes who or what is doing the learning (Miner and Mezias, 1996; Fiol and Lyles, 1985). Learning is not strictly an individual mental process; instead, learning can occur at the level of the individual, group, organization or population of organizations. Importantly, learning at the organizational level is not equivalent to the sum of each member's learning. Organizations may have learning systems embedded in organizational structures or technologies that influence individual members, and these may transmit learning processes to others both between and across subunits of the organization. Organizations may learn practices from one another (Levitt and March, 1988), whether through the diffusion of technologies, codes, procedures and similar routines (Zucker, 1987); through broader coercive, mimetic, or normative institutional processes (Meyer and Rowen, 1977; DiMaggio and Powell, 1993); or through tacit or explicit knowledge transfers (Nonaka, 1994).

What causes radical learning? Some point to the need for a crisis, such as a new leader or dramatic change in environment (Miller and Friesen, 1980; Starbuck, 1978). Others relate organizational learning to organizational structure. Contingency theory in general (Thompson, 1967; Lawrence and Lorsch, 1967) argues that formal organizational structure influences internal communication processes. Recently, Popper and Libschitz (1998) argued that organizations can have 'organizational learning mechanisms' operated by individuals that allow the entity to systematically collect and use information, thus bridging individual and organizational learning levels. These authors present case study evidence of such organizational learning mechanisms in the Israel Defense Force. As in Adler and Cole (1993), organizational learning mechanisms are concrete organizational structures that affect learning and the learning environment in the organization.

However, these studies do not relate different structural arrangements to their effects on different types of learning, such as incremental versus radical learning.

The empirical study of organizational learning is relatively limited. Questions that have been addressed include how organizations learn practices from one another, particularly through the imitation of high-profile organizations (Levitt and March, 1988; Huber, 1991; Zucker, 1987; Meyer and Rowen, 1977; DiMaggio and Powell, 1993). Some empirical studies have focused on organization 'learning curves' in production, specifically studying the effect of cumulative production on production costs in the service and manufacturing industries. Studies of chain affiliation (Darr, Argote and Epple, 1995, and Ingram and Baum, 1997) imply that components within chains should learn faster than independent components. However, in these studies learning is the independent variable that affects a performance outcome. In contrast, states are seeking to identify mechanisms to promote the outcome of learning itself.

Motivated by states' struggles to contract with the most effective organizational form for a given policy purpose, this study provides an empirical test relating radical learning to both changes in institutional forces and choice of organizational structure. In contracting for services, states impose external forces through regulatory pressure and can choose the preferred organizational type to achieve radical learning and induce changes in care delivery patterns. We empirically test the effect of external pressure and organizational type on learning. In particular, we focus on differences in radical learning that can be achieved by having units join a single chain rather than remaining freestanding.

Background and hypotheses

Over the past few decades, organizational forms and relations in the public sector have diverged in range and type, and the archetypical bureaucracy that represents traditional government agencies has undergone restructuring if not downsizing (Scott, 1998). Many public agencies have adopted hybrid structures. One such structure includes contracting-out certain tasks to private companies, regardless of their profit status, and imposing financial incentives to improve the efficiency of governmental services (Scott, 1998; Osborne and Gabler,

1992; Brooks, Liebman and Schelling, 1984). In particular, states have reconfigured their contracts for public mental health services with providers in order to achieve better outcomes for mental health clients and to lower costs.

With this trend, public mental health systems face a new set of institutional pressures. In state policy and research arenas there has been strong support for the coordinated delivery of a flexible array of services to respond to mental health clients' multiple needs (Stroul and Pires, 1997; Stroul, Pires, Armstrong and Meyers, 1998; Goldman *et al.*, 1992, 1994; Provan and Milward, 1995). Historically, delivery of mental health care to clients was viewed as fragmented with mental health providers taking a narrow clinical view of their clients' needs. In contrast, newer models of coordinated delivery of services, as exemplified by the Program in Assertive Community Treatment (PACT) for severely mentally-ill persons, reflect a conceptual model of multi-service coordination and has been shown to be effective in various settings (Morrisey, Tausig and Lindsey, 1986). This has led to greater normative pressure from model mental health programs for providers to deliver care according to integration and coordination principles.

The PACT model of care is a significant departure from previous organizational practice in mental health. In many cases organizational changes or adjustments do not necessarily reflect the existence of learning. However, the case of shifting from traditional mental health care delivery to adopting the PACT model of care requires a dramatic change in philosophical view and interpretive scheme, from one that is individual provider-focused to one that is client-focused. In this sense, we assume organizations that adopt a PACT model of care represent evidence of successful radical learning.

Regulatory and legislative pressures from the states have reinforced mental health service delivery in this integrated manner. In other areas outside of health there has been evidence that state mandates through regulatory pressure result in more rapid adoption of normative practices (Tolbert and Zucker, 1983). To exert pressure on providers, states have changed funding arrangements to further encourage delivery changes. Aside from improving client outcomes through coordinated service delivery, states also hope that greater coordination of services will ultimately lead to greater efficiency and lower public costs. In the United States, more than half of state Medicaid programmes have implemented policies termed 'managed care' for the delivery of publicly funded mental health services (National Academy of State Health Policy, 1999). Managed care is a policy intended to increase the emphasis in service delivery on prevention, coordination of care and less restrictive service settings, while promoting accountability and reducing costs (Freund and Lewit, 1993). A major component of managed care is the implementation of risk-based payment to providers, in addition to implementation of routine performance monitoring systems. Furthermore, normative pressure increasingly exits for providers to model service delivery according to integration principles.

This study explores how providers, in this case community mental health centres (CMHCs), respond to external pressures to change service delivery brought about by new funding mechanisms. Normative pressure from accumulated research and a so-called community service ethic, along with regulative pressures, may lead to changes in provider behaviour and organizational practice (Provan and Milward, 1995; and Weiss, 1990). Furthermore, the change in funding mechanisms underscores the need for radical learning as the shift in financing has demanded a fundamental change in the framework in which the organization operates, requiring adoption of new norms, assumptions and strategies. Consequently, we hypothesize that:

Hypothesis 1. CMHCs will respond to external state pressure and increase service coordination and integration.

In addition to changing funding mechanisms, states have rearranged public services delivery by contracting with new forms. One new organizational form in public mental health is the corporate chain. States may favour chains over freestanding providers for several reasons. First, transaction costs decline for states because a single contractor substitutes for multiple individual providers (Williamson, 1979). Second, radical learning may occur more effectively across units that become part of a formal chain than it does across organizations that remain separate and freestanding.

The chain consists of components organized for functional reasons whose relationship reflects pooled interdependence (Thompson, 1967). Pooled interdependence requires rules for standardizing communication and decision effort, and the formalization of protocols and procedures is essential in standardizing these processes.

To coordinate service delivery, a capacity to manage information flow is critical to impel adoption of new processes but also to promote radical learning. Information flow and knowledge transfer occur on two levels. First, information flow must take place between the contracting company that executes administrative tasks related to the state contract and CMHCs that conduct service delivery. To do so, decision-making must be centralized. A clearly defined decision-making hierarchy is necessary to quickly solve problems. This entails peripheral components to send information to the centre of the chain for a decision to be made and then sent back out to the periphery (Scott, 1998). Consequently, we further hypothesize that

Hypothesis 2. Formalization of protocols and centralization of decision-making apparatus will increase among CMHCs belonging to a chain.

Entities that become part of a chain may more effectively benefit from learning at the individual and organizational levels, relative to entities that remain freestanding. Centralization in chains may promote stable interactions among staff (Vroom, 1969), potentially leading to greater opportunities for knowledge transfer and radical learning across individuals. In addition, radical learning may also occur at the organizational level across mental health clinics. Although it is possible that freestanding organizations respond to environmental uncertainty by forming cooperative relations with other similar organizations and sharing information and operating philosophies (Galaskiewicz, 1985), we argue that such transmission will occur more swiftly among formal components of a chain as a result of formalized and centralized structures.

Hypothesis 3. Radical learning at the organizational level will occur more readily across CMHCs that become part of a chain than across CMHCs that remain freestanding.

Taken together, these hypotheses contrast the effects of new funding pressure against the effect of chain affiliation on radical learning.

The Colorado experiment

In 1994, the State of Colorado instituted an innovative new contracting arrangement for Medicaid mental health care services. The initiative, called the Colorado Medicaid Capitation Pilot Program, is a mental-health carve-out programme, which began paying contractors a fixed price for each Medicaid client rather than for each mental health service delivered. The mental health contractors in turn became the single entry point for clients needing services. Contracts were signed with seven Mental Health Assessment and Services Agencies or MHASAs.

Under risk-based financing providers are paid a fixed amount per person per month without regard to whether the client actually uses services, and without regard to their specific diagnosis or condition. (Payment rates for MHASAs varied by regional historical use and by clients' eligibility states.) With this amount the provider can deliver a flexible set of services, with fewer limits on the amount or type or service than under traditional service payment. Under traditional payment, also called fee-for-service, providers may only bill specific amounts for approved services and typically face limits on the amount or type of services allowed.

Capitation covers all inpatient and outpatient mental health services, excluding medication and nursing-home coverage. Full financial risk was transferred to the MHASAs upon implementation with no reinsurance or other protections from high-user risk (Bloom *et al.*, 1998). Because MHASAs are not paid if their client costs exceed the fixed price, they have an incentive to reduce reliance on inpatient care in favour of less costly community-based care.

Another unique aspect of the Colorado pilot programme is the use of two different organizational modes. In one area, primarily the northern section, the state contracted with six existing not-for-profit community health centres, which act as the managed care organization. Each community health centre (in one case, an alliance of three centres) is responsible for a different geographic area. We referred to this arrangement as the 'free-standing' model. In another area, primarily in the western and southern parts of Colorado, the state contracted with joint ventures between a single for-profit managed care company and either one or several community mental health centres. We refer to this arrangement as the 'chain' model. The chain with which Colorado contracted is a national chain with extensive experience contracting with three other states and numerous private employers for mental health services.

Three mental health centres remained under the existing fee-for-service system and serve as the comparison group. Capitation began in the 'freestanding' area on 1 August 1995 and started a month later in the 'chain' area.

Managed care encourages implementation of a service coordination philosophy because capitation financing provides incentives to reduce future costs by shifting care away from institutions to less costly community settings, and emphasizing prevention and early intervention (Catalano, Libby, Snowden and Evans Cuellar, 2001; Frank, McGuire and Newhouse, 1995). Capitation financing may give providers the financial incentive to implement effective interventions that require coordination, such as PACT for adults or multisystemic therapy for children (Henggeler, Melton and Smith, 1992; Henggeler, Melton, Smith, Schoenwald and Hanley, 1993; Henggeler, Schoenwald and Pickrel, 1994).

There are also potential unintended consequences of capitation in mental health services. When clients interface with multiple service systems the capitated providers may find opportunities to substitute other health and human services for mental health care. Under capitation of a fixed set of services, there is an incentive for providers to shift care – and subsequent costs – to sites where payment is not capitated. This cost-shifting would be defined as one agency reducing its own expenditures by inducing another agency to pay for similar services. Cost-shifting from capitated to non-capitated health services has been demonstrated in studies of adults (Norton, Lindrooth and Dickey, 1997a,b) and children (Libby, Cuellar *et al.*, 2001).

Previous studies from the Colorado experiment have focused on how the change in financial incentives has affected patients' receipt of care or their clinical outcomes. One study found both reduced inpatient utilization and outpatient utilization among a sample of adults with serious mental illness (Bloom *et al.*, 1998); others examined the effect of capitation on indirect aggregate measures of prevention activity (Catalano *et al.*, 1999). Findings were mixed with proportionally more children and those of younger ages seen in the for-profit sites compared to the fee-for-service sites after capitation, while there were no significant differences for not-for-profit sites. Another study found that innovations in service configurations and increased service capacity occurred within the capitated sites relative to the fee-for-service sites (Cohen and Bloom, 2001).

The natural experiment in Colorado provides an important opportunity to study learning. Unlike previous studies, this one contrasts the effect of external pressure from the capitation experiment against the effect of chain affiliation on radical learning.

Research methods and data

The normative pressure in mental health services delivery is towards integration, coordination and consumer focus. This new direction in service delivery requires a fundamental philosophical shift for providers. We examine the effect of external financing pressure from managed care and the effect of chain contracting on several outcomes, which indicate whether a CMHC's overall programme philosophy and organizational characteristics are consistent with a shift toward integration, coordination and consumer focus. The programme philosophy measures capture employee's perceptions of the CMHC's focus on clinical team building, interagency relations, types of preferred therapies, and client and family roles, whereas the organizational structure is captured through employee perceptions of formalization and centralization. To examine the effect of external pressure from managed care on employee's perceptions of these key organizational outcomes, a general regression model is specified as follows:

Outcome = f(managed care, organizational characteristics, individual characteristics)

In addition, we argue that the external pressure will be mediated by whether the centre is freestanding or part of a chain. Consequently, we model this effect as,

Outcome = f(managed care*chain CMHC, managed care*freestanding CMHC, organizational characteristics, individual characteristics)

Employees in 17 CMHCs in Colorado were interviewed at two separate time periods, once before the experiment (1994) and once after (1996). The CMHCs were selected by balancing counties from different geographical areas in the treatment and comparison groups and matching on percentages of poverty, ethnicity, degree of rurality and comparable industrial bases (for example, a geographical area whose major industry is mining versus one that is primarily ranching).

Employees responded to two questionnaires, (1) The Community Program Philosophy Scale (CPPS) and Organizational Structure and Climate (OSC) Survey, which were administered at similar time periods. The CPPS data sampled 10 to 12 staff members from each of the 17 selected CMHCs at one-year intervals. The CPPS scales, which assess various components of coordinated, integrated community care recognized by mental health professionals to be necessary, were computed to describe the overall philosophy and approach to the programmes. This CPPS has been developed to assess and compare programmes that serve clients with severe mental illness; it has been found to be valid and reliable and has been used successfully to differentiate programmes (see Scheid and Greenley, 1997). In addition to subscales on programme components and approach, the CPPS also contains five subscales modified from the

Moos Community-Oriented Programmes Environment Scale (Moos, 1974) that assess aspects of the organization's work climate. The Moos scales, however, aggregate measures across employee roles. As an enhancement of the Moos scale data, a separate survey was conducted, the Organizational Structure and Climate Survey (OSC). The OSC collected data from both administrators and clinical staff on organizational structure, culture and staff morale.

Variables

To assess radical learning, we measure changes in a variety of measures from the CPPS, reflecting employees' perception of overall philosophy and approach to programmes. For our study we used individuals' responses on seven scales from the CPPS, each of which consists of four items. The ranges for the CPPS subscales are 4 to 20 in our data.

Team model measures the extent to which a team or individual provider cared for the individual consumer. The staff were asked to evaluate the extent in which the following occurred: (1) single treatment person assignments were used rather than a team approach; (2) several staff members, beyond medical staff, were assigned to work as a team with each client; (3) individual consumers eventually got to know most programme staff; and (4) individual consumers usually got to know only one programme person very well.

Interest in more severely ill clients measures a CMHC's interest in this subpopulation of patients using the following items: (1) staff find it rewarding and challenging to work with very disabled clients; (2) staff feel effective in addressing the multiple needs of severely-ill clients; (3) staff prefer to focus most of their work on insightful, psychologically-minded clients; and (4) staff prefer to work mostly with clients who are willing and able to be employed.

Substance abuse orientation measures the extent of service provision for mentally-ill clients with alcohol or drug addition. The staff was asked to evaluate the following four items: (1) existence of organized services for mentally-ill clients who also abuse alcohol or street drugs; (2) efforts made to encourage mentally-ill clients not to use alcohol or street drugs; (3) goal of the programme does not encompass mentally-ill clients who also abuse alcohol or street drugs; and (4) aiding clients with alcohol/drug problems is not a major focus at the CMHC.

Emergency Access measures coordination with emergency services as responses to the following items: (1) the programme has on-call coverage outside normal work days; (2) we work closely with emergency room or hospital staff when one of our clients is treated there; (3) when clients enter the emergency room or hospital we may not learn of this for several days; (4) we advise clients and families to go to the emergency room for crises outside normal work hours.

Referral Advocacy measures degree of client assistance in linking with services provided by other agencies. The items include (1) when making referrals or placements, staff accompany clients on their first contact; (2) when making referrals or placements, staff usually allow clients to follow through on their own; (3) transporting clients to needed services is an appropriate staff activity; (4) helping clients with the application process in other agencies is rarely done here.

Users exercising power measures CMHC's philosophy regarding client advocacy. The four-item scale assesses: (1) staff give first priority to being the client's advocate; (2) staff do not support client-empowerment or advocacy viewpoints very strongly; (3) clients' views about the programme are systematically documented; and (4) staff make major treatment decisions without consulting the client.

Longitudinality of services measures the CMHC's view on long-term relationships with patients with the following: (1) the programme emphasizes maintaining long-term regular contact with most clients; (2) staff help clients through a crisis or a transition without continuing to see them indefinitely; (3) it is common for the same staff person or team to see clients over many months or years; and (4) most clients receive brief treatment aimed at termination within a few months.

We also measured *formalization* and *centralization* scales from the OCS. Formalization is measured by the extent to which policies and procedures within the organization are formal and explicit (Daft, 2001). It was measured by a 10-item scale, based on inquiries about the perceived explicitness of policies and procedures in the agency (Comstock and Scott, 1977). Centralization is measured using an index on the centralization of authority. The index represents the extent to which decision-making authority and power are concentrated at top levels of the organization, rather than being decentralized or dispersed throughout various levels of the organization (Daft, 2001). This scale is measured by 10 items which ask about the level of input given by programme directors into four specific administrative decisions, such as hiring of staff, decisions about disciplinary actions regarding staff, care delivery policies, and the size of staff; and six specific clinical decisions, such as the agency's emphasis on service provision, decision to add a clinical service, frequency and format of charting, medication-related issues for consumers, and ancillary services to be offered to consumers (Comstock and Scott, 1977).

Our explanatory variables include the time period (pre, first post-period, second post-period) and whether the CMHC was in the managed care group or not (freestanding or chain). Because employees are nested within CMHCs, independence cannot be assumed, and consequently we incorporated fixed effects to account for clustering of individuals within groups and corrected standard errors for clustering. We measured dependence on government resources as the proportion of a CMHC's revenues from Medicaid. We also controlled for other organizational characteristics, such as organization size and learning environment. The size of each CMHC was determined by the total number of staff. Whether learners can absorb knowledge through the periphery of communication depends on the overall *climate* and *culture* of the organization (Brown and Duguid, 1991). Organizational climate is important because it signifies an organization's social layout and its affective ambiance (Morris and Bloom, 2002; Reichers and Schneider, 1990; Sousseau, 1988; Schneider, 1975; James and Jones, 1974). The climate could be transmitted in a social context via informal relationships, and therefore, we controlled for work climate measures such as provider perception of organizational innovativeness, involvement in job, clarity, cohesion of the work group, and supervisory support derived from the Moos scales in order to distinguish effects resulted from the chain affiliation versus those attributed to organizational culture and climate.

Analyses and estimation

The analysis uses a quasi-experimental, pre-post design with non-equivalent comparison groups. The observed change is the conversion of public CMHCs from fee-for-service to capitated managed care. Non-equivalent comparison groups refer to managed care areas (one with a corporate chain and one with freestanding CMHCs) and 'fee-for-service' areas. These are not equivalent groups, because enrollment into plans was not randomly assigned, but rather results from phased implementation of managed care on a geographic basis determined by the state.

Table 14.1 presents results showing the effect of external pressure on employees' perceptions of the CMHCs' programmes and philosophy. These specifications test the first and second hypotheses. Increases in these measures reflect adoption of service coordination and integration practices consistent with PACT and radical learning. The key variable measuring the effect of the state financing change are the interaction terms for chain*post and freestanding*post. These variables measure the

244

Table 14.1 Effect of external pressure on employees' perceptions of programmes and philosophy

	(1) Team model	(2) Interest in SMI users	(3) Substance-abuse orientation	(4) Emergency access	(5) Users exercising power	(6) Longitudinality of service	(7) Referral advocacy
Post	-1.16	0.13	0.1	0.39	-1.25	-0.37	-1.08
	[1.40]	[0.96]	[1.20]	[1.19]	[1.36]	[1.26]	[1.28]
Chain	-1.5	-0.15	-0.47	0.52	-0.77	-0.33	-0.82
	[0.63]*	[0.43]	[0.54]	[0.53]	[0.61]	[0.57]	[0.57]
Freestanding	-1.5	0.25	-0.18	0.41	-2	0.19	-0.53
	[0.68]*	[0.46]	[0.59]	[0.58]	[0.66]**	[0.61]	[0.62]
Chain*post	0.1	-0.16	0.46	-0.79	0.49	-0.28	0.45
	[0.94]	[0.64]	[0.81]	[0.80]	[0.92]	[0.85]	[0.86]
Freestand.* post	-0.45	-0.8	-0.08	-1.15	1.41	-2.17	-0.06
	[0.99]	[0.68]	[0.85]	[0.84]	[0.97]	[0.89]*	[0.90]
Clarity	-0.08	0.01	0.03	0.07	0.11	-0.15	0.01
	[0.07]	[0.05]	[0.06]	[0.06]	[0.07]	[0.07]*	[0.07]
Staff cohesion	0.21	0.2	0.05	-0.09	0.04	0.29	0.2
	[0.09]*	[0.06]**	[0.08]	[0.08]	[0.09]	[0.08]**	[0.08]*

	(1)	(2)	(3)	(4)	(5)	(6)	(7)
Innovation	0.31	0.3	0.15	0.16	0.32	−0.07	0.2
	[0.08]**	[0.05]**	[0.07]*	[0.07]*	[0.08]**	[0.07]	[0.07]**
Involvement in job	−0.04	0.04	0.06	0.12	−0.03	−0.05	−0.14
	[0.09]	[0.06]	[0.08]	[0.08]	[0.09]	[0.08]	[0.08] +
Supervisory support	−0.01	−0.02	−0.03	0.01	0.03	−0.02	0.05
	[0.08]	[0.05]	[0.07]	[0.07]	[0.08]	[0.07]	[0.07]
% Medicaid revenue	−0.05	−0.01	−0.01	−0.02	−0.02	−0.03	−0.04
	[0.03]	[0.02]	[0.02]	[0.02]	[0.03]	[0.02]	[0.03]
Total #staff	0.01	0	0.01	0	0.01	0	−0.01
	[0.00]	[0.00]	[0.00]**	[0.00]	[0.00] +	[0.00]	[0.00]**
Constant	7.78	7.57	10.88	11.66	2.81	14.97	13.68
	[2.32]**	[1.59]**	[1.99]**	[1.98]**	[2.27]	[2.09]**	[2.12]**
Observations	242	242	241	242	242	242	242
R-squared	0.24	0.38	0.22	0.15	0.23	0.16	0.23

Note: Standard errors in brackets. + significant at 10%; * significant at 5%; ** significant at 1%. Coefficients on discipline dummy variables not shown.

average change in outcome variables resulting from a change in the financing mechanism relative to the areas where no policy change occurred.

We found no effect of external pressure from managed care on employees' perception of the CMHCs' programmes and philosophy when we combined chain and freestanding CMHCs as one experimental group (data not shown). We then examined whether the effect of managed care might be different for chains versus freestanding CMHCs, a mediating effect. As shown in Table 14.1, the analysis found very few statistically significant changes as a result of managed care. The only significant changes were that employees in chains perceived that CMHCs reduced their reliance on intensive psychotherapy, while employees in freestanding CMHCs perceived a reduction in user contact outside the programme office and reduction in longitudinality; that is, users seen over several years. The effect of dependence on government resources was statistically significant in only two cases and very small. Even if some individuals' perceptions became more PACT-like, these were offset on average by individuals who perceived a move away from PACT.

We also found little support for the second hypothesis: freestanding CMHCs showed no statistically significant changes in the overall extent of formalization or centralization as a result of managed care (Table 14.2). Somewhat surprisingly, CMHCs that became part of chains also did not evidence greater formalization or centralization.

Discussion

Our results show that external pressure from changes in financing had little effect on average for radical learning measured as changes in employee's perception of a CMHC's programme and philosophy characteristics. Employees perceived little change whether they were in freestanding CMHCs or in chain CMHCs. For the few changes that were statistically significant, the direction of the effect in freestanding CMHCs was counter to integration, coordination and user empowerment. Employees reported a perceived reduction in user contact outside the programme office and reduction in longitudinality. It is possible that deep learning requires a longer time period than the two years captured in our study. Alternatively, the external environment may have changed so dramatically that learning could not take place (Lawrence and Dyer, 1983; March and Olsen, 1975).

Table 14.2 Effect of external pressure on formalization and centralization

	(1) *Formalization*	(2) *Centralization*	
Post	0.39	0.01	
	[0.44]	[0.36]	
Chain	0.22	0.23	
	[0.22]	[0.18]	
Freestanding	0.15	0.07	
	[0.22]	[0.18]	
Chain*post	−0.11	−0.04	
	[0.27]	[0.22]	
Freestand.*post	−0.42	−0.07	
	[0.26]	[0.22]	
% Medicaid revenue	0.02	0	
	[0.01] +	[0.01]	
Total #staff	0	0	
	[0.00]*	[0.00]	
Constant	3.11	4.3	
	[0.44]**	[0.35]**	
Observations	221	211	
R-squared	0.18	0.04	

Notes: Standard errors in brackets. + significant at 10%; * significant at 5%; ** significant at 1%. Coefficients on discipline dummy variables not shown.

The data and methodology used in this study attempt to identify whether individual-level or organization-level learning is promoted by external pressure or collective organizational features. However, this study does not attempt to identify the individual mental or organizational microprocesses that lead to radical learning, as these are not observed in our data. For example, we cannot observe whether the learning that occurs across subunits that becomes part of the corporate chain is due to vicarious learning, generative learning, inferential learning or experimentation (Miner and Mezias, 1996). We observe only that the process, whatever it may be, appears to be facilitated by the chain structure, relative to free-standing units. Extensive case studies were also conducted in Colorado and we hope to provide more insight into microprocesses based on this qualitative research in future work.

Further, this study does not evaluate whether the learning consistent with PACT is good from society's or clients' perspectives. Other studies, cited previously, have addressed the cost effectiveness of PACT, here we take the perspective of governments that have already made a decision to promote learning toward a PACT model of client care.

While the pressure from states is ultimately to change services provided to clients, our outcome measures reflect employee perceptions of CMHC programmes and philosophy, consistent with our focus on radical learning. Although the employee-based data provide a better perspective on radical learning, additional evidence on actual client service patterns is needed to measure whether practices changed. However, results of our study provide preliminary lessons for state governments and policy-makers. We find that funding pressures and organizational type alone had little effect on radical learning at the individual level in the short-run. States may take this into consideration when designing their contracts and implicitly encouraging different organizational forms.

References

Argote, L., Beckman, S. L. and Epple, D. (1990) 'The Persistence and Transfer of Learning in Industrial Settings', *Management Science*, 35: 2, pp. 140–54.

Adler, P. S. and Cole, R. E. (1993) 'Designed for Learning: A Tale of Two Auto Plants', *Sloan Management Review*, 34, pp. 85–94.

Argyris, C. and Schon, D. A. (1996) *Organizational Learning* (Reading, MA: Addison-Wesley).

Banaszak-Holl, J., Mitchell, W., Baum, J., Berta, W. and Bowman, D. (2000) *Chain-to-Component Transfer Learning in Multiunit Chains of US Nursing Homes, 1991–1997*. Paper presented at the Academy of Management Annual Conference, 2000.

Bloom, J. R., Hu, T-W., Wallace, N. T., Cuffel, B., Hausman, J. and Scheffler, R. M. (1998) 'Mental Health Costs and Outcomes under Alternative Capitation Systems in Colorado: Early Results', *Journal of Mental Health Policy and Economics*, 1: 1, pp. 1–11.

Brooks, H., Liebman, L. and Schelling, C. (1984) *Private–Public Partnership: New Opportunities for Meeting Social Needs* (Cambridge, MA: Ballinger).

Brown, J. S. and Dugui, P. (1984) 'Organizational Learning and Communities-in-Practice: Toward a Unified View of Working, Learning, and Innovation', *Organization Science*, 2: 1, pp. 40–57.

Catalano, R., Libby, A. M., Snowden, L. R. and Evans Cuellar, A. (2000) 'The Effect of Capitation Financing on Mental Health Services for Children and Youth: The Colorado Experience', *American Journal of Public Health*, 90: 12, pp. 1861–5.

Cohen, E. and Bloom, J. R. (2000) 'Managed Care and Service Capacity Development in a Public Mental Health System, *Administration and Policy in Mental Health*, 28: 2, pp. 63–74.

Comstock, D. E. and Scott, W. R. (1977) 'Technology and the Structure of Subunits: Distinguishing Individual and Workgroup Effects', *Administrative Science Quarterly*, 22, pp. 177–202.

Daft, R. L. (2001) *Organization Theory and Design*, 7th edn (St Paul, MN: West Publishing).

Darr, E., Argote, L. and Epple, D. (1995) 'The Acquistion, Transfer, and Depreciation of Knowledge in Service Organizations', *Management Science*, 41, 1750–62.

Darr, E., Argote, L. and Epple, D. (2001) 'The Acquisition, Transfer, and Depreciation of Knowledge in Service Organizations', *Management Science*, 41, pp. 1750–62.

DiMaggio, P. J. and Powell, W. W. (1983) 'The Iron Cage Revisited: Institutional Isomorphism and Collective Rationality in Organizational Fields', *American Sociological Review*, 48, pp. 147–60.

Epple, D., Argote, L. and Devadas, R. (1991) 'Organizational Learning Curves: A Method for Investigating Intra-Plant Transfer of Knowledge Acquired Through Learning by Doing', *Organization Science*, 2: 1, pp. 58–70.

Fiol, C. M. and Lyles, M. A. (1985) 'Organizational Learning', *The Academy of Management Review*, 10: 4, pp. 803–13.

Frank, R. G., McGuire, T. G. and Newhouse, J. P. (1995) 'Risk Contracts in Managed Mental Health Care', *Health Affairs*, 18: 5, pp. 214–25.

Freund, D. and Lewit, E. (1993) 'Managed Care for Children and Pregnant Women', *Future of Children*, 3, pp. 92–122.

Galaskiewicz, J. (1985) 'Interorganizational Relations', *Annual Review of Sociology*, 11, pp. 281–304.

Goldman, H. H., Morrissey, J. P., Ridgely, M. S., Frank, R. G., Newman, S. J. and Kennedy, C. (1993) 'Lessons from the Program on Chronic Mental Illness', *Health Affairs*, 11: 3, pp. 51–68.

Hedberg, B. (1981) 'How Organizations Learn and Unlearn', in P. C. Nystrom and W. H. Starbuck (eds), *Handbook of Organizational Design* (London: Oxford University Press).

Henggeler, S. W., Melton, G. B. and Smith, L. A. (1992) 'Family Preservation using Multisystemic Therapy: An Effective Alternative to Incarcerating Serious Juvenile Offenders', *Journal of Consulting and Clinical Psychology*, 60, pp. 953–61.

Henggeler, W., Melton, G., Smith, L., Schoenwald, S. and Hanley, J. (1993) 'Family Preservation Using Multisystemic Treatment: Long-term Follow-up to a Clinical Trial with Serious Juvenile Offenders', Journal of Child and Family Studies, 2, pp. 283–93.

Henggeler, S. W., Schoenwald, S. I. C. and Pickrel, S. G. (1994) 'The Contribution of Treatment Outcome Research to the Reform of Children's Mental Health Services: Multisystemic Therapy as an Example', *Journal of Mental Health Administration*, 21: 3, pp. 229–39.

Huber, G. P. (1982) 'Organizational Information Systems: Determinants of their Performance and Behavior', Management Science, 28, pp. 135–55.

Huber, G. P. (1991) 'Organizational Learning: The Contributing Processes and the Literatures', *Organization Science*, 2, pp. 88–115.

Ingram, P. and Baum, J. A. C. (1997) 'Chain Affiliation and the Failure of Manhattan Hotels, 1898–1980', *Administrative Science Quarterly*, 42, pp. 68–102.

Lawrence, P. R. and Dyer, D. (1983) *Renewing American Industry* (New York: Free Press).

Lawrence, P. R. and Lorsch, J. W. (1967) 'Differentiation and Integration in Complex Organizations', *Administrative Science Quarterly*, 12: 1, pp. 1–47.

Levitt, Barbara and March, James G. (1988) 'Organizational Learning,' *Annual Review of Sociology* 14, 319–40.

Libby, A. M., Evans Cuellar, A., Snowden L. and Orton, H. (2002) 'Substitution in a Medicaid Mental Health Carve-Out: Services and Costs', *Journal of Health Care Finance*, 28: 4, pp. 11–23.

March, J. G. and Olsen, J. P. (1975) 'The Uncertainty of the Past: Organizational Learning under Ambiguity', *European Journal of Political Research*, 3, pp. 147–71.

Meyer, J. W. and Rowan, B. (1977) 'Institutional Organizations: Formal Structure as Myth and Ceremony', *American Journal of Sociology*, 83, pp. 440–63.

Miller, D. and Friesen, P. H. 'Momentum and Revolution in Organization Adaptation', *Academy of Management Journal*, 23, pp. 591–614.

Miner, Anne S. and Mezias, Stephen J. (1996) 'Ugly Duckling No More: Pasts and Futures of Organizational Learning Research,' *Organization Science* 7, 88–99.

Moos, R. H. (1974) *Evaluating Treatment Environments: A Social Ecological Approach* (New York: John Wiley & Sons).

Morris, A. and Bloom, J. (1980) 'Contextual Factors Affecting Job Satisfaction and Organizational Commitment in Community Mental Health Centers Undergoing System Changes in the Financing of Care', *Mental Health Services Research*, 4: 2, pp. 71–83.

Morrisey, J., Tausig, and Lindsey (1986) 'Interorganizational Networks in Mental Health Systems: Assessing Community Support Programs for the Chronically Mentally Ill', in W. R. Scott and B. L. Black (eds), *The Organization of Mental Health Services: Societal and Community Systems* (Beverly Hills, CA: Sage).

National Academy of State Health Policy (1999) *Medicaid Managed Care: A Guide for States*, 4th edn (Portland, ME: National Academy of State Health Policy).

Nonaka, I. (1994) 'A Dynamic Theory of Organizational Knowledge Creation', *Organization Science*, 5, pp. 14–29.

Norton, E. C., Lindrooth, R. and Dickey, B. (1997a) *Cost Shifting in a Managed Care Plan* (Chapel Hill, NC: University of North Carolina at Chapel Hill).

Norton, E. C., Lindrooth, R. and Dickey, B. (1997b) 'Cost Shifting in a Mental Health Carve-out for the AFDC Population', *Health Care Financing Review*, 18, pp. 95–108.

Osborne, D. and Gabler, T. (1992) *Reinventing Government* (Reading, MA: Addison-Wesley).

Popper, M and Lipshitz, R. (1998). 'Organizational Learning Mechanisms: A Structural and Cultural Approach to Organizational Learning' *Journal of Applied Behavioural Science*, 34(2), 161–79.

Provan, K. G. and Milward, H. B. (1992) 'A Preliminary Theory of Interorganizational Network Effectiveness: A Comparative Study of Four Community Mental Health Systems', *Administrative Science Quarterly*, 40, pp. 1–15.

Scott, W. R. (1998) *Organizations: Rational, Natural, and Open Systems* (Upper Saddle River, NJ: Prentice-Hall).

Shaw, R. B. and Perkins, D. N. T. (1992) 'Teaching Organizations to Learn: The Power of Productive Failures' in D. A. Nadler, M. S. Gerstein and R. B. Shaw, eds, *Organizational Architecture* (San Francisco: Jossey-Bass) pp. 175–91.

Starbuck, W. H. (1983) 'Organizations as Action Generators', *American Sociological Review*, 48, pp. 91–102.

Stroul, B. and Pires, S. (1997) 'State Health Care Reforms: How they Affect Children and Adolescents with Emotional Disorders and their Families', *Journal of Mental Health Administration*, 24, pp. 386–99.

Stroul, B. A., Pires, S. A., Armstrong, M. I. and Meyers, J. C. (1998) 'The Impact of Managed Care on Mental Health Services for Children and Their Families', *The Future of Children*, 8: 2, pp. 119–33.

Thompson, J. D. (1967) *Organizations in Action* (New York: McGraw-Hill).

Tolbert, P. and Zucker, L. (1983) 'Institutional Sources of Change in the Formal Structure of Organizations: The Diffusion of Civil Service Reform, 1880–1935', *Administrative Science Quarterly*, 28, pp. 22–39.

Vroom, V. (1969) 'Industrial Social Psychology', in G. Lindzey and E. Aronson (eds), *The Handbook of Social Psychology*, 2nd edn (Reading, MA: Addison-Wesley), Vol. 5, pp. 195–268.

Weiss, J. A. (1990) 'Ideas and Inducements in Mental Health Policy', *Journal of Policy Analysis and Management*, 9, pp. 178–200.

Williamson, O. E. (1973) 'Organizational Forms and Internal Efficiency Markets and Hierarchies: Some Elementary Considerations', *American Economic Review*, 63: 2, pp. 316–25.

Zucker, L. G. (1987) 'Institutional Theories of Organization', *Annual Review of Sociology*, 13, pp. 443–64.

15
Summing Up

Sue Dopson and Annabelle L. Mark

The upsurge of interest in leadership in the English National Health Service (NHS) is a response to the government's belief that stronger leadership is needed in the public sector. This is because strong leadership is seen as critical to navigating transition and uncertainty on the scale that is currently seen within the NHS. Further, albeit lesser, reasons for emphasizing leadership include the need to rekindle the interest of professionals, especially clinicians in health care, in participating in these roles in the context of a renewed interest in leadership across all sectors of the economy. Is this upsurge of interest in leadership justified? Is it desirable?

Contributions within this book suggest it is justified in health care because clinical and managerial posts contain an element of leadership, which is greater in times of rapid change and in new organizations. An example is the significant need for NHS leadership in the new Primary Care Trusts, because both management and organization at this level are unfamiliar territory. However, contributions also suggest a downside of this 'switching on' to leadership, namely an inflated expectation of what it can achieve. Certainly, effective leadership can drive significant progress, motivating, managing and overcoming challenges, but it is in danger of being seen as a cure-all, at the expense of other more fundamental elements. For example, it could lead to less attention being given to the essential managerial tasks of ensuring there are good systems of checking that things are working properly.

There is tremendous cynicism at NHS grassroots level regarding the gap between current government rhetoric on leadership and the reality of what is needed on the ground. A case in point is the dominance of professionals, particularly clinicians, who are deemed to occupy the leadership roles with most power in local health care contexts. What is urgently needed is also a system where leadership responsibility is awarded according to personal skills in order to broaden and deepen the overall leadership cadre and to foster a more transformational or consensual approach to the leadership role.

The issue within the current government leadership debate is that it encourages too much emphasis on vision and inspiration and too little on the need for understanding the complex context in which leadership in health care takes place. So what is the future for health care leadership? How have successful health care organizations approached the issues and what are the lessons we can draw from them? Crucially, too, why is the disparity between government policy and grassroots reality continuing to grow?

The selected chapters in this book reflecting on international health care contexts suggest that health care organizations which have successful leadership in place can certainly be said to have commonalities. Typically, leadership is distributed within the organization, professional power is understood, the complexity of social relationships within the organization is acknowledged and discussed, efforts are made to harness talent, and the contribution of different sorts of perspectives are valued and utilized. From this approach and from analysing the challenges ahead for health service leaders, Sir Alan Langlands, former Chief Executive of the NHS, laid out some key points for the successful foundation of leadership development in his keynote address at the conference held at Saïd Business School, Oxford. He noted the following points:

- Small working groups with complementary skills are important in achieving progress.
- A diversity of leadership needs to be introduced both in terms of occupational base and hierarchical level.
- Personal skills are often more important in leading change than formal status or rank.
- Continuity of leadership is key – particularly during times of change.

What is puzzling is that such advice is not being effectively communicated to government policy-makers. Current research is providing useful information on the success of different leadership methodologies and the experiences of health care services in other countries also hold valuable lessons about the way ahead. Perhaps it is the responsibility of those involved in research to make the government more aware of their conclusions and to bring policy-makers on board in order to influence decisions to better reflect the needs of the NHS. It is also of course the responsibility of policy-makers to listen.

The contributions captured in this book highlight a further set of questions that could be usefully considered:

- The importance of considering the question of leadership, of what and for whom?
- If leadership is an emergent property, how can we be sure it will emerge, and will we recognize it as such when it does?
- What are the implications of the expanding gap between the rhetoric and practice of leadership in health care systems?
- What are the dangers of seeing leadership residing in single individuals? What might be the consequences of the inflated expectations governments have of what leadership can achieve in managing such complex social process as those involved in health care?
- Is the continued dominance of clinicians in leadership processes within health care appropriate, and what are the alternatives?

There are significant methodological issues in comparing leadership issues across different cultures to ensure that comparative outcomes are valid. The contributions in this book suggest that the more robust studies are characterized by:

- the use and development of organizational theory;
- a clear presentation of research design, methods used, database and rules for analysis;
- a substantial empirical base so as to allow underlying patterns to be uncovered; and
- that previous studies/ literature/ findings inform analysis.

Discussions of the research designs that enable further insights into leadership processes are quite underdeveloped at the present time and merit renewed interest if we are to make further progress in the study of leadership. The relative failure of researchers in this area to influence policy-makers in their thinking about leadership requires researchers to consider new strategies in disseminating the results of their research.

Contributions also suggest that leadership is not one thing but many, but the recognition of its appropriateness, as the introductory keynote speech for the Oxford Conference by Professor Beverly Alimo-Metcalfe Professor of Leadership Studies at Leeds University pointed out, rests most accurately with followers and not those elsewhere. As she further indicated in her presentation, research now suggests that the best predictor of successful leadership is proving to be the opinion of subordinates and not peers or superiors. The appropriate response to this by organizations may indeed energize the whole organization by recognizing the role of all participants in developing and maintaining the leadership process.

Once leadership of health care organizations is better understood, a further important task will be the identification of the future issues that leaders of those organizations will face. Sir Alan Langlands identified five key challenges for leaders of health services in his conference address. These he defined as:

1 *The swing from the collective towards the individual.* 'The erosion of collective values in society generally will occur to such a degree that all health systems might eventually have the same three-tier structure: a top tier of fee-for-service medicine for the very rich; a middle tier of insurance-based managed care covering the middle classes; and a third tier of publicly funded "rough and ready" care for the poor.'

2 *Advances in biomedical research.* He argues these will result in 'new forms of diagnosis and treatment: eg gene mapping and gene therapy, ultrasound treatment of tumours; intravenous treatment at home controlled by a chip; advances in nanotechnology – the science and technology of creating working machines on a molecular scale – allowing nanometer-sized chemical agents to repair damaged cells. The amount of information uncovered by the human genome project is staggering but it is only a step towards answering the real question – how do genes in the genome work together in a human being? Progress is in two directions blending molecular biology and clinical practice and taking the basic science to a further level of detail.'

3 *Media developments such as digitalization and other advances will result in a proliferation of news and information on health.* 'Health care is excellent quarry, particularly health care in a system like the NHS for which a party political angle to news stories can be used. The new media also means that the public are seeking out and becoming familiar with research based information – sometimes in a controlled manner (like NHS Direct), sometimes not. One recent paper from the US estimated that more than 70,000 websites disseminate health information and more than 50 million people seek health information online. We are only beginning to understand the long-term consequences of this on health systems.'

4 *The imbalance between supply and demand.* 'Regardless of the actual level of supply and demand (which none of us can measure very easily), the *perceived* difference between supply and demand will grow as expectations rise. The answer can't just be more of everything.'

5 *Changes in the burden of disease.* 'Attention will continue to focus on the impact of ageing and the growing inequalities in health and the demand for health care between rich and poor. There will also be changes in the nature and prevalence of disease (e.g. AIDS, CJD, tuberculosis) increased resistance to antibiotics and threats from changes in the physical environment. Global travel will increase the risk of transmission of infection and risky behaviour, particularly amongst the young, which may have profound effects in the future.'

The general conclusion from the reflections on leadership in health care documented in this book is that leadership is not best characterized as a noun, but is more appropriately captured as a verb. Furthermore, leadership undoubtedly involves the use of power in the face of great uncertainty. Given this, perhaps leaders should seek to embrace and question this uncertainty, rather than deny it.

Index